Lenient Times preceding Tribulation

www.lenienttimesprecedingtribulation.com

LENIENT TIMES

PRECEDING TRIBULATION

JEREMY N.

PRIMIX
PUBLISHING
THE WRITE CHOICE

Primix Publishing
11620 Wilshire Blvd
Suite 900, West Wilshire Center, Los Angeles, CA, 90025
www.primixpublishing.com
Phone: 1-800-538-5788

Published by Primix Publishing   07/25/2022

ISBN: 978-1-957676-35-7(sc)
ISBN: 978-1-957676-36-4(e)

Library of Congress Control Number: 2022914171

1

It is a warm, humid summer night. An automobile enters the premises of the estate. The twosome within arrive at the wedding reception. Ashley turns her head to check all the mirrors to ensure that the car is exactly within a safe distance from all the other surrounding cars. Shifting the gearstick to 'park', Ashley takes one final look at her own reflection and then proceeds to vacate the car. The couple begins to make their way into the hall of celebration.

The banner reads "Congratulations Patrick & Rachel"

As the couple enters the hall, they hear and see the merry cheers and laughter of others. The clinking of champagne glasses pierce through the steady hum of many conversations going on simultaneously. As Michael and Ashley make their way through the magnificent hall, friends greet them. They stop from time to time for pleasant chatter and sentimental hugs.

Eventually, Michael and Ashley make their way to their seats.

Benjamin:	It's a party now!
Michael:	What's going on?

Michael greets all at the table and gives Patrick a hug. Michael slips Patrick a box evidently concealing a significant gift. Michael leans in and whispers to Patrick.

Michael:	A present fit for a King. Congratulations my brother.

Michael gives Rachel a kiss on the cheek.

Michael:	Congratulations.

Ashley and Rachel squeal merrily at the sight of each other.

Ashley:	Baby you look gorgeous! I am so happy for you!

Rachel:	Thank you baby! You look amazing as well.

The entire party consists of Patrick's friends and family. It is a grand ceremony. The guests at the main table consist of Patrick, his sisters, his father, Rachel, Michael, Ashley, Benjamin and Jasmine. These are the individuals that occupied Patrick's inner circle of trust. There is a profound and intimate reason as to why each individual has a seat at this table. His father and sisters are bonded to him by blood. Rachel is his lover and fiancé. Michael and Benjamin were his two best friends. Jasmine and Ashley are significant others of theirs. These three couples had been bonded in amorous relationships since they were young, and had thrived as they grew up into adulthood.

Michael and Benjamin gently but yet soundly tap their champagne glasses with their spoons.

Benjamin: My brother is all grown up! I still can't believe it. He has everything he could ever want, a beautiful woman to marry and support him. I am so happy for you boy! Success and nothing less!

Michael: I have known you for most of our lives and I have never seen you so happy. From one brother to another, I am happy for you. I am always going to be here for you my brother. You deserve this day.

Michael and Benjamin walk over to Patrick and playfully embrace him while messing with his well-placed hair. Patrick, who is smiling from ear to ear, gets up and hugs them both. Patrick then with his face blushing like a rose turns toward the crowd.

Patrick: I love these guys. Seriously, love them to death. For as long as I can remember, we've been brothers, and you guys are the best friends that anyone could ask for.

Patrick turns to Rachel.

Patrick: And baby, I can never imagine what I would be without you. I am the luckiest man in the world. There is no dollar amount that can show how much you mean to me. I cannot wait to marry you.

Patrick takes a bow. The crowd gets fired into a frenzy. Loud raptures of applause thunders out as the elated couple share a kiss for all to see.

Patrick: To love and marriage!!

Crowd: Love and marriage!!!

Patrick shudders, as if an arrow is shot right through his lungs. He felt starved of air.

The music starts to blear, celebrants begin to take to the dance floor. Patrick heads out to the balcony on the higher level for a smoke and a quiet sip of wine on his own. Michael and Benjamin notice their brother exit the room, they decide to join him.

Michael: What are you doing out here all alone?

Benjamin: You alright man?

Patrick: I'm alright, I'm alright. Don't worry about me.

Patrick looks distant and dismissive.

Michael: You know you can tell us anything right?

Michael says so as reassuringly and as affirmatively as he can possibly do so.

Patrick: It's nothing, just thinking about some bullshit.

Benjamin: Don't tell me you're still thinking about Amy or whoever? Forget that stuff Patrick! Go see whoever tomorrow if you really need it that bad!

Michael: Shut up Ben! Seriously?

Michael takes the wine glass out of Patrick's hand and tosses its liquid over the edge of the balcony.

Michael: Now it's time to look forward to the future. Tonight's a night for celebration alright?

Benjamin: I know man, you're getting married!

Benjamin says so as he shakes Patrick at the shoulders. Almost as if to awaken Patrick. Patrick sighs and looks to the stars in the sky.

Patrick: It's just stuff you know? None of this will mean a thing if we get arrested next week.

Michael: We won't. Don't worry.

Patrick: How do you know?

Michael: I just know. We're invincible. We were meant to do this! Anyone who dares to come into our way, I feel sorry for those fools.

Michael's conviction brings about determination within Patrick.

Michael: Now trust me alright! Trust Ben! When have we ever failed you?! We're all we got.

This is not an uplifting guarantee that Michael was offering to his friend, Patrick. To Michael however, this is a factual truth.

Michael lights up his own cigar and offers Patrick one.

Patrick hesitates for a moment. Then he forcefully snatches the cigar and accepts Michael's celebratory initiation.

Patrick: Alright! Thanks for everything!

Patrick lights it up.

The celebration progresses into the night, with the serving of food and drinks, every single person is thoroughly enjoying themselves. It has turned out to be the gala that everyone had been anticipating it to be. The Night remains young, and they are going to celebrate and live while they were young! Reckless abandon for time and space, all that matters is this current moment. Food, alcohol, music, dancing, it is truly a blissful night.

As dusk turns to dawn, the celebration and its attendees slowly transition back to reality. It is now time for everyone to turn back to their real lives.

2

Rain pours down on the land below. Michael, Patrick and Benjamin leave a car and go ahead to meet their partners in crime, Victor and Travis, their brothers in bloodshed and mayhem. Numerous encounters with violence and death had hardened these young men's souls and robbed them of all sympathy and empathy. They have no regard for the worth of human life, especially the lives of their enemies. Their only loyalty is to money and nothing else. Mark, one of their brothers in arms had been slain by their rival, Nicholas. Nicholas was a sworn enemy of theirs, a rival, a competitor who has to be eliminated at all costs.

They sit in the car outside Nicholas' house. They are armed and ready. The impact of what they were about to undertake would be of extraordinary significance. If successful, they would attain vengeance while robbing all the riches that Nicholas has to offer. Both objectives are of equal importance.

Patrick: Ready for this?

Travis: I've been ready for a while.

He asseverated with a steel glare of a man possessed. Everyone else nodes at him in silent consent, they are all salivating at the sweet scent of vengeance.

Patrick: After this, we're done.

Victor: No doubt.

Benjamin: I want to kill him myself.

They smash down the door of Nicholas' residence. They are fully concealed with masks, hunting for their prey. Screams emanates from all the throats of each dweller within the residence. The intruders can sniff out the fear pulsating through each screamer's veins. The blood brothers quickly secure the perimeter of the compound. The brothers in arms swiftly overwhelm the residence and those who live within. Those who live within are left sobbing in disbelief and stiffened with fear. The intruders pilfered, trampled and rifled through the house, searching for their prizes. Eventually, they find Nicholas, he is in a drunken slumber.
They forcefully land strikes upon Nicholas. He tosses and turns, incredulous with pain. Nicholas is defeated.

Patrick withdraws his stance to soak in the moment even further. Then he reasserts himself by returning to his former stance, with no hesitation.
Patrick elects not to take Nicholas' life. Thus, allowing Nicholas to live on as a cripple. Patrick makes sure to inform Nicholas of this transpiration. And that this was nobody else's fault, but Nicholas' alone.
Nicholas looks into the eyes of his assailant, numbed by

pain, scanning his own thoughts and memories trying to figure out what or why this was happening to him.

Nicholas' wife screams in horror, their children shriek uncontrollably. The intruders follow to assail the rest of the family, feeding on their fear. They proceed to extract a substantial amount of cash and continue to pilfer the house of all items of value. The blood brothers are content with their accomplishment. They had obtained what they came for. The blood brothers catch themselves in their ecstatic elation and realize that they could not leave any witnesses alive to reveal their deadly resolve here this night. So one by one, the witnesses fall. And as quickly as the blood brothers entered the house, they are gone laughing into the night. Their reckless abandon for reason and sentiment for life had claimed yet another horrified set of victims, indelibly scarred for life. It was as if their victims' submission to their will made them stronger, and they were determined to gain their victims' surrender by any means. These blood brothers are servants to their own recklessness and their warfare has many vain intents.

3

They return to their house, exploding with pride and excitement. It is a rush they had felt one too many times. Thrill had consumed every fiber of their entire being. The financial compensation and the satisfaction of vengeance, so sweet it was. The blood on their hands is of a badge of honor. It is a symbol of the willingness and temerity to do what is necessary to defend one's own pride and honor. They have no hesitation or pity to do what they thought was right. They crave it.

Benjamin turns to the liquor cabinet and pulls out some tequila. He hands out some beers to his blood brothers.

Benjamin: You realize what just happened? We really did it back there!

Victor: No doubt, no doubt!

Patrick raises his drink to give a toast.

Patrick: Listen, this is to you guys.

                I never thought I would say this but as of now, I am truly happy. I love you guys.

                We are brothers forever!

Travis: They got what was coming anyways

Their vast greed for money has proliferated into every action that they take. Money supersedes everything in their mind.

Patrick: Forget those people! Tonight is about us! And nothing else!

It is the greatest night of their life. How could it not be? They have got drinks, food and beautiful women who are not their significant others to enliven their lusting hearts. They indulge in a night of alcohol, sex and drugs, something they have alas, done one too many times and far too often. But this night stands alone and preeminent in great significance and magnificence because of their accomplishments.

Patrick slips away secretly from his brothers' coronation of each other's treacherous achievements.

4

Hours later, Michael awakens from his drunken daze. He looks around at his friends, who are still deep within their slumber. Taking a deep breath, he cherishes all that the moment has to offer, he grows fond of the new memories he and his brothers had created. He remains blissfully certain of the future. His throat is parched, so he decided to take a sip of water. As the liquid gushes down his throat and down through his system, he feels refreshed. Everything is going to be alright.

Benjamin walks into the room where Michael is resting.

Benjamin: Hey, where's Patrick?

Michael: I don't know? I just woke up.

Benjamin: What time is it?

Michael: Six.

Benjamin: Damn. Last night was amazing.

Michael: I know

Patrick returns hours later, his face concealed with a mask, he opens the door, he immediately overpowers Victor and Travis. Victor and Travis stood no chance as they were in a deep slumber upon the couch. The elimination of Victor and Travis buoyed Patrick's resolve. For if the night ever were to turn ill for Patrick, chances are that it would have been because of those two, for they were skilled in the arts of physical combat.

Patrick had come to satisfy a burning desire. He could care less about how many lives he took. And he is willing to sacrifice his own life for this achievement. Everybody involved could very well lose everything.

A surge of calm concentration spreads through Patrick's body, he walks forcefully through the doorway intently focused on finding his two remaining 'blood brothers'. He could sense the reaching of his goal and attaining of all the grand riches that it offers. He wants the riches all to himself. The propitious sum of cash will take him to another level of bliss. He needs the money to sustain the affluent lifestyle that he has established with Rachel. Expensive clothes, outings and belongings. This plunder will undoubtedly secure his and her future. The greed and the perception of need possesses Patrick and forces him to sever all bonds of brotherhood and commit wickedness in cold blood.

Benjamin and Michael were shocked out of their wits as they see the masked man round the corner towards them.

Benjamin: What the?!

Michael remains silent as this atrocity unfolds before

him. The masked man takes aim in their direction, they duck and hide under the kitchen counters, they outlast the first wave of attack from the masked man's gun. They unveil themselves from their hiding area and retaliate. A fierce battle ensues within the kitchen.

In the heat of battle, the masked Patrick tries to make a run for the cash. Michael and Benjamin realize the motives of the assailant. They then fervently defend their prize. A skirmish of untamed animalistic aggression unfolds. Both sides desperately need prevail and are willing to take out their enemy to gain the upper hand.

The masked man heads for one of the false walls and retrieves a weapon. Michael and Benjamin are incredulous that the mysterious attacker knew where it was, a nauseating sensation brews at the abyss that was their minds. Michael and Benjamin know that something is not right here.

Michael and Benjamin try to hide for cover once again, they both go for the same corner, but Benjamin is there first and gets to the spot underneath a desk where another weapon is concealed, Benjamin inadvertently shoves Michael aside. The primal beasts within them are revealed. In the fight for survival, sworn brotherhood can be tossed aside like a grain of sand in the long road to self-preservation. This leaves Michael vulnerable to the masked man's assault. Michael is then greatly overwhelmed. Michael lies on his back, staring at the ceiling.

The masked Patrick realizes that Michael is no longer a threat and is as good as dead. He turns his attention to the existential threat that is Benjamin. The uncertainty and fear is grossly thickening in the air, almost strangling in its control over thought.

Benjamin: What do you want?!

He shouts at the top of his lungs' capacity.

The sheer angst and desperation of his voice bellows from the depths of his diaphragm. The masked assailant unleashes another wave of attack. The attack penetrates the safe confines of the overturned living room table. Benjamin recognizes that there is a pause in the assault of the masked attacker, Benjamin, recognizing that this is his opportunity to retaliate, immediately springs from beneath the table, all bets are off, either the attacker's relentless assault will eventually claim Benjamin's life, or Benjamin would be the aggressor and end this predicament on his own terms.

As the masked Patrick prepares to begin another wave of aggression, Benjamin's aggression brings him Patrick to the realization that his enemy is not yet defeated and is coming in strength.

A fight continues. Benjamin eventually strikes the masked Patrick in a strategic area of the body, a sharp cry of agony and shock emanates from Patrick, Patrick falls. Benjamin moves in once more, realizing that his enemy no longer poses any immediate or fatal danger to him. Benjamin carefully approaches the masked man, placing one hand on the mask and pulling it off to unveil his wounded foe.

It is one of his closest friends, Patrick, gasping for air. It is quickly materializing into reality that these are to be his final moments. Benjamin is at a loss of words, all of a sudden, he is thrown into the process of losing a dear friend, a brother in arms. The aggressive acts of both were in accordance to all that Benjamin believes. These beliefs were deemed by Benjamin to be correct and good up to this point in his life. Trespassers and betrayals were to be dealt with, acted upon with swift vengeance and no mercy. Benjamin is entranced by the shocking revelation, he shudders and stumbles backward, all his best friends laid motionless on the floor which is stained with battle scars. In his bewildered state, Patrick launches one last assault against Benjamin which hurts Benjamin.

The wounded Benjamin then snaps out of his trance and shock, he falls back, he gathers his thoughts, the emotionless animal within him awakens to strike back against Patrick. It is an insatiable creature that is eventually satisfied by the sight of a wounded Patrick backing away for cover and clinging on for dear life. In realizing that the battle was lost, Patrick musters all that remained within him and flees for his life. Patrick suffered multiple wounds. If he had not fled, he would have surely died. He is now in a state of profound aesthetic decrepitude. He barely trots off into the night, he hopes to find help wherever he goes.

Benjamin takes a deep breath and sits down. His attention then turns to his own immediate state of health. He takes off his shirt to wrap his wounds. After the open wound is no longer critical or life threatening, Benjamin surveys the room, he realizes that Michael is gasping for air. Common sense gnaws at him to take Michael to the nearest medical facility. However, the scheming and ever-calculating criminal mind within him separates him from all reason and human attachment. "Those damn medical facilities and authorities ask too many questions." Benjamin thinks to himself.

He gets up and limps towards the money and stashes as much of it as he can into the biggest bag he could get his hands on. Throughout the frantic moments of packing and stashing, he does not turn to even look into the eyes of his ailing friend Michael. Is it the guilt of his deeds that drives him into profound shame and avoidance of Michael? Or is it the sheer concentration of a materialistic and malicious man who is so consumed by the urgency of the moment to extract the money and flee the scene and the consequences of his actions? In all honesty, neither the former nor the latter is clear.

"Why would I risk my freedom for another man? What use is he to me?" That is the question and statement that prevails in Benjamin's process of reasoning.

Freedom. That is the chief tone that is striking within all these blood brothers. No one knows what the future holds, for they are blood brothers no more.

Michael lays less than ten feet away from the frantic Benjamin, Michael is a picture of frailty. Every breath is a struggle, he is incredulous at what is transpiring. He is witnessing Benjamin's blatant and complete avoidance of his presence and plight. And like the gentle breeze of the cold autumn night, Benjamin leaves the premises. These actions occupied all of Michael's concentration. His focus floats around the room, he sees the wreckage of battle all over the room, he also sees the richly adorned decorations of the room, plus the heavily affluent belongings that they had collected and maintained through their relatively short time on this world. It all means nothing to him now as he fades. Michael starts to think of his relationships and his dearest kinsman. He is full of regret, but strangely, he is able to immediately discard the burden of this regret to peacefully resign to the inevitable fate that is now all too real. His vision begins to blur.

This is it, he knows it in his heart. He is going to die. A tidal wave of sensation envelopes his body and all his sensory nerve ends. All substantial and existential pain is numbed out. Nothing else mattered, all his past misdeeds became irrelevant, all his deep psychological and physical pains past him by and washed away from his mind. Everything is of utter quietness.

As he feels his life-force beginning to flee from his existence, so too does all that burdened him with great weight. He does not know what this is that is enveloping him. There was no pain, no sorrow. It is calm and serene, even though

Michael knows that he is in pain and sorrow. It just feels real, but also far away from him. He does not think of the past, he knows that he has a past, but it has no effectuality. He is in touch with a great excitement. This feeling envelopes and flows through Michael. As It courses through Michael's very being, Michael's body seems to lose all sense of mass and sensation. A part of Michael panics at this onslaught as he senses that he is on the precipice of trotting upon new territory. Fear and panic eventually gives way, due to an actuality of a growing glow of quietness. Michael's mind begins to feel a great elation that his being is experiencing such euphoria. And then, Michael's mind senses that his body is not losing mass or sensation. Rather, it is just getting overwhelmed by many sensations that the body is having a difficult time orienting itself to. His mind begins to grasp on to the moment. As Michael enters this new plain of existence, he is made to know that this Space here, it is the Space of the Mind. Every man, woman and child in history has passed through this Space. It is thus, infinitely vast beyond measure. For every one of them have a Mind, and thus, all in history will come to this Space. And Michael is to know that there is so much that happens in a Mind that is out of the mindful control or will of the person. This significance flows through Michael, he does not know yet what it means. He tries to see it. He wants to get a grasp of it. Then at the moment of sublime balanced continuity, Michael is revived.

He had found peace.

All turned to a quiet stillness.

Michael thinks about how he was once told that the Dead know nothing, for their bodily functions have lost its source of impetus. Michael thinks, the Space of nothingness could be the lightening feeling that he has now espoused as sweetness.

5

Michael's eyelids peel open from a slumber of which its duration is unknown to him. His complexion is pale and sullen. He stares blankly at space. He has no idea where he is. He has no idea what time or place he is occupying. He notices that he is connected to a series of intravenous drips and equipment. Alas, Michael realizes that he is in a hospital facility.

In that moment of mild confusion, a woman dressed in a healthcare uniform enters the room and checks the equipment by his bed. She checks off several things on her checklist. She has what Michael thinks is an adorable haircut. After ensuring that everything is in order, the woman tends to Michael's wounds cautiously with great care. She makes sure that there are no signs of infection or excessive bleeding. Her intense focus is disrupted from the sight of Michael's inadvertent gaze at her.

Nurse: Oh hello sweety. How are you feeling?

Michael: I'm ok.

His voice is so silently subtle that it is almost undetectable.

Nurse: My name is Irena. I'm just checking your
                      wounds and all your vital signs honey.

She has a delightful tone to her voice. There is so much
warmth in her every breath.

Michael: Alright, thanks.

Michael is experiencing a moment of perplexing light-
hearted confusion. The compassion and unconditional love
for another, it was and still is an aspect of humanity that he
had completely overseen in days gone by. He greatly desires
to express his immediate and profound gratitude towards
Irena. However, this act of pure unfiltered good will that is
being sent forth his way from Irena is too overwhelming for
him to comprehend or digest. And so, silence and rigidity
continues to dominate his disposition.
      Irena continues to dutifully organize his bedside so as to
make it more presentable. Then she turns back to Michael.

Irena: Would you be needing anything honey? A
                      drink? A blanket maybe?

Michael: *No thanks.*

Michael whispers.

Irena: Alright then, have a good night, I'll be
                      around to check on you every now and then.

She turns and exits the room.

Michael lightly exhales a scant, cramped breath. He had barely breathed the entire time he was experiencing Irena's care. He takes a moment for inward clarity and to collect his thoughts. The goodness of humanity had exalted Michael with its righteousness. He is experiencing a sort of tranquil light-heartedness, like the one he was brushed with in what he presumed to be his last moments on this world, only this time, he harbors the cognitive and physiological ability to truly appreciate its every drop of hallowed and lucid brilliance. It reminds him how fleeting life can be, he wants to feel this magnificence permanently. It is now his life's goal to replicate and perpetuate this grand sensation.

As he wanders through his thoughts, the unfortunate truth is that his mind does not intrinsically understand what it is to be free. At this point of his life, there are too many unresolved issues that needed validation of some sort, there are far too many questions left unanswered. To him, freedom is only a sense, a feeling that is unequivocal in the ocean that was life. He seeks to navigate through those waters, but lacked the sense of direction. It is frustrating to not be able to feel the way he wants to.

As he orientates himself to this empty room, he cannot help but realize that there are no visitors to commiserate with. This unsettling nature of this loneliness triggers all the negative emotions and soon enough, the dreadful memories begin to insidiously creep its way back into his mind, leaving an unpleasant sting. He begins to be paralyzed by those haunting memories, his body convulses uncontrollably with each passing vision relative to episodes of vitriol and violence done unto him. He feels a tide of wrath within him. He claws at the pillows and bed sheets. He has a pounding in his heart that is intensifying his focus on one singular intention, revenge. He needs blood to set right all that was wronged upon him. He loses sight of the reason for him to be alive and breathing. He has tunnel vision on this need for vengeance, he cares not about how or why he is lying in this bed and enduring the commencement of rehabilitation. His mind and thoughts are raging with a truly rotten hatred for the individuals he formally professed to be blood brothers.

As Michael shudders and convulses, the mind unconscionably and forcibly flashes images of that horrid event before Michael, enslaving him to relive it time and time again. Michael sees Patrick being possessed by greed, Patrick's irises demonically searing Michael with its gaze as Patrick blasted Michael relentlessly without hesitation. Michael remembers being filled with incredible pain and confusion. Michael remembers being petrified, yet calm, as he awaited his newly anointed foe to stand over him and deliver the kill-shot that never came.

Then, the focus of his memory shifts towards Benjamin, who vanquished the imminent threat that was Patrick, but refused to even acknowledge the very presence of a dying Michael. In the periphery of this vision, was Patrick fleeing with debilitating injuries. An agonizing and profound regret that Patrick had not perished that night flows through the progression of Michael's thoughts. Patrick did not deserve to leave that room with his life. Patrick did not even deserve to live.

The faint prospect of Patrick's continued existence aggravated Michael. In being coupled with the betrayal offered up by Benjamin, this ultimately sums up in further venom to Michael's fresh searing wounds. Their every breath insults Michael. Michael is experiencing a very clear hindsight. Michael dwells upon every verbal and non-verbal form of communication that he ever experienced with those two foes. All that had happened seemed to have had telling signs of this current inevitability, its consequences were now amplified by the morbid realization that there is now no turning back. This reality incessantly grips on Michael's body, his body turns cold, he cannot even find the capacity to scream or shout in frustration. At this point, the convulsions have progressed into an unnerving stillness. There is a glistening of the body with the copious amount of sweat caused by the unveiling of this violent truth.

Nurse Irena returns into the room, at first glance she is taken aback at how much Michael had perspired.

Irena: O my goodness, are you alright? You're sweating so much!

Michael stays quiet.

Irena: Let me check your vitals!

Irena checks all the readings on the machines.

Irena: Well, your temperature seems fine, but your pulse is through the roof. Are you experiencing any pain?

Michael: I'm fine. I'm just a little cold.

As Michael says these words, his focus leaves the situation. As his mind races, it hinders his ability to slip into a slumber. Michael lays down in detachment from himself, he recognizes that this racing within his mind has been extended and prolonged for far too long. He then sees how his thoughts have raced over all his events, past and present. He decides to no longer resent that rapidity of his thoughts as a burden barring him from a sleep which he will wake up from. Rather, Michael decides to appreciate his mind's ability to put forth such a fluid and smooth force within him that stands proficient and dexterous. As he stops resenting it, he finds an appreciation of this gift of being able to not only process, but also welcome situations. Michael sees no benefit in trying to curtail or abate this gift. Instead, as he presently lets it flow, he finds that the rapid processes of his examinations have already begun to bring a semblance of peace and quiet to his mind.

Irena: O I see, it's just the withdrawal effects of the morphine that you've received for the operation. It's quite common. Just try to relax. I'll get you some juice ok honey?

Michael: Ok.

Irena: Let me know if anything changes my dear?

Michael feels faint and shudders. He had expended a significant amount of energy. He falls into a deep slumber.

When he awakes again, he sees a carton of juice by his bedside. His early morning vigor is immediately brought down to a certain morose despondency. It is a feeling of purposelessness. He is a Man in need of direction, and Michael has none to speak of. Now that he has had time to absorb the vicious blows that his life had laid upon him, he felt shattered and broken. Sleep, it seemed had brought him no peace.

All that he had known to be true was full of lies and deceit. All his life, his social surroundings had lauded the traits of greed. Michael was taught to savor the blandishments that a relentless drive fuelled by greed would provide. That was all he had come to appreciate, he understood no other meaning of life. This fatalistic view of life further compounded his misery, because as of this moment, there were no blandishments, he had nothing, he is nothing, all is lost. And what is worse, he has no one to help weather this malicious storm. Neither his body nor his mind offers him the quietness when he seeks solace and repose. There is nowhere he can run to hide from this searing truth. All is lost.

All he can think of is to get even with those who had done harm unto him. His thirst for revenge is not just limited to Patrick and Benjamin. He wanted to lay waste to them and their families. Through his rehabilitation process, he realizes just how broken his body is and was, the act of ambulation was an arduous process which at times brought tears to his eyes. The very need for revenge weighs heavily on him, it drains him of a great majority of his energy, and it continuously occupies most of his thoughts. He wants it so bad with a great desire. It is slowly consuming him.

Every miniscule event or occurrence seems to trigger an unflinching chain of memories and flashbacks that serve as horrible thorns that are the bane of his existence. It is insidiously robbing him of all pleasures in his life. It is his entire world that now hovers over him, casting a long shadow that obscures what bit of hope that is left in his mind.

Days pass seemingly without grace, and it takes a grinding toll on Michael, he is a helpless prisoner of circumstance. He is broken. He regrets waking up every morning. Inevitably, the thoughts of suicide creeps from the darkest shadows of his mind. It is not long before it frequents the forefront of his thought process, emanating as a favorable solution to all his hardships.

One day, this fatalistic attitude drives him to search out and find a weapon. Michael can no longer take the subjugation of his own mind to these imprisoning memories. Every passing moment makes him weaker. In his desperation, he holds a weapon and prepares to take his own life. In anticipation of affliction, he retracts the weapon from the fear of an inordinate amount of pain. It is in this very moment that it dawns upon him, it is just the thought of the finality of death that seems like a potent escape to resolve his very plight. However, this realization did serve as a distraction that took his mind off his hellacious reality, even if it is just for a brief moment, it is a welcomed event. In a bizarre turn of events, when experiencing times of heightened stress, he would almost find a fortuitous solace in that thought of death. It is in the end, not suicide where Michael finds solace. for he now knows that he does not harbor the will to take his own life. In his mind, it is a pain that he is not willing to bring upon himself, no matter how laden with appalling circumstances his life develops to be. He now ascertains that he will never meet a self-directed demise as his end, he is obstinate in this belief.

As time passes, he forms a clearer perspective in which to perceive the events that have been consigned unto him. He now meets memories with a more reflective thought process, rather than an irascible need to find an immediate solution or a way out, such as having revenge or taking his own life. He realizes that his now timorous heart has been morally debased at the very core of its foundations of beliefs. These beliefs have seemingly blindsided him, and he is now left with the remnants of what he had formally considered to be a full life.

All his life, he had followed a set of beliefs. It had evolved over his years. But the general direction of those beliefs had been sculpted by his individuality that was in turn influenced by those around him, his blood brothers. They were the pillars and foundation of the edifice. In one fell swoop, his foundational beliefs and support were ripped away from him, and he almost paid the ultimate price as a consequence of his petulance.

As he surveys the ruins of his current predicament with his newly found intrinsic sense of reasoning and knowledge, there is nowhere to go but travel inward to overcome the cravenness that is churning within.

As he journeys inward, Michael realizes that his spirituality is teeming with strife and is incongruous in nature. He is a lost soul, so to speak. It is volatile in temperament, constantly sending itself into a torrent of unrest with haunting visions of the past. It is a constant state of unrest. Try as he may, he simply cannot block out the images of unhappiness. When he does try to forcibly redirect his thoughts, it only triggers a more vicious onslaught of pain due to his failures, and thus, further bludgeoning him with contradicting incongruity. His abrasive approach with failure is yielding no rewards, peace continues to elude him.

Irena comes back into his room with her usual pleasant disposition.

Irena: Hello,

Michael looks at her with astonishment and relief. Astonishment because she is advantageously pleasant on the eyes and relief as she has once again rescued him from the torture of being imprisoned by his own mind.

Irena is slightly taken aback at Michael's response for a brief moment. She is an experienced caregiver and recognizes the angst on his face. Therefore, she uses a lighter tone of voice and touches his hand.

Irena: Today is the day. Are you ready?

Michael: For what?

Irena:	For your rehab my dear. You're getting discharged. You can go home.
Michael:	Oh I see.
Irena:	You alright?
Michael:	Yes.

Michael pauses to think for a moment.

Michael:	Yes, it's just that you caught me off guard there. And, I guess I'll kind of miss this place.
Irena:	I see. Well, you could always come and visit. Let me just do one last check on all your vitals ok honey?

All his vitals check out fine. Another man comes in with a vacant wheelchair to wheel Michael to fetch a ride. Michael is immensely grateful for Irena's benevolence towards him. As he sits down in the chair, he looks up at her, his voice crackles up, raw with nostalgic gloom.

Michael:	Thanks for everything.
Irena:	You're welcome sweetheart. All the best in the future.

As Michael departs the room with the man wheeling him, Michael is evidently lighter in mood. All the tension in his mind is temporarily put at ease. The care and compassion that he feels is greatly resonating warmly within him. He hitches a ride on the hospital's transport service that carries him safely to the rehabilitative care facility. He spends the entire ride fixated upon the good will of humanity. The kindliness of the fresh spring morning embraces Michael with its tender soft touch. Hope is beginning to spring within Michael's mind.

6

Michael sets foot upon the rehabilitation center's premises. His eyes behold the welcoming sight of a freshly manicured garden adorned with a multitude of colorful plants surrounding a fountain spring. All about the garden traverses people with visible physical impairments accompanied by what one would think are caring companions. Patients and visitors also lounge upon the lawn furniture to sit and congregate with one another.

Michael is then wheeled into the facility and is passed on from the hospital transport worker to a rehabilitative facility worker. As he is wheeled down the halls of the facility, the facility worker and he engage in standard conversational acts of rudimentary acquaintance levels. Michael notices that with each inhalation, there is a distinct but peculiar scent in the hallways. Michael is then subsequently introduced to the team of care workers. They follow to introduce themselves. There is the physician, physical therapist, psychologist, social worker and then the nurse in charge of all care in the facility.

After an extensive conversation and executing all the

insipid administrative work with the medical team, Michael was brought to meet his fellow patients. The therapists believe that when it comes to reparations of a holistic nature, it is safe to assume that establishing a social support network is to be an effective strategy in nurturing each patient's healing process.

As Michael is brought in, it is just in time for afternoon tea. The opportunity arises for Michael to meet all of his fellow patients, staff and volunteers on the unit. Fellow patients vary along the spectrum of pleasantry, some were heavily blight socially and emotionally, while others were pleasantly outgoing in conversations about their diagnosis and history, and then there were those who were pleased to meet his very acquaintance. Michael forges fateful bonds with them in that split second, and while it proved to help pass the time during his therapeutic treatments, there is a certain unfulfilling nature about their bonds to him in Michael's mind.

Perhaps it is because Michael never fully discloses his life's story with them. He has not and will not shed any light upon his true malcontent with life, about how he is exasperatedly screaming on the inside, that he has a venomously malicious will to achieve homicidal deeds. It is due to this fallen nature that Michael never experiences a complete mutual compassion with these companions. It continues to be purely superficial in his mind, too shallow to be substantial. He gingerly treads around each conversation, constantly remaining guarded about the truth and details in his life, attempting to seem normal and content. All this fortification however, takes its toll on Michael. It is emotionally draining on him, each passing day would become more and more suppressing in nature. On occasion, when experiencing hardships in his rehabilitation, he would explode in a paroxysm of rage inwardly as well as outwardly. These incidences were purely demonic in nature. From Michael's understandings of the medical team's explanation of this issue beforehand, when it did occur inwardly, his blood pressure would spike in a perilous fashion, his body temperature would rise inexplicably, blood vessels would constrict to cause varying levels of discomfort, anger, panic and loss of rationale or logic in his outward behavior. Michael's state was hazardously being bludgeoned into despondency. Almost all experiences in his daily life are being steered through dreariness, he especially has an unyielding disdain towards what he thought to be the condescending sympathy of others, every episode of interpersonal communication is comprehended as having some level of negative connotation attached to it.

He is slumping in stagnation. It is a vile state of mind that offers him no solace or comfort. He cannot seem to appreciate joy. The effects of sorrow seem so much more amplified than it should be. In the premises of his mind exists the ever present need for retaliation and vengeance, which only aggravated the inflamed wounds of body and mind. Every fiber of this the body and mind is being arduously gnawed upon by his vitriolic fixation and obsession with the past. He feels an unyielding shame for his current state, he wishes for no one he knows to see him like this.

This intrinsic thought process leads to a very lonesome existence. Relationships of all sorts in his life fall into decay as he is both incapable and unwilling to maintain them. Even though Michael will not admit it, he continues to be grief-stricken from the loss of previous bonds. He also lacks the cognizance and willingness to form new ones.

Out of the darkness one Thursday afternoon, while Michael is on his way to the physical therapy room, the same room which he had been reporting to for the past few arduous weeks, the grace of humanity decided to pay Michael a charmed visit. There she is, a nurse in a lime green uniform and long flowing hair. The loose nature of her uniform does not hide her natural feminine curves. Her complexion is picturesque, and her hair is fluid like nectar. Within this line of sight, Michael realizes that one of his fellow patients needs help getting up from his chair. He is an elderly man and from the looks of it, he is recovering from a lower body weakness. From the way he leans, Michael sees that the elderly man is not able to hinge upon his legs and feet to rise into a standing position. He seems to struggle with each attempt to rise out of his chair. Michael ceases this opportunity to acquaint himself with this nurse.

Michael: Um, Nurse,

She turns toward Michael, her beauty descends upon Michael, seeing this however, Michael remains in complete control of his composure and instantaneously replies,

Michael: I think he needs help.

He says so calmly, all while pointing at the man. She proceeds to tend to the patient, helping him up to his feet and escorting him out of the room. Michael walks with them. After assuring himself that this is all that is needed of him in this moment, he musters the gumption to speak to the nurse again,

Michael: Sorry about calling you 'Nurse'.

Nurse: Oh that's ok.

Michael: By the way, what is your name?

Nurse: It's Darcy.

Michael is taken aback by the crack of a smile that Darcy hints as she introduces herself.

Michael: I'm Michael. Nice to meet you.

Darcy: Nice to meet you too.

Her mild gaze holds Michael captive for an instant. Both of them seemingly beholds the other with a certain delight. He smiles back and continues towards his area of treatment after saying goodbye. On his way to the designated area, Michael realizes that through his time spent in the facility, he no longer notices the distinct scent of the hallways which he immediately detected when he first came to the facility. It no longer stands out to his perception anymore.

In this designated room, he continues to suffer the hardships of having a precarious and fragile mindset. Pain is the preeminent tone of this particular room. In this room, there was much physical failure and shortcomings that is to be experienced and has been endured. Michael scantily trots through another hour of therapy. At the end of his session, he is in mental and physical anguish. He is not what he used to be. He wants to feel no pain in doing ordinary activities such as walking. He just wants to feel like the normal self he was before all these unfortunate circumstances presented themselves to him. He is bitter that such unfavorable circumstances had befallen him.

As he walked through the hallways of the facility towards the familiar exit, there Darcy is, on her way to the bathroom. They cordially stop at the sight of each other.

Michael: I guess I'll see you around Darcy.

Michael utters this with an amorous tone while tapping her shoulder.

Darcy: You're leaving? Hold on! Follow me.

They went into her assigned unit to retrieve a box.

Darcy: I'm selling chocolates for my brother.

She said with a gleeful smile.

Michael: Oh. How much is one?

Darcy: Two dollars.

Michael: Well, anything for the children right?

Darcy: Thanks.

A gentle pause takes place as they both absorb the moment and Michael hesitantly picks out a chocolate.

Michael: How old is your brother?

Darcy: He's ten.

She says this while looking out the window.

Michael: Well, you tell him to stay in school ok?

Darcy: I will.

Michael: What time are you working until?

Darcy: Seven.

Michael: Well, don't work too hard alright?

Darcy: I won't. Thanks again. I'll see you around.

That exchange took place faster than Michael would have preferred for it to have taken. But given the fact that he was reeling from therapy, he lacked the capacity and will to carry out all his desired interactions. However, he is satisfied with his new acquaintance. Michael feels a great enticement. Everything about her leaves a pleasant occupation of Michael's mind.

Michael was infatuated with her from the moment he first met her. Her scent was pleasant. Her eyes lit up with a wholesome but yet, seducing outlook at each interaction no matter what the situation. Her accent was distinctively unique and amiable. Her voice was soft and tender. Her smile was unequivocally fair. Her skin was smooth and firm, sultrier than any other that Michael had ever touched. Michael could lose himself within her.

But as the moments wore on along his way home, the soreness in his muscles began to resurface at the forefront of his mind. This path of healing was indeed, going to be a process.

Michael has had to learn to reactivate all the muscles in his body. Muscle weakness and atrophy had overwhelmed Michael's physiology through his operation, sedation and prolonged state of being bed-ridden. He had taken all his past neural cohesiveness and muscular flexibility, strength and endurance for granted. In his weakened state, it was all too prevalent from his perspective that substantial losses were continuing to mount in his life. And with the continued failure experienced in therapy, it only leads him down a path of additional bitterness and anger. The aforementioned precariousness that is his current state of mind, takes from him all the capacity to coalesce socially with any factions of peoples. He is in a horrible and constant state of unease internally. He became overly sensitive to seemingly normal interactions, constantly misconstruing or misunderstanding the intentions of others, this apprehension often lead him to obscure messages of a neutral or positive tone into that of a negative or detrimental nature. These anemic forms of comprehension leads him to endure decrepit forms of communication, always demonizing people in his mind, always expecting the worst for their intentions. At least inwardly, fellow patients' remarks would constantly reinvigorate a vile hatred within him. He had not quite understood what that hatred was supposed to be directed at. Whenever he was alone in a room, his mind wandered. At some level, channeling his former self in terms of vile urges regarding violence, he just wanted to bring harm upon everyone that ever begrudged him on any level. It did not matter to Michael whether or not it was intentional or unintentional on their part. It just seemed like the only way out. It seemingly brought him instantaneous relief of the mind. The mental image of carnage being spilled seemed to appease some part of him. These thoughts brought further complications to an already internally contentious mind within. Michael is languishing in the fall, obscured in a dispirited prison of the mind with absolutely nowhere to run to. These negative thoughts were his mind's way of coping with his situation. These were delusions of grandeur, it brought some sort of internal comfort to his mind, that's why he did it. He allowed himself to revert to a previous adaptation of his life's doctrine. There was no rhyme or reason why he dreamt of bringing tyranny upon strangers. He did so and felt a sluggish comfort in doing so. However, it did not bring him peace of mind, just a temporary relief from strife. That is why he continues to search for alternative methods of comfort. Peace however, would continue to elude him.

He is his only outlet for dialogue and deliberation. It is a self-antagonistic form of problem solving. All his perspectives lacked insight or objective perception. Sorrow evolved into voracious anger. He beholds his past with a venomous disdain, an unctuous weight it is, strangling him and dragging him down to the bottom of the abyss. With each new day, he feels he sinks to a new low. With each new day, Michael regrets waking up. He feels the consignment of sorrowful feelings to be a pathetic weakness and grows to detest it. Michael will seek to eradicate them.

He becomes so overwhelmed with angst and desires to inflict pain upon those who ever caused him harm in his life. He is driven to restless madness by the inane memories of past betrayals. He remembers what he can of his experiences. Somehow, even past events with no semblance of correlation or prevalence to his current situation, end up being disturbingly modified in context by his mind into acts of betrayals against him. Unfounded hatred is then engendered within this very same mind towards indiscriminate past relationships. Most of the revulsion is directed towards those in his closest inner social circle of family and friends. As a result of that engendering, he begins to act in accordance of this thought processes and isolate himself even more. He eventually comes to the conclusion that in order to make peace with all that has been imposed upon him, he will have to take the life of the one whose betrayal aggravated him the most. The one whose wound infliction is the freshest. In his mind, the fulfillment of this task would set him free. With that freedom, he will be able to grow. Finally, his contentious past would come to an end.

He begins to meticulously plan an attempt on Benjamin's

life. He methodically completes steps towards his murderous goal. His mind continues to be subjugated to torrents of despondency periodically. However, the flaming need for suicide and self-flagellation are no longer an option, rather, a stronger more intense focus on reality has prevailed. He hungers for the ability to muster the courage to bring this plan to fruition.

He reconnects with common friends that both he and Benjamin share to learn of Benjamin's whereabouts. After accomplishing this, he fashions an itinerary of events to consummate revenge. That is Michael's sole express purpose. In Michael's mind, Benjamin had the life that he, Michael, ultimately needed. Michael desperately wants to bring balance and justice to the situation as he saw fit. He hangs on to this need, his mind would not allow him to let this grudge go. In a sense, he needed revenge to satisfy the rage within him.

However, in fraternizing with these friends that now seemed more like strangers, Michael felt that it brought upon him a nauseating sensation to his inner being. Their morals, etiquette and mannerisms came across to him as sickening and depraved. These traits were attributes he once called his own. He once was a prideful member of this faction of society. When the deduction of this logic began to form, he was reviled at his former self. This additional hatred energizes his grim agenda to right the wrongs in his life even more.

He then begins to obtain weapons that would help in delivering the act of revenge to fruition. Now, he is both physically and mentally prepared. He must have run the hypothetical scenario through his mind thousands of times, studiously envisioning possible shortcomings or obstacles that might arrive against him. In the fear of those aberrations, he continues to bolster his arsenal of tangible and intangible weaponry. All of which he will sought to use in laying an assault upon Benjamin. Michael makes a conscious choice to consistently harden his heart and mind, turning cruelty into a habit. He is ready.

On the day of orchestration, it is a warm summer's afternoon. The warmth of the time and space is completely antithetical to the bitterness and resentfulness that brews within Michael's heart and mind. He surreptitiously enters the premises of Benjamin's residence, walks into the room where he knows Benjamin will be. Michael slams the door shut and locks it. Benjamin turns around absolutely astonished by Michael's presence. Once he took a moment to digest the fact that Michael is indeed present and in the flesh, Benjamin's expression changes to that of relief. It is almost as if Benjamin knew that he was being hunted by Michael. There was and is no doubt that this was to be Michael's course of action, Benjamin did leave Michael for dead, robbing him in the process. Silence emanated within the room. Piercing gazes from both parties. Both of them had energy surging within their veins, they were beginning to realize the potency of this moment. Michael is relishing an opportunity to attain vengeance against one who had caused him so much pain. Michael's plans are coming into fruition.

Michael: You had to know I was coming for you.

Michael snares with a distinct grin of satisfaction in the moment.

Benjamin: You better kill me if you get the chance boy!

Benjamin retorts back instinctively. There are no more words that need be spoken between the two, just anger, hatred and violence.

Before Michael could act, Benjamin charges forward relentlessly to launch a preemptive strike. There is nothing to it in Benjamin's mind, only one is going to live, and he is hell-bent on ensuring his continued existence. The brawl is consuming them. In the corner of both of their minds, they know that the loser would suffer the consequences native to the pain of death. Neither of them is willing to submit to the other's will.

Bonds of brotherhood and fellowship were shattered and discarded permanently forever more in this very moment. Each moment that the tussle continued on with seemed like an eternity in Michael's mind. As the fight lingers on, Michael's mind begins to stray. It was up for grasp. Michael does not know whether it was being from the lack of oxygen to the brain, fatigue or exhaustion from constant movement. Maybe it was even the repeated blows that were either absorbed or blocked. That was all currently beyond Michael's fathomable domain. Either way now, it seemed like he was just swinging blows for the sake of the cordiality and courtesy of the occasion. The actual cause of this violence seemed to be lost upon him. All actions right now were purely under the instinctual autonomic commands, with no emotions or reasons banded to it. The pace of the altercation was distinctly lessened as more time elapsed. Michael's perception of passing moments began to slow down, his reflexes and body awareness began to stir and take over. His breathing patterns began to steady. He is now engaging Benjamin with relative ease, rather than it being the grotesque struggle that it initially was.

As Michael began to soak in the moment, he is privy to the complete demolition of Benjamin's former facade, followed by the full disclosure and affirmation of Benjamin's true appreciable nature.

It was as Michael had realized all those months ago, laying upon the floor that was mangled by battle. Michael was a victim of a murderous rampage and left for dead due to

Benjamin and Patrick's greed. In the months following that haunting occurrence, he surveyed the aftermath that was his life and attempted to pick up the pieces of a shattered existence. In doing so, he conveniently hid the truth from himself when he gazed upon its unsightliness. Michael begrudgingly interpreted how he had lost close friends through vicious bloodlust and got betrayed by another friend. He grieved and toiled in agony for what seemed like an eternity, contemplated suicide vehemently. He uncompromisingly sunk to never before trodden lows continuously that were devoid of grace with each passing moment of existence.

It was in this moment of vulnerability and weakness, where peace and happiness seemed completely out of his reach. He panicked and seemingly forgot all the human benevolence that he had experienced in the past months and thus, blindly miscomprehended his association with Benjamin as the representation of his sole remaining bond which was worthy of being deemed as a friendship. The fact that Benjamin's acceptance of friendship is no longer existent or pertinent was unthinkable to Michael. Internally he thought, how horribly decrepit and lonely of an existence would it be to have if it were known that all bonds forged throughout his life were lost and never again to be retrieved. Was he not worthy of a bond? There was now a deep sense shame, an overwhelming sense of loneliness grew over him. Michael was stricken with grief and panic for himself in regards to what his future holds.

He was at the height of his disorientation and was in great need of a sense of direction. Fortuitously, it came from within. The truth was unbearable for him to behold. So for the sake of self-preservation, he searches for pleasantries within those asperities to elevate towards the forefront of the situation to masquerade as presentable and acceptable truths. A part of him still wanted to believe that Benjamin was still his friend, that the man he knew for so many exultant and jubilant years of friendship was the same person that stood before him. And so, Michael let that thought process thrive and emanate within him. He allowed himself to believe those doctrines, trading it for a moment's peace.

The thought that he is once again worthy of one's friendship brought him a glimmer of solace and warmth. It did not matter to him that these thoughts were rooted in absolute absurdity.

As this comforting absurdity began to resoundingly rouse a sense of calmness within him, he began to understand the truth for what it really was. He no longer anxiously discards it petulantly in panic and helplessness. Benjamin's true conviction was and will always be that he scorned Michael feverously, it was cemented in his ardent physical attempts to inflict pain and devastation upon Michael coupled with his barbarous visage that showed itself throughout this altercation. It began to resonate within Michael's core that after all these events have unfolded, there was going to be no love lost on Benjamin's part. Michael promptly makes peace with this revelation. It is now in Michael's hands to reciprocate. The absence of love channeled a malicious effect within Michael. Michael wittingly silences his conscience and hardens his heart to stone. In this moment, his capabilities and intentions are impossible to predict. Within this trance-like state, Michael summons every fiber of his being into trouncing Benjamin physically by any means necessary with no vacillation or hesitation.

Michael overwhelms Benjamin with an onslaught perpetuated by calmness, instinct and iron will. Each attempted blow on Benjamin's part was turned into a lost cause, as Michael's blows of retaliation ascend insurmountably in force. It is in this moment, where Michael executes a move which entirely capitalizes upon Benjamin's erroneous position and stance. Benjamin falls to the floor violently. Michael is ready to deliver the killing blow with his weapon. Benjamin lays there in exhaustion and hopelessness, resigning to his fate. It is his time to die. Michael did not start this, but he sure would have felt damned if he were not to be the one to end this once and for all. Vengeance will be his. Michael stands over Benjamin, realizing that this passing moment was distinctly significant. All that he had hoped and dreamed for was standing right in front of him and coming to fruition, he had achieved his goal. He had a look of steeled resolve and vengeance, unaffected by all that surrounded him. His conviction for revenge had never been stronger than it is in this moment.

The ascendency towards a dominion over the situation gave Michael some clarity. He saw within Benjamin with a debilitating sense of spitefulness towards others. Benjamin had allowed this spitefulness to consume him entirely. Benjamin had lost his way. Spitefulness, it is all too prevalent in the world. People will act out of spite just to put their object of disdain in the place they wish for it to be in. Their pride consigns others to be relegated to a position that is inferior to them. And in accordance with this sentiment, they seek to denigrate if not destroy all oppositions utterly. Those are the foundations in which Michael and Benjamin were both languishing in. Imprisoning themselves in the bondage of servitude to the endless discord connected with being governed by vengeance and retaliation to bring themselves satisfaction. And thus, filling that perceived void in their lives. Benjamin is a person that had committed heinous acts which victimized Michael. Leaving Michael in desolation. And in retaliation, Michael chose to subjugate Benjamin to a place that was even more barren.

In Michael's mind, his entire life is and had always been leading up to this moment. All the hardships and pain became part of an acceptable chain of events within a simple sequence of actions. A sense of satisfaction coupled with completion and nostalgia grew over Michael, his intuition advises him to relish this moment in its entirety. He recognizes that this is unfolding to be a turning point in his life, one that he would remember until the day of his death. It was as if he came to recognize that this act of sweet vengeance was the reason for his existence. He felt that killing Benjamin was his purpose, one that would bring closure and validation for all past events, and thus, a good and happy ending.

In a paradoxical turn, Michael felt a whiff of sorrow for the man before him. Benjamin lived a life that was without regard from or for others, a life that was also without the principles of compassion. His life had no hint of a relevant solace, purpose or contentment. Benjamin's life was completely governed by greed and pride. As a result of these traits, all that Benjamin seeks is to gratify himself as a form of positivity and validation, nothing else mattered to him. Benjamin held within him an iron will to fight Michael to the death in a conflict perpetrated by Benjamin himself. And as it turned out, Benjamin was now on the precipice of his own death at the hands of Michael. Michael initially resisted this new found pity for Benjamin. He tried to renew his vile agenda forcefully in his own mind and perform the act he so desperately craved to execute for so many days. It was beginning to prevail in Michael's mind that attaining vengeance would only gratify an insatiable side of himself that would only need to be appeased to a larger extent on some inevitable future date. This appeasement would lead to the further purging of solace and compassion on that later date. The desecration of these warm sentiments would result in a cold and angst-filled mind that would only spread its frost throughout the rest of Michael's entire being. Michael leaves the scene, never to return again.

Upon executing his exit, regret and anxiousness begin to crawl into Michael's mind and slowly but surely, overwhelms him. As an aftermath, Michael begins to go back and forth in his mind about whether or not he did the right thing. His mind sways violently in both directions. He tells himself that the act is over with, that there is no turning back from here on out for himself. Michael begins to ponder his life before all these brothers he considered to be friends showed themselves. He needs to search out the reason to go on. With a heart full of bitterness, he surmises that fate had always been against his favor, he never stood a chance at happiness. His thoughts turned to his parents. In his mind, they were never competent enough to have him as their child. They were never prepared to have, love or care for a child in the way a child needed to be. Their priorities were not in place for such a task and commitment. They would often lay hostility upon Michael for deeds which they themselves were flagrantly guilty of in their own past. Their constant exercising of poor judgment repeatedly led to premature uprooting of stable situations for Michael, they made premature, but permanent decisions with Michael's needs relegated to irrelevance. It was their incapacity and indecision that led to his instability. This inescapably confounded him to this life of his to be rife with turmoil. All they cared about was their personal goals and priorities. They saw him as a dull creature in their possession, rather than as a child and a person. Everything was centered upon their own priorities.

Michael's livelihood was molded in the form that best matched the status of those priorities. He lived a life hopelessly bounded into submission. His voice was smothered, his family's preferences and discretions stifled him. He felt weary from these thoughts.

In this life of maddening desperation, it stripped the mind of reason and perspective, Michael lingered on resentfully, depleted by their lack of trust and strove to find acceptance elsewhere. He found a sliver of it within deceitful foes masquerading as exuberant acquaintances. His perception of life was so skewered that he did not see them for their true identities, thus, slipping further into other forms of bondages. He willingly submitted himself into servitude and loyalty towards these cohorts and wore these submissions as badges of honor with great pride. This obtuse reality became a satirical source of joy for him.

"They drove me to this point. This is the end" he asserts to himself.

Hate and anger begin to fill his veins. He cursed and damned his parents for what they had done to him. He could care less for what their true intentions were. They drove him away with their sundering hostility and ignorance. In his desperation, he was driven into the arms of those prodigal cohorts to establish new meanings of home and companionship. He had to fend for himself in a cruel world that eventually brutalized him. Michael just simply cannot get these thoughts out of his head.

He got home and all that he desired to do was to lay in silence. He is in need of repose. He climbed into his bed and laid himself down for a moment. However, in this stagnancy, the banks of his memories begin to stir again. He recalls it in torrents, the vivid acts of blatant deprivation that his parents used to impose upon him to achieve their priorities. He would have to endure periods of isolation when they would discard him as unworthy of their attention. Many a times, they seemed to intentionally induce harm, embarrassment and denigration upon him through incessant admonishment and castigation. And in some cases, they would banefully berate and degrade him subtly in private moments within the comfort of their home, resulting in Michael crumbling inwardly.

He grew to absorb these blows internally. As a child, these degradations would result in paroxysms of rage outwardly, resulting in conflicts. Repetitive conflicts would drag Michael through tumultuous episodes of circumstances. In time, he no longer harbored the patience to endure it. Eventually, he learned to absorb those bludgeonings internally and exude a phlegmatic visage while burning on the inside.

He felt anger in recounting these events. Anger turned into hate, hate turned into hopelessness. He lays in stillness. He feels a chasm where his heart is.

Michael feels great discomfort. He finds it hard to breathe. Panic-stricken, he tries his best to sooth his disheveled mind and heart.

It feels like there is a growing gaping hole in his heart, he felt cold all over. In his growing desperation, he places his right hand over his heart to sooth the pain, an act to cover the emptiness of that chasm, hiding it from himself. It does not heal or sooth the vacuity which he suffers. However, Michael finds that it does lend some warmth and sensation to this cold and numb chasm. It does ease the pain for a moment. To his despair, the frigid numbness continued to linger. And now seemingly getting obtusely stronger, overwhelming the effects which the warmth from his hand had offered. He turned over to lie on the front of his chest, pressing his rib cage firmly into the mattress so as to relieve the numbness. He gradually begins to feel his heart beating and thumping. This repetitive tone commences a rhythmic composition into his mind and correspondingly, his thoughts.

His thoughts begin to settle and focus on one hopeful acknowledgement. He acknowledges that his heart is functioning well. Michael acknowledges that his heart is and always was a part of the one thing that remains true, his body. It was always here. Michael's mind begins to settle some more. He begins to feel the warmth of his breath ricochet off his bed sheets and into his face where he absorbed it mightily and cherished it for its comfort and alleviation, as even his face was cold. With the warmth that he felt from his every breath and steady auditory beats of his heart, he begins to further contemplate these moments.

Suddenly, his mind ruptures, he finds himself sorely pitying his own existence. Life should not be like this, rife with pain and anger. He begins to mourn how his parents should have taken his sickly childhood as a sign.

"How did it ever come to this?" he regretfully ponders toward himself.

"I should have died in those early years as a child" he thought to himself. "Maybe that's why my life feels empty. Maybe it's because I shouldn't even be here."

In his sorrow, he finds himself pitying his parents for not appreciating what was in front of them and prioritizing other agendas. What is left of his being is fractured even more so from this realization. There is no forgetting or reconciling what has transpired here. He can feel himself slipping and languishing away.

7

His mind is now a cold, damp and desolate place. No longer did it harbor any hopes or dreams. It is filled with poison, all forms of warmth and goodness are extinguished. Warmth and goodness are both beyond his reach. It is a deluge of flagrant anger and intolerance. In his solitude, he will often have no choice but to ponder the past events of his life. More times than not, these reminiscences will leave him full of regret and anger at his own choices throughout life. He blames himself ceaselessly.

"Why didn't you turn back when you had the chance you fool?!" he would often furiously excoriate himself.

And he knew that there were plenty of chances to turn back. He really had no lingering desire to live on.

However, this lackluster aspect of him was a side of him that never revealed itself, he was deeply aware of its social impropriety. And the more he strove to hide it, the more it dominated his thoughts and focus. The only outlet he had for this building tension was to attack his continued physical rehabilitation with a vindictive anger which he had built up within. His anger was slightly subdued with social contact and his need for outward propriety in front of others.

With each physical improvement achieved, Michael would exude a certain silent apprehension of the moment, and yet internally consummating it with vindictive satisfaction. Many a times within the rehabilitation facility, this vindictive satisfaction would show a clenched jaw and eyes sternly focused with intent, as sweat flows from his scalp onto his face. The entire area might be bustling with activities, but it does not sway his intent.

Michael finds that these substantial gains would momentarily satisfy him. His renewed focus on his rehabilitation meant he had to come into contact with the facility's staff and volunteers once again. As he continually draws more contact with them through his defective lens of perception, their unknowing ignorance in communication begins to aggravate Michael again. Malice and tension insidiously begin to mount within him once more. This unknowing social circle of altruistic but communicatively-flawed volunteers and ignorantly selfish fellow patients, who were themselves going through times of tumultuous pain, gives rise to covert cruel intentions within Michael's mind which begin to slowly inundate Michael's entire being. He begins to consciously withdraw socially in order to save himself from those cruel intentions. In other words, he wants to prevent himself from committing a heinous act, whereby leaving his victim in a position that could not possibly be indemnified. He wants to realign his focus inwardly. These thoughts of cruel intentions would often sneak into his mind where he remembers and recalls how he turned away from indulging in his impulsive need for vengeance against Benjamin. The thought of attain vengeance against Benjamin and its possible aftermaths remain ever present in varying degrees of severity in his mind. On occasion, he would rue his course of action taken. It was in those moments where he despised himself for that imposition upon himself. It deprived a certain part of him from perceived happiness. That part of him was ever present in the corner of his mind wrestling to break free to dominate Michael's psyche and actions. It was and is a constant struggle for Michael to keep that malice in shackles.

After most of these sessions of physical therapy, he would often come across Darcy the Nurse, their unlikely bond of friendship continues to grow with each passing conversation and interaction. With each embrace that they share, the atmosphere mysteriously intensifies. Her gentle touch helps assuage the tumults that toil in Michael's mind. Michael's infatuation with her deepens. She begins to occupy a significant portion of his daily thoughts, bringing to him a sense still placidity.

But his life is becoming a series of unstable and violent sways between the extremes of vitriol, affection and everything in between. Michael is losing a grip on his own life. He begins to realize that in order to attain an autonomous state of peacefulness, and being in control of his negative or positive passions, he has to change his internal processes of perception. Therefore, that is what he begins to search for, a source that would change his thoughts.

He begins to frequent the library in between his therapeutic sessions. He begins to read and examine a book on the human body's systems. In the book of the body works, there are many poignant facts that illuminate his mind about the nature of the human body.

There was a microscopic view of the simplest cell of the body, comprehensively explaining its parts and their inherent functions. Through a session of light reading, Michael is enthralled by the simple cell's mechanics of its self-propelled brilliance, managing all aspects of its own existence. Concomitantly, it also dawns upon him how precarious the nature of its structure was and is. If any of its constituents are anything less than perfect, the cell itself will fall into horrible listlessness. The body's wholeness, vitality and balance hinge upon microscopic fluctuations of infinitesimally microscopic volumes of matters and motes which as singular entities could be essential or injurious to the body. The biological and chemical balance that the body strikes within itself is nothing short of extraordinary. The possibilities and likelihoods for infirmity of any kind is endless, and in accordance of that nature, sickness does grab a hold one's normal life functioning. Such as reproduction, this can occur at any level of existence. Even at the microscopic level. And at any level, the process is deeply subjugated to the mercy of seemingly infinite amounts of infinitesimally subtle factors' ability to coalesce.

The next topical section is the body's outer most layer, the system that is the skin. It offers every and any organ or component a layer of protection. It also withholds the ability to communicate within itself and its ancillary mechanisms. It has the ability to regenerate itself and all its byproducts with a sustainable pace. Also, it acts as an important regulator of the body.

In scoping through the skeletal section, Michael finds that he had previously undervalued the body's bones' acts of sustainability and functionality through anatomical means.

He then forwards himself toward the section on the muscular nature of the body. He realizes that the muscles' nature as a complex fabric is in constant need of maintenance and sustenance through physical and dietary means, equally so with the bones. The main benefit which the muscles offer the body is rescuing it from complete inertia through the power of initiation. It is also ironic how the system in itself is rife with fragility. It is satire which he is experiencing first hand through the marvelous hilarity of the physical rehabilitation setting. A simple and quick turnaround of one's circumstances can slide such a capable entity, that being the muscular system, into decrepitude and languor with relative ease.

As he continually builds up his knowledge of the human body, he begins to perceive his feelings and desires in a much more sagacious light. The book continually draws him in and materializes as a serviceable escape from what to him, is an undesirable life, manifesting as an oasis in the desert, hydrating a mind which is parched of knowledge and sense. His life is no longer a source of joy for him. In his mind, his sole focus is to seek respite and repose, aiding the healing process, and go from there. "I just need to get better." That is what he keeps telling himself.

He then arrives at the section that thoroughly describes the brain and the nervous system. At first glance, he is mesmerized by the intricate matter in which the system is formed. The brain is a work of art within the masterpiece of creation that is the human body. The vertebrae and the cord of nerves within it, as fragile as they are, it serves a high purpose, and the microscopic individual nerves and nerve ends can be the most pivotal hinge of which all humans' existence rests upon. It powers and sustains everything. Its mere functioning to deliver movements, thoughts and emotions are all acts of sheer marvel and wonder. It takes the great precise filtration and drainage of the brain's fluids, this stirring and maneuvering requires whole other networks of bodily tubes. Michael recognizes the inordinate discipline and regimens of the systemic nature within the nervous system, the coordination of blood vessels to bring about nutrients and the conductivity of biological electricity which is the energy that powers and controls absolutely everything. In other words, Michael knows that he would be nothing without the flow of this minuscule current. The coordination of blood vessels would include the conducive nature of the walls of the blood vessels to hold up as tubes within the system. It would also require the valves within the vessel to hold up to ensure the effective flow of blood. Knowing now what he just learned about the body and its sustainability, Michael is in awe of this system's structural deliverance of nutrients and its mechanisms of protection and maintenance over the entirety of itself and the rest of the body for that matter. This system enables a human being to deal with many plights. The system itself also exemplifies sympathy for its fellow body matter by rightfully changing properties within them to give them the necessary resources to combat what may come. It is through this deliverance of nutrients that enables a self-propelled existence of the system. An existence which withholds functioning abilities that is both innate and phenomenal. As he continues to peruse through the book, his gaze lands softly on the divisions of the brain, and the different functions it holds. It is privy to him that there are many levels of cognitive functioning. It is also revealed to him that there are biological and chemical reasons behind the behaviors and feelings within, which can at times be unpalatable and intractable. Minuscule secrets of the nature of things were slowly enriching his life. In knowing the physiology of these parts of the body, and how they are by nature exhaustible and fragile, not withholding the ability to regenerate, it appears ever more so poignant in his mind to accumulate the strategies of maintaining this very system. As unfortunately, it will deteriorate with the attrition of time, as all things do. Physical regression is inevitable. All it takes is the passing of time for infirmity to be unleashed.

The five senses are the next piece of delicacy that is offered up for interpretation. The organs that enable the ability to utilize these senses as tools are the skin, eyes, ears, nose and the tongue. The sheer amount of layers and components contained by those organs and the complexity that lay within those layers are fascinating to Michael. Not to mention, it requires the flawless execution of the blood and its vessels for healthy functioning at the very core and periphery of the five senses.

Next in line is the endocrine system. It romanticizes the nature of hormone production by glands with the relevant purposes of those hormones. Michael inexorably draws from these readings that the human existence would be crippled without the proper functioning of this system. And in some of the diagrams, it shows the hampering results of either the over or under-production of hormones. The absences of these glands are unthinkable. It allows for vital interactions between bodily organs to maintain a critical balance within itself and the entire body. The balance within a body is so precarious and volatile, it is susceptible to change at any given moment. There are no bounds to the depths which a body could and would get thrusted into should it not be balanced chemically, not to mention physically. Physical wellness and growth are deeply affected by the hormonal presence. In his ongoing physical therapy, there was plenty of emphasis placed upon the physiology of his anatomy in Michael's mind. And in so doing, it dominated his priorities and thoughts. This inexorably drew his attention away from the other dominant aspect of his existence, the chemical side. Michael remained unaware and ignorant of this side, despite having come into contact with its account and portrayal a few many times. Before Michael can begin to loathe himself for this ignorance, he consciously immerses himself within the words before his eyes. He sees that the hormones and glands are not to be taken lightly. They too, are critical divisions of the body. To truly master his course of life, he first has to recognize this complex division of his body for what it truly is and always was. And that being a structure of organs that in reaction to certain triggers, readily produces chemicals into one's bloodstream, invariably causing for a wide range of shifts in one's mental state. Some triggers that come to the forefront of Michael's mind are the horrible flashbacks which haunt him up to this day, or the somewhat distasteful interpersonal interactions that he experiences with his fellow acquaintances garnered within this rehabilitative process. The sensations and emotions felt by one as a result of those very shifts could be countless. A very potent emotion is love, and Michael was devoid of it. Emotions and sensations form impulsive needs, which lead to certain actions to come to fruition, actions which Michael above all else, wishes he could take back. But he cannot do that. Michael feels that he needs to accept and recognize triggers for what they truly were in his life, thoughts of the past. That was all they were. And in terms of actions, Michael sees that he needs to discern impulsive desires from realistic needs. The impulsive desires, Michael now knows it to be inner feelings formed by the hormonal chemicals proliferating in the bloodstream. Michael grasps the pertinent and realistic need to steer clear of any reaction whatsoever from himself, he knows this to be true and reasonable. He needs to bide his time and let things unfold. When he experiences his flashbacks of malicious moments shared with Benjamin and Patrick, there was a part of him that needed vengeance and seething with anger, it is now within his power and recognition to choose what course of action to take. Will he choose to be governed by bodily chemicals, or will he allow for truth and reason to prevail?

Truth and reason have always been kind to Michael. He remembers that kindliness fondly.

The next chapter is about the blood and the system which it resides within, the cardiovascular system. In his readings, it became clear to him that blood is the fuel, source and reason behind existence. It delivers life sustaining nutrients to body parts, has the ability to help a body absorb external assailments and enables the body to thrive under injuries. It is the body's power of regeneration. The system however, withholds the need to be catered to in order to perform admirably. Maintenance of the system's organs, vessels and muscles should be the person's primary agenda in order to ensure and assure the system's act of deliverance. There is also a convoluted simplicity to the heart acting as a provider, with the aid of simple fibers running through its core, acting as an impetus behind a self-sustaining mechanism of self-preservation. Proper maintenance through selective and conducive acts enables proper performances from the heart and its vessels. The heart and its vessels, it can be the giver of life, or the harbinger of terrible sicknesses.

Michael then browses through the pages about the body's immune system. He finds certainty in this system's potency as the body's defender against infirmity. However, this system does not stand alone as a sole entity. It has its functions unfathomably rooted within and assisted by our dietary choices. It is a system with highly complex and intricate mechanisms with too many moving parts to manage with the conscious mind.

In moving on, he arrives at the system that allows for breath, the respiratory system. The lungs are the loading docks for oxygen. The lungs alone possess the proper features for its own protection and functioning. There is an elaborate process in which the lungs absorb and extract oxygen, the body's other systems then use the oxygen for energy. To the rest of the body, the lung's elaborate process is absolutely vital. In order for adequacy, these other systems need this vitality and proper maintenance. Diagrams that follow are of the chest cavity, it impresses upon Michael this system's proximity to and coordination with the heart, in addition, that very diagram shows Michael that the blood running within the heart always departs from the heart and flows directly to the lungs. It is a running flow which is indicative of the existential need for cohesiveness within the body. It is all intertwined.

He eventually gets to the digestive system. There is a subtle inconspicuous physical and chemical brilliance in the significance of the digestion and absorption of foods on a microscopic level. The focusing on the absorption of foods coerces Michael to hearken back to the saliency of which the foundations of a human's immunity defenses against ailments are built upon. The safeguarding of this system propels the body to proficient functioning and adequacy.

Finally, he arrives at the section of the human reproductive systems. The urinary function of this compartment is essential in eliminating waste. This utility is frequently undervalued as an essential trait of the body. The unimaginable and unsightly decrepitude the body would go through without this ability arises within Michael's mind. The body would become a toxic and uninhabitable wasteland. Kind of like a mind that does not purge itself of negativity. The reproductive functions and diagrams indicate to Michael the system's complexity. On a microscopic level, it is an unbelievably arduous journey just to begin one human life. Uncountable numbers of unconsciously controlled situations have to coalesce to enable a healthy gestation.

This refined outlook on his body gave him a few reasons, when in doubt, to continue on with his rigorous physical therapy. There were times where he did need the extra motivation to get to the facility.

As part of his rehabilitation, he takes up meditation sessions offered within the facility. This greatly enhances his understanding of his mind's conscious control over the body. The breathing and stretching techniques teach him to quiet his mind and eliminate any and all external distractions. His internal perspective on life morphs into one that is constantly in regeneration and replenishment of energy and focus in each fleeting moment of the day.

Michael continues on. In doing so, he ponders reality. Michael sees that Benjamin held a malicious disdain for him. Michael progressively grows more congruency with that reality. Time begins to mend the wounds.

Back in therapy, Michael sits down with the wife of a handicap patient in the waiting area. This patient's medical problems run deeper than most. Chances of him regaining full mobility in his legs are next to none. This inevitably casts a heavy burden upon the lives of both husband and wife. The wife, Annabelle, is a peculiarly stern lady whose countenance seemingly bores a frowning set of eyebrows and a stiffened upper lip. She always seemed to have her medium length hair stiffened backward with heavily scented products. On some days, her hair would fashion itself in an uncontrollably convoluted manner, one that would not be tamed by Annabelle's iron-clad efforts. Today is one of those days, and concomitantly, Annabelle's visage furrows even more so. She and Michael begin their conversation as they always do. Many people dislike her for her forceful attitude and her need for tampering with the affairs of others. Michael finds her to be tolerable. Michael finds her blatant and crude honesty to be refreshing. In most of their conversations, she would talk to Michael about her daily accomplishments that brought her great personal satisfaction. Michael would just listen, most of the time she would ramble on about the simplest of things, where she would then subconsciously look to Michael for subtle validation and consent. Michael tolerates her eccentricities because he once saw her in a private moment of weakness, one which was not meant for the eyes of another to see, one that Michael will not soon forget, and thus, caused him to sympathize with her plight from there on out. And then, she was surprised by her visiting granddaughters. Michael takes his leave from them briefly to allow for them to focus on and spend some quality time with each other. The grandchildren were very adorable. They begin to bustle around her, playing with their toys as Michael remembers how he once did before as a child. It is picturesque. Annabelle smiles and seems elated. Michael is glad for the alteration of Annabelle's mood, he finds it refreshing.

However, once they leave, Michael sees her take a brief moment for herself. She blankly stares into space despondently as her eyes well up and eventually glisten in the light. She then begins to claw at her face incessantly with her hands in frustration and sadness. Her misery is palpable. Michael knows that Annabelle, being the strong-willed woman she is, would never concede to address these emotions. In front of everyone, she always portrayed herself as a lady with an unbreakable conviction.

Michael patiently waits for Annabelle's episode of inward angst to subside outwardly before he makes his return to accompany Annabelle once again. This is where the two of them pick up on another conversation. As they continue to converse with one another, the dialogue eventually stumbles upon Darcy and how Annabelle offered her a new skincare product that greatly helped with the dermatological care of her child.

Michael: Darcy has a kid?

Annabelle: Yes, a son. He's like ten years old I think.

His mind and body flusters. But strangely, a part of him had always known this to be true.

Michael: I see.

He takes a moment to digest that information. It is intriguing to him as to why Darcy would convey herself in such a way to him. Nevertheless, as these facts sink in, he refuses to allow Darcy to fall off that pedestal he had placed her upon in his mind. She is unblemished in nature in his mind. His passion for her delved deeper than any such physical sensuality. The fact that she is married with a child does not sully his opinion of her, he is just thankful to be around her. Her presence is calming to Michael, he feels a prevailing goodness in himself when he is with her. Through this revelation, Michael holds no ill will towards Darcy's situation, he sustains an appreciation for her entire being, more than even he could consciously know of at this juncture in his life.

As the conversation with Annabelle concludes, more patients and family members stroll in, all of whom are familiar faces to Michael now. Michael would sometimes lack the supplemental energy to even attempt to match their emotions in order to make out for fruitful interactions. It was in those moments where Michael would strive superfluously to masquerade any inefficacies on his part. These moments would gnaw upon him significantly. In time, Michael learned that affluent bonds could still be generated from a reserved sense of captivation on his part towards the other. All it took was a solemn display of interest to those who engaged with him, it offered much appeasement to the general surroundings, and helped Michael to cope with the undulating mode of communication and emotion, both internally and externally.

Michael enters the therapy room, he had entered this room many times before, but this time, he enters with a deeper sense of appreciation for the kindness experienced here. As Michael realizes this, he fondly looks back on the time he had spent here. The fair memories greatly exceeded the memories which were foul, and in retrospect, the memories which were foul seemed more like illusions rather than realities. It held no weight of significance. It also held no bearings on the past, future or present. He sees now that no one human is faultless, to expect complete appropriateness of every situation was an erroneous pursuit. All that matters to Michael now is the warmth of goodness, and there was an abundance of that here. He had come to greatly treasure and cherish the bonds of friendship and intimacy formed here. There is much transparency here. The bonds are translucently pure and good.

He looks around. He sees many faces, some show elation that the body is on the mend, some looks show distress under the weight of failure. He performs physical routines to constantly improve his physical state. He exemplifies satisfactory levels of improvements and progress. He converses with fellow patients around him as he performs his many routines. He finds their wide spectrum of emotions to be undeniably fascinating. This fascination raises about a singular appreciation for the extent of the human capacity. Overt responses were just ways for the mind and body to cope, that was all it was. Every action has a reason behind it. Michael is at peace with that.

He is content in the moment. Within his body, Michael can sense favorable hormonal outputs from his physical activities. It is currently sustaining and strengthening this pleasant contentment. He appreciates it. He takes a seat, his session has culminated. Seated next to him is a fellow patient, George.

George is a man of many attributes. He had been attending physical therapy since before Michael joined. He had witnessed Michael's entire rehabilitation from the beginning. He had lived many years, far more than Michael could currently lay claim to. George was not perfect, nor did he try to come across as such. He is completely comfortable in his own skin. His employer requires him to attend all his therapeutic sessions, and so he obliges, that is all this group knew about him. He seemingly never desired to disclose any other facts about himself.

George, like Michael, is also full of perspiration from a successful session. And just like Michael, he too seems satisfied with his very own performance. They both modestly acknowledge each other's presence with a slight nod towards each other. They then turn their attention to the television which is on the news channel for all the patients' viewing pleasure. They hear of many of the world's current events.

George smirks distastefully at the current broadcast's fine points and lets out a sigh of subtle apathy.

George :   That is ridiculous. Nobody is perfect.

Michael realizes George is talking to him, and so Michael responds,

Michael: How do you mean?

George: No Man should be given the authority and power to judge another Man. It's against nature, bullshit really.

Michael sits still in contemplation of George's statement.

George: All these god damned politicians, they don't care about anything but themselves. And we give them the power to run our world. Society is all gone to hell. It's impossible for things to run smoothly, some imbecile always has some stupid agenda that screws everything up for the rest of us. Democracy my ass! What choice do we have when all you have to choose between is that from a conglomeration of human scum? We are prisoners who are told that we have the freedom of choice and expression. We are told this, so we believe it to be the truth and continue to empower this shame of a system with our silence. What choice do we have when the only way of peace and order is to subject your own livelihood to the unspoken oppression from those who only stand to gain plenty from your acceptance?

He portrays a level of bitterness in all that he says. Michael begins to surmise that George is a Man that has seemingly been worn down by Time. All events in his life seem to fan the flames of his apathy and disinterest. George has seen much that this world has had to offer, the wealth of experience seems to have morphed his reality into one that is insipid and mundane. He is no longer taken aback by situations that arise. Rather, everything is perceived by him to be a variation of something else that he has already seen before. Michael then realizes he is catching George in a candid moment of George's unfiltered outlook on the world. No one has ever seen this side of George. Michael decides to continue to listen to this speech. It is after all an intriguing perspective, neither refreshing nor dull.

George: What ever happened to just treating others the way you wish to be treated? Have everybody develop a little insight, proceed with a little caution and let everything run its course. I know, it is impossible, wishful thinking really.

George says this to comfort himself. A brief moment of silence envelops them both.

"Self-governance, it is a dream. To treat all with the civility of humanity. To not allow outer circumstances to taint one's actions. Can this dream be truly gone from us?" Michael asks himself. Michael realizes George gives him a unique perspective of the world. It is knowledge from another, Michael treasures it. Michael takes a moment to formulate an applicable response.

Michael: Maybe all we need is a little imagination. You know, creative ways to steer the course of the future.

George: I hope I will see it in my lifetime son. The fact is that this system we live in is one that victimizes many and will continue to do so. There is a lot of pain in the world Michael, livelihoods are destroyed everyday.

Michael is surprised to see that George knows his name to be Michael. Michael can hear the tone of George's voice crack a little with palpable despair. George's expression begins to furrow. George is obviously speaking of some form of a personal experience. It is most likely a wound that is still tender and raw. Michael has no response for George, silence lingers.

George: In life, you will come across many people who will treat you in a manner that is judgmental to the point of cruelty. They will impose upon you as they see fit, they will disregard your beliefs. You have a job kid?

Michael shakes his head.

George: I've been working since I got out of school. Got married, bought a house, had kids, put them through school, watched them grow into adults. In all my years, if there's one thing I can tell you, it's that nothing in this world is ever black or white. Everything is a shade of both. I've had people wrong me in life. Looking back, I've given it some thought. If someone mistreats you, they do so to benefit themselves. In their mind, they are heading towards a goal. They do not see the wickedness it sometimes creates. How could they? Their need to achieve their goals is consuming them. It lessens their awareness of their actions and its repercussions. Now given, some people do see it but prioritize their wishes over kindness and act to their own advantage. Personal wishes are a highly personal thing. All people will strive to attain it through different means. There are many reasons as to why a person will be unkind to you. For some in their mind, they are serving something higher than themselves. And with that, they look for ways to confirm their bond to that loyalty. Some when aggravated, will hit back without thought, and in doing so, they fail to see the meanings of their actions. They end up hurting those who they should love. But it is up to you to see them for what they really are, that which is completely consumed by raw ill will and spite.

There are some people who are so cunning towards their victims. They battle to get to a superior position of knowledge and power, just to wear down victims to the point where they can even dictate their victims' thoughts with designed actions. They do so for personal gain. These people are hunters of terrible greed. They will do anything to get what they want.

Every one of these hunters should burn.

Michael feels a grave connection to that hateful sentiment. However, he sees George's anguish and discontent. He does not want this for himself, he has been down that road of wanting vengeance, and there was no peace there. His memory of it, now in hindsight, portrays that pursuit as rather meaningless. Experience and understanding seemingly saves him from ruining this present moment of his life.

Michael's expression is one of monotony. However, the overall monotony fails to veil the visible scars of tension that Michael continues to show. Michael subtly twitches with a grimly secluded petulance. Parts of Michael feels diminished with a slight disquiet.

George finds a certain unease in his confidant from the conversation. George tries to relieve the built up tension in Michael's mind by further explaining his thoughts.

George: These hunters seek to terrorize the weak in compensation for the lack of something in their own lives. What we should try to feel for them is pity really. Imagine what a life it would be to live, if you had to terrorize others because you had nothing worth holding on to.

George finds himself to be growing with calm surety in confiding to and caring for Michael. George sees frailty within Michael and thus, tries to embolden Michael with the courage to let go of whatever festers in the mind.

George: Imagine if you were desperately searching for happiness and trust. The need for safety is the explanation for most of the deeds you would do. That is their life. That is why they choose to act against you, because you are in the way of that place of safety.

Michael finds George's speech distinctly relevant. Michael finds that the words pierce right through him. Michael becomes grateful for his decision to spend some time with George today. It made them both better Men. They both had the will to act as they normally would not, it just took the arrangement of circumstances for them to ingratiate each other.

George: The values of a dog-eat-dog society makes it hard to live an honest life, especially when self-gratification is the highest priority. If One were to coordinate their beliefs as such, there would be many reasons not to act with kindness. These reasons restrain

One from goodness. When One has restraints, kindness will seem burdensome. Why would anyone who seeks to gratify themselves give up an opportunity to advance their standings, especially if Life is a competition of vanity to them?

Michael: Have you ever given up any chance for advancement for kindness?

Curiosity grabbed a hold of Michael. He was intrigued by the Man behind all these facts which were being presented to him. This was his opportunity to get to know George a little better.

George: Yes.

It seemed like such a dismissively vague synopsis of his life. Despite all his warmth and honesty exemplified over the past hour, George seemingly caught himself once he realized that he was becoming too transparent. However, George feels the need to vent further.

George: Those who desire good will through selflessness endear themselves to the sentiment of second chances. One chance is all treachery needs. Deviants feast upon that leniency. The world's crimes and functions are too broad of a matter to be governed by codified laws within books. Constant change is invoked in systems of laws. However, one element can always be composed in order to contradict some other component of the code.

Both Men take a moment to acknowledge their past experiences with a deafening silence.

Michael: Is there a perfect system to rule?

George: Yes there is, it is where the dreams of personal gains do not exist. Where there are only circumstances and happenings.

Michael thinks to himself that George is an unequivocal idealist who rues the shortcomings of the world, thus, leaving George in exhaustion and with unrealistic hopes.

George: Where there is no need for crimes because there is nothing to gain from it. When no crimes occur, there is no need for vengeance. Thus, there is no ill will. There is no need for law or enforcing justice. The more effort we as People invest into trying to govern the thoughts and actions of other People, the more of ourselves we lose in the process. The world was fine before all of our control mechanisms, and it'll be fine long after we are all gone. The Human race as a species has an innate nurturing and caring ability in our psychological processes. It is when we attach perceived values of our possessions and desires, that we allow our thoughts to dictate our actions. Through the influence of our social environment, we add previously unknown needs and desires to our contemplation of our own existence.

It is within these contemplations of desires that give rise to so much pain in the world.

George's mannerisms and expressions are that of heightened emotion and exasperation.

George: It is unkind to impinge upon the thoughts and actions of another Man. It is the exercising of cruelty. From the day a Man is born, they should be free of the greed and scheming of hunters. We were not meant to be preyed upon on this world. Our existence is solely our own.

Schemers seek the passing off of their burdens. They are determined to cover their expenses by drawing upon the resources of others. These Others may be aggravated by these losses. This leads to a tireless cycle of aggression against each other. Innocent victims will be accumulated along the way. I have seen many People of gracious warm sentiments have their hearts turned to stone as a result of trying to repel treachery, thus, emerging from these affairs and losing a part of their humanity.

Even one hunter or schemer is far too many for this world Michael. Their effects are devastating.

George's exhaustion is truly prevalent at the uttering of this statement.

George: Rulers and leaders of Men utilize the flows
of trade and currencies in and within their
constituting parts to seek to tip the balance
of power back in their favor and away from
any and all competitors. In addition, they
seek to enhance a failing order by creating
more laws, the same system of laws which
are undone by criminals. Men continuously
add multiple layers of words of law in an
attempt to govern every aspect of every
situation, thus, creating loopholes and
safeguards, which can be exploited. Blatant
acts of corruption can be conceptualized
and nullified in the words of law. The same
mechanisms of defense can be utilized as
weapons of defiance and aggression. Those
who seek to gain an upper hand can achieve
it through that conceptualization. The
greed for more power corrupts authoritative
personnel. We need protection from these
corrupt officials. There are no subtle
tactics or broad interpretations to take on
animals ruled by a desperation and self-
centeredness.

Some cannot escape from the clutches of
those we all need protection from. Over
the lives of those who need to escape,
stimuli of all kinds have caused them
to become progressively susceptible to
follow leaders that have lead others astray
in the past. Bureaucratic decisions are
constantly executed that implement deeds
of lesser evils, ultimately harming some

for the greater good. And even if one sees the folly, the system of laws ensures that one is obligated to contribute to corrupt leaders' causes. For those leaders control the funding. Funding and focus on certain segments of our civilization can result in the hindering of the livelihoods of some helpless peoples. Miseries of some have reached suicidal lows, and even worse, creating new hunters that prey upon the innocence of even more weak ones. When hearts are broken in that manner, those responsible view these as necessary sacrifices and keep their objectives fixed upon the Greater Eventuality.

George takes a moment for himself.

George: The slightest hint of misery brought upon anyone is unnecessary. Every women, child or man means something to somebody else. Every one person is the child, friend and loved one of someone else. That sentiment is more than enough of a reason not to violate another's life, no matter what.

There are some violators that will never see past their own needs. And they live only to serve themselves. Their entire focus is on attaining what they want. Once they attain this, they will protect it with all their might. Some believe in redemption of past offenses. I consider myself as one with that thinking. Some violators feast upon that leniency through treacherous means. There is no way to tell one's future deeds, you can only let Time tell its story.

Michael has a newly-found admiration for George and his idealistic beliefs. He is by no means perfect, but even in his folly, there is wisdom. In Michael's mind, George has seen the decay of society for what it is and is unwilling to accept it. The tone of George's voice exudes a wave of pain and anger. It seems as though there is nothing for him here, nothing worth staying for, but yet he lingers. His reasons for staying were only known to George himself.

Michael: Is there any way to do what is necessary? Do solutions exist in the world today?

George: Of course, there is always hope. It is up to everyone to want to hope.

Michael sees within George a hint of hope and conviction. But there is an absence of the will or determination to act.

Michael leaves that place in a contemplative state of mind. Walking through the hallways, he begins to ponder the world and the unabashed statements of George. The common widespread approach is that a person needs to respond to asperities with a vigilant anger, an act to balance the situation. However, in Time, the true face of Asperity is a void, Michael sees that. There is nothing to balance or respond to. Feelings of love and joy are both results of brainwork and reflection. Both of these belong exclusively to the mind. Michael has felt himself calmly steer that exclusivity before. The pursuit of permanency and prestige is an errand that will leave One running in endless circles. Some miniscule element will always upset that pursuit. Michael has seen that One can and often will feel the need to hold on to some animate or inanimate object in Time. This need to hold on is predicated upon the thought within the mind that One's existence would somehow be lessened if One were to be without this object of fondness. One's body by birth and its essential functions are distinctly vital to the self, other attachments that One may hold on to and perceive as salient are what they are, accessorial. And no matter how much delight it offers the mind, it is all by nature, completely and undeniably severable. And when the time comes that they are indeed severed, One's primary biological form will still be as it always has been since the day of birth. All the pain and scars that One endures from these severances are true in the moment as well as hurtful in nature. Attachments are not the primary substance of existence.

How could they be?

Michael ponders.

If it were, it would be against its very nature. Every object has its own nature within Time and Space. Eventually, the body, mind and conscience begin to understand that all it will ever need, lays within its primary self. Michael sees that now. If One allows for what is natural to take place, Time can be the greatest natural gift to balance anything that can be thrown at One in Life. In that Time, the choices One makes will shape One's life. It is up to One to examine the effects of the actions taken in life and ensure that it steers clear of denigrating another's life. Eventually, One becomes part of Forever. Michael knows that now.

Michael goes around the various therapeutic centers and sees the choices people make that are a testament of intense endearment. In this walk, he sees real pain. He feels the sorrow of others as he contemplates their misery. He is neither burdened nor invigorated by the misfortunes of others. Rather, he feels a steady tone of nature unfolding in the only way it can. Supporting loved ones choose to be there for the downtrodden patients. Comforting them. Commiserating with them.

He sees an old friend, Madaline, a volunteer. She is changing the television channel for the viewing pleasure of others. She was the ideal volunteer, a provider of warmth for the patients. She really was. However, she recently lost a close loved one and has consequently allowed her life to gradually deteriorate through general apathy for her own well-being. Due to the current lifestyle she leads, she stands as a high risk of all sorts of ailments. She looks haggard and is experiencing a degree of self-neglect. She has detached herself from society and all its implicit overtones. She speaks contentiously about how she could drop dead at any moment and there would be absolutely nothing wrong with that. She also speaks of Life and her daily routines with a bland dissension. She is bitter at her pain, and comprehends other people's acts of reassurance as acts of condescension. She will not allow for Time to heal her wounds. When she interacts with people now, there is a palpable sense of frustration and desperation in every move she makes. Her initial intentions and motivations when she first joined this facility was to comfort those in pain. She has now unwittingly become the exact opposite of those hopeful designs, for her mindset has evolved. Not only does she impose an unpleasantness upon others around her, but in a regrettable way, her actions seem to bring a sense of satisfaction to her for having the ability to release some of her inner tension. She could not perceive her acts as unkind, this was the only way she knew how to act, in her mind, she was doing no harm. In her mind, she was just doing what she could to get through the day.

Michael feels that in a strange way, she is doing exactly

what her inner being needs. Her perception of the world is one that is leaden. A huge part of her has been severed from her. It does not matter to her how or when the course of her existence will culminate. Whenever her life does end, she will know that she has had the chance to address her feelings of resentment about her surroundings. Michael knows there will be no holism on her path. She will experience upheavals in life. And when she does, she will seek to strike down those perceived barriers hard with a recognized vigilance. A sheer aggression. This internal conflict and inability to accept Life for its neutral resolve will leave any One exhausted, as their hopes and dreams are not attainable. They are at war with an enemy that does not exist. In states of war, there is no peace.

Peace, it is often pursued by many. Michael thinks of Nicholas and how that life passed unhurriedly without peace. Nicholas' last memory was an understanding of himself staring helplessly into the eyes of his murderous and triumphant enemies, watching them experience the venomous elation at his demise. In that moment, nothing could have angered him more than that sight. There was absolutely nothing he could do in that moment or forever more. Michael attempts to imagine the anguish that must have been felt by Nicholas in that moment. It is unbearable. Michael feels responsible for Nicholas' fate. He apologizes to Nicholas profusely. Michael has never felt more guilt for his own actions in his life. Michael knows that Nicholas is not here, but somehow, Michael hopes that some part of Nicholas hears his sincere apology.

Michael continues to look around. He sees real existential pain in front of him. Patients were visibly worn down by anxiety and fear of their medical state. Sick children look desperately to their parents for protection. Their parents can offer no such safe haven. As their fate closes in on them, there is a great rising disquiet of the unknown. As their diseases begin to unmask its true potency, patients and their families are horrified by its true nature, for its terminal forms cannot be overcome or diminished. All around, it closes in on the patients and their loved ones. Patients seek to do whatever it takes to stave off death. But as the body begins to break down, the only aspects of themselves that can be nourished are their minds and hearts. And when they do come face to face with their end, the focus of the mind and heart becomes their only protection from fear, doubt and distress which closes in all around. Without a fair focus, they will certainly crumble. And in the last moments that Life has to offer, their focus of the mind and heart are all that steers them unconsciously through the transition to death. Michael has been guided by this steering force before.

Michael thinks about that transition that they will undergo, they should not be afraid of what is to come. For a Mind and a Heart that is steadfast does not and will not betray One.

In this adversity, they do not want to be alone. Some are no longer able to sleep in peace. They find a dire need of sleep medication, which unyieldingly leads to a severe medicative dependence, thus, further entrenching them in their troubles while trying to repel fear.

Visiting families and friends constantly hold patients back from falling before they absolutely must, gingerly safeguarding the patients, hoping to savor every last existing memory of this continuation. Some visitors demand that the patient deal with their crisis in a certain way, a way that the visitor deems as appropriate, at times, even appearing to be obtrusive and demanding. However, within the core of these visitors' many actions, is the ambition to help their loved ones. As he looks around, Michael had witnessed some visiting family members coaxing and convincing their loved ones to ingest medications deemed as necessary through prescription. Coaxing would come in the form of many promises of an untroubled still for the patient. Both patient and family member know this ingestion will bring griping antagonistic side effects to relieve the patients of their abundantly more severe primary pain. With these promises, Coaxers had to inadvertently exercise some form of cruelty in order to help these patients. Cruelty, because the aforementioned side effects broke the body down in grievous and excruciating manners. Had these Coaxers neglected to exercise that cruelty, they would then have to watch their loved one go through a deeper agony as a result of their negligence. Michael knows there will be no comfort down that road. Michael knows there is no easeful consolation down the alternate route. He has talked to many people that are willing to commit solutions to drugs, and relegate any other possible alternative to nullity. It is an act of desperation.

Patients desire neither of those paths, but are petrified of the thought of succumbing to their disease, and thus, do what they must. As patients continue down their paths, support is constantly offered at every turn. The deepest one being companionship. Friends and family protect their frail bodies from harm in helping them through simple tasks such as walking and sitting. The provision of amicable treats always brings a smile to the patient's faces. Michael could tell that these visitors were adamantly putting up brave faces through the adversity in order to rescue the patients from deeper miseries. Visitors selflessly cast off their own fears and apprehension in the solitary goal of bringing joy to their afflicted loved ones. Visitors constantly put themselves in harm's way, emotionally and psychologically. As long as they steady the mindset of the patients, that is all that matters. Michael watches these interactions in deep silence. As their diseases close in, the power of touch and safety becomes infinitely more prevalent and pertinent. As all events transpire, there is a constant harrowing uncertainty from all parties emotionally invested in the situation. And it is exemplified in the deeply furrowed visages all around. Michael can see that, the sight of it all delves into his mind. Michael also perceives that the minds of those visages dream of the day where life will be reverted to normalcy and the existence of hardships will crumble to the ground. Where they can gallivant in the comfort of their loved ones' accompaniment without worry, towards a destination unknown, for the prospect of arrival will bear no burden.

At these junctures in life, Michael sees that it is fluidly easier for One to swallow their pride and offer a fair countenance.

> *"This will be the way I will behave from now on. Why wait for a tragedy to occur before caring in such a way for Another."*

He tells himself.

In watching these acts of humanity unfold before him, Michael remembers suffering from the constant struggle he shared with petulance due to the failures he experienced in life. Michael remembers how he had to agonizingly keep petulance from being showed due to the fear of exhibiting impropriety in front of another person. Now, he finds a nullity in that strained circumstance. This restrained petulance had prevailed over Michael a few many times. The worthiness of watching stirs within him. Michael continues to learn. Each moment is a renewal of all that had preceded it. Michael recognizes that, and in his recognition, Michael acknowledges that if One were to so choose, any past moment could have absolutely no wearing burden upon One's present circumstances. If One chooses to devote each moment to simple acts of stabilizing their surroundings, all that comes inwardly towards themselves and the foundations of themselves, then troubles and disturbances could be weathered by One for as long as they live.

Michael hearkens to the past.

I've committed many acts of wickedness. Atrocious deeds that should have deemed me endless punishment and torment, a place of no return. It took even deeper acts of malice and betrayal to bring about peace in my life. I am in harmony at how this has all unfolded."

As he soaks in the moment, Michael is pleased.

Michael sees that there are Some in this World who are very well fitted to care for Others in their Lives. This World would be under greater care if They were the Leaders. The care they give is Whole. Michael sees that They, who are very well fitted, could have been Some who would have engaged resources in the place where it will better the World.

With each new epiphany of existence, previously segregated parts of his being gradually begin to coalesce. This continues to add to his progressive stability. He is now progressing on a stable chartered course, not restless in an overwhelming agitation of unawareness. Emotions and actions were subtly controllable, constantly steered in the direction of warmth and fellowship, not vengeance or hatred. As he continues to strengthen his body's health through the care and love of nutrition, companionship and rest, it amplifies his mind's stability. A physically and chemically balanced body offers Michael a firm platform of existence. This allows for his mind, heart and conscience to expand and venture with stability. Michael knows that this harmony needs to be assiduously cared for and cannot be ignored into gloom.

When he did come into contact with foul degradation, it

seems holistically artistic the way he shrugs off its irascible petulant nature. To Michael, it is effortless and routine because of the foundations he assiduously laid in his care for his body, conscience and mind. He will always hearken back to the understandings he gained from that Anatomy Book which he stumbled upon while at therapy. The body's functions and possible ailments were plain and simple to him. Time was offering him a pleasant disposition. The natural unfolding of its course brought him to a comfortable state. He had no control over It. All he did was receive It as an open concept and with a comprehensive mind.

The help he was given in that space and time solemnized in his mind the importance of self awareness. When One knows the Self, One will be free of carelessness and exists with mindfulness. One would care for others as Beings of plain existence, be aware of natural boundaries and live a life that does not impinge upon others in any way. Michael can see that those were the ways which he had received his help.

In experiencing the fellowship and companionship of others, Michael grew inexplicably weary of his own growth. He is ever cognizant of the indecency of his past, thus, he never let anyone know his past deeds. He made sure that the villainy would never be uncovered. Constantly guarding these secrets and not letting friends completely in required extreme levels of emotional strength and endurance. In addition, he took it upon himself to be outwardly compassionate to others. The cumulative burden of secrecy is a significant load to bear. He needed to find some technique to alleviate this mounting tension that was building in his body and mind.

Michael discerns that the tension which he feels is that of a palpable physical nature. He feels it in his body. When a body is tight and taut with tension, stretching out the many parts of the body ought to relieve this tension. He searches out different stretches for various parts of the body.

He finds stretches that relieved tension which had accumulated within his body's muscles. Coupled with the comprehensive breathing techniques taught to him in this search, the alleviation of tension calmed his mind. A quiet mind coupled with the relaxation offered by stretching was a great antidote for Michael's anxiety and apprehension. Momentary instances of peace gave Michael the ability to find some solace within the day. And due to his previous readings, he now holds the understandings as to how and what was occurring within his body when it does attain peace and relaxation. From there, he garnered a deeper enjoyment and appreciation for his body. It was not just a random amalgamation of emotions and sensations in restfulness. Rather, there was a defined method behind this hard-earned tranquility. He now understands that the entire body and its many singular compartments were all interconnected and interdependently brilliant. This made his peace so much more profound. Connections forged between his body, mind and conscience were cherished ever so much more by him. It shows in his interactions with others, he is at peace with his own existence. He is no longer despondent in the face of deluges of unfavorable emotions, for he knows it now to be the completely controllable compensations and reciprocations of hormones within his body. Those compensations and reciprocations are in place to help him in life. With that understanding, Michael senses the capability to calm internal storms, no longer crumbling internally or externally with the either deliberate or inadvertent assaults from the external entities. These assaults came in all sorts of varieties and natures. No matter the situation, he is always able to put up a visage of strength and fortitude whenever its need arose. The capability to calm is effortless. Michael feels no strain upon his will of mind. His mind has grown. He is without a doubt, a different man from the one that had entered through the doors of the medical facility, a man who was physically and emotionally shattered. He now has the gift of perspective. Through his metamorphosis, he is able to empathize and sympathize for someone else who walked another path in life, he could feel their joys and sorrows, and in so doing, he could discern a reason behind every act of benevolence or feat of infraction, whether it was committed knowingly or unknowingly. This new found connection to reality is only nurtured more so by Michael's interactions with his fellow patients and volunteers as he continues to return to the Medical Specialist's office for regular check-ups. He knows how to share parts of himself with others. Interactions seem so much more meaningful and forthright. The nature of this social atmosphere he shares with the patients and volunteers is one of restoration and ease, as well as one of generosity and kindness, many social stigmas that would have normally hindered interactions did not seem pertinent in this given situation. They forged bonds rooted in altruism. Michael's newly found governance over his emotions enables him to forge significant paths in life, he ventures in and around his new friends' social circles, daring to reveal himself to a certain extent, intrepidly embarking upon crossings of love with those he grew amorous of along the way.

These relationships and bonds that he found were precious to him. He always interacted with them wearing a pleasant disposition. Those relationships and bonds became the integral impetus behind his happiness and ease of mind.

On one of his regular medical appointments, he is offered to formally join the social support structures within the hospital's network, there are many support groups offered, Michael humbly agrees to join. As he begins to make strides forward within this new endeavor, he gives a conscious effort to get to know his fellow patients and support group members. He learns that his new acquaintances are a very diverse group of individuals. To Michael, they are all surprisingly honest with their individual assessments of their own lives. The honesty is refreshing to Michael, who had kept all the tumults and disorders of his life strangled within. Their honesty gives Michael strength. However, it did not inspire him to be completely transparent with them. Because of his past, Michael fortifies himself within himself. He would have a facade of emotional neutrality toward his fellow support group members. To them he is a picture of peacefulness with a pleasant disposition. To some of the group members, he is a source of strength and warmth. For Michael does not impose his opinion upon anyone or anything.

Within the support group, there is wealth of characters. There are patients with all sorts of infirmities recovering at varying rates. There are cancer patients, orthopedic patients and fellow physical therapy patients. There are also volunteers who just want to lend a helping hand. Michael maintains his attendance in these many rendezvous. Meetings would entail a gathering that would serve as a distraction for the patients. It serves as many opportunities to get away from the hardships that their conditions burden them with. Their gatherings brought an extensive stabilizing effect to Michael's life.

Group members would divulge their circumstances to Michael. He grew to hold a mindful admiration for them. Their stories were teeming with anguish and adversity. The preeminent emotional response is sorrow for those involved. He sees how distraught his fellow patients are and commiserates with them. He embraces them in the hope to bolster them with courage to face what is to come. Michael understands their plight, he sees parallels with their experiences and his own. However, he did not feel burdened by the circumstances that had surrounded him. In a fortuitous way, the deep physical and psychological wounds he suffered from his unyielding past had clearly numbed his emotional perspective. And in so doing, this increased its threshold. He carries the memories of that ominous night ponderously and will do so for the rest of his days. It was both a gift and a curse. From time to time, it either haunted him mercilessly with flashbacks whenever triggered, or it strengthened him by providing him with foresight and the calm poise of discernment due to his experiences of the lessons learned. It was a traumatic experience for Michael to have to endured. Michael had to adjust, lest he would languish in misery. He willfully and forcefully shifted his life's conceptual paradigm drastically. It entailed an act of extreme uprooting of his many viewpoints as to what he regarded as true. He had to allow a part of himself to grieve the past, and yet, shed off all the parts that can and will drag him down. He had to experience and validate these events with the sense of anger, mourning and need for retaliation. But yet, he also had to peel off a new part of himself to ignore the atrocity and adopt new principles to embolden his entire existence. The former was deluged with emotions, including despondency. The former mostly left him without vigor, for he spent most of his energy yearning for frivolity, which he sees now was in essence, an unavoidable part of his personal healing process. The latter part of him which he peeled, had to consciously step back to discern effective decisions and learn appropriate ways to heal from within, such as meditation and selective distractions from the unfortunate realities. Capricious torrents of cravings had to be denied by sagacious will and discernment through fortitude and distraction. The denying of those yearns initially masqueraded as intractable rejections of the heart's desires, dragging him down like ponderous deadweights, stirring up repugnant emotions within his mind, body, heart and conscience, causing further derision within himself. As he stepped out of his paradigm through developing and nurturing his bonds with others, all while contemplating situations from all angles and perspectives, he learned that his actions reverberate outwardly. His actions were individual events in a long chain of singular affairs. And what action he chose was his choice and nobody else's. It was completely within his power to execute however he so pleased in the here and now, and in doing so, it would be a part of forever.

Forever, it is a very long time. Michael had felt its warmth and magnificence through his journey to the precipice of his mortality. Things that seemed insurmountable now were just transitory and existential events in the odyssey through Time. A warm glow emanates through his body as these rationalizations proliferated through his mind. This warmth brought tranquility through his heart and soul.

He was light hearted in every sense of the word, he gazed upon life through the lens of sympathy and empathy, the act of aversion from those vengeful urges soon attained congruency with his intrinsic thought process. In time, it seemed effortless and spontaneous.

This onslaught and retrieval of his wellbeing taught Michael that one's Being is made up of the mind, body, heart and soul. They are volatile interdependent compartments of One that are open to change, just like the biological systems of the anatomy.

When passing through possible triggers nowadays, Michael looks at it with calmness in the memory of his grief-stricken self, no longer is he dejected by the events that occurred. Rather, he solemnly ponders about how it seemed like another life. Michael stands by himself. Michael cares for and comforts himself. Michael is here for himself. And even still, he remains enlivened by the chain of singular reactions which had preceded. Each progressive one seemingly has a greater influence in Time.

The time has come to coalesce with Forever. This much

he knew to be true. Whatever that is left of him will willingly exist in mindfulness of the moment. Michael knows a certain significance is presently shifting and forming within. He is free. This gift of freedom is to be cared for with a light-heartedness, that way, it will last in Time.

Michael goes into the world with this thought of freedom and complete surety that everything in existence is a gift. Not to be measured against something else for the determination of its worth. This surety helps Michael grow.

Michael walks into a meeting of the support group. This time, there is a pious man that is brought in to lead the session. He does his usual quoting and expounding of scriptures. The pious man also presents reasons to establish or restore faith. This pious man affirms to the group members that they are not alone in their hardships. This pious man is eloquent in his ability to address salient issues of the infirmed. This pious man is decidedly aware of the tenderness of damages incurred in the patients' lives, and is able to make his audience aware of the path of healing by articulating the appropriate statements at the fitting time. From the expressions on their faces, Michael can tell that group members feel as though all they need is this pious man's presence and wisdom. In and during his dialogue, the raising of spirits is inexhaustibly palpable through verbal and non-verbal means. Michael is distinctly aware of and impressed by this pious man's effect on the group. This pious man seemingly distributes spiritual sustenance at will. This pious man spiritually and emotionally fashions his oratory to uplift his audience and instills hope within them. Through his message's dramatization and climax, this pious man gives his audience's existence a significant and pleasant purpose and finality, all while hinting at subtle and possible opportunities for the near future. This pious man shows appreciation for the group's fellowship and companionship at the culmination of the gathering. Michael sees that this pious man dedicates himself to cleanse and bring nourishment to others. He has chosen the theological route to serve this purpose. Those intentions were laudable and distinguished. In the solemn and respectful nature of the room, Michael had not noticed Darcy's presence, as her head was bowed down in intense concentration. As of late, Michael had not seen her frequent the patient area that often.

Michael sees her and registers her presence in his mind. Michael takes a moment, then proceeds to walk over to the pious man and strikes a conversation centered on faith. The realm of their conversation seemed to be immediately abundant with trust in and recognition of each other, both persons were kind and open with each other. Michael gently steers the conversation toward his initial objective and inquires with the pious man about how theology existed before the time of disciplines, where Intermediaries acted as interpreters and ambassadors. This pious man tells Michael that Man always believed that their divinities existed in ways that were supernatural and beyond themselves as humans. Over time, theological documents and accounts reflect Man's historical culture and grasp of knowledge on the subject of Faith. Their knowledge has always been directly affected by their exposure and comprehension of faith. At the center of all dilemmas and conundrums, and at the heart of every congregation the world over, there exists a varying portion of each individual's intrinsic being that is aware of the simple and profound bond that a Man's existence shares with their divinities. Thus, revealing the bond's sheer brilliance.

Michael's attention then turns to Darcy. Michael cannot help but be unsure of himself in the moment as he approaches her. She remains seated and looks at the man that approaches with a conspicuous sense of forbidden ardency. As he approaches her, he gazes over the table that stands in front of her seated body. There it is, her slightly protruded abdomen, clearly indicative of a woman with child. Michael stands there and surveys the moment. Each passing second continuously strips him of his buoyancy and self-assurance. Each passing moment seems like an arduous grind. Eventually he catches himself from sundering and valiantly speaks words. His words did not have to carry any deep meanings. Michael knew it just had to carry the conversation.

Michael: Hey, how've you been?

Darcy: I'm alright.

They both seem slightly bashful.

Michael: Haven't seen you in a while.

Darcy: Yes I know, they've got me pretty swamped at work.

Michael: I see. How is your little brother?

Darcy: He's good. He's alright.

She continues to speak of her young child as her little brother so as to hide the truth from Michael. That she is a married woman and a mother of a growing family. Michael muses over what is transpiring. She continues to invest deeply into this image that she has portrayed of herself to Michael.

They both continue to speak toward each other, an insignificant conversation really. Darcy and Michael take great care not to deliberate over what stands there in accentuated circumstance. And as for Michael, he tries his best not to be caught gazing at her abdomen. He is ashamed of his feelings for Darcy. He is embarrassed of how he and Darcy both were carrying on with this act.

Fortuitously, he feels strangely thankful for this experience. This conundrum that exists provides him with a comforting solace. Michael feels that he has met Darcy at a fitting time in both their lives. It is not just a mere coincidence. The unique dynamics of their relationship energizes Michael. Their bond is vibrant and animated with lure, repulsion, surety and adoration. Michael recognizes that if he masters this encounter, he will be prepared for much more in Time. Michael continues to grow and thrive because of this experience. It brings a sense of buoyancy to his balance.

The relationship continues to grow with steady health and vigor. He feels he is a better Man for it, she calms his internal storms. She neutralizes any anger that may stir with acidity inside of him. This acidity, which is born out of distress and strain, would otherwise harm his body. The more time he spends with Darcy in delightful companionship, the more he feels his appreciation for life expands. Simple things take on deeper meanings than they normally would. Her demeanor and mannerisms continually strengthens the passion Michael has for her. Reasons for discontent and animosity diminish until it bears no significance. The deeper appreciation of another being's life has swallowed those reasons entirely. The reasons' venom presently seems like a distant quandary, but the deluging fluctuations that Michael had experienced in life leaves him with the weariness that inner spite can always be triggered back into relevancy, for it is the absence of appreciation. It is the ever present nature of a deviant, the dearth of appreciation enables them to defile any object of their hatred, no matter how subtle or profound. Their perspective is as such. They cannot feel the pain that ensues. If a person has damaged nerves and is being burned, they cannot feel the burn.

The experiences with Darcy instill all this into his mind. He thinks back on his course of action in the face of lustful revenge, and how he failed to consummate vengeance, and how he flagellated and excoriated himself with rage for that choice in the moments after. He knows now that had he turned onto the path untaken, Darcy and he himself would be hard pressed to accept that selection. The absolving of Michael would have been impossible. At this juncture, he feels warm and ripe with companionship and truly has no regrets to burden him, he remains thankful for the unfolding of events. Who knows where he would have landed had he wandered down that untaken path of murderous rampage, continuing to spread the frost of hate that has so deeply pronounced his psychological pain and anguish in the past.

Darcy's presence has evidently transfigured Michael's life in all domains of his existence. The surreptitious affection they share warms the lens with which he comprehends life with. Patience exists where petulance formally stamped as its stronghold. Empathy and understanding far outweighs pride and ignorance. Selflessness thrives where self-centeredness once reeked. Sentiments withheld by vanity no longer stand preeminent. Rather, an appreciation for the natural course of Things rests at the forefront.

Michael now treasures the attachment he has with Darcy. The frequency and subtlety of their dalliances begin to increase. Both were beginning to accept their feelings for one another. They boldly begin to show it in every interaction as it comes forth. This was harmoniously pleasant for Michael. However, the burden of this lust begins to sear the stability of Darcy's domestic life. She knows it is wrong yet she cannot stop. This inner clamor reveals itself in the way she carries herself. She shows a considerable unease with her professional environment. The work seems overwhelming as her efficiency declines. The eyes of others seem unnecessarily judgmental in her mind. Agitation is prevalent and preeminent, which is amplified by her irascibility. She yearns for relief from all that closes in on her.

Michael observes the noticeable decline in Darcy's spirit and drive. He knows that this very same bond that has caused him to flourish has shackled Darcy in a cycle of punishment within her own being. This grieves Michael. He knows what he has to do.

After a pleasant visitation with the existing patients, Michael gathers the courage to walk up to Darcy. This visit seems like a blur, he only did it to pass some time. It empowers Michael with the necessary fortitude. As he walks towards her, he ponders the subject of Darcy. She has been more than a physical fascination in his mind. The infatuation he had for her saved him from certain death, the distraction granted him release from the imprisonment that was his mind. He is grateful for all that. They amble towards each other, Michael reads the angst that is written all over her face, which seems to be permanently as such lately.

Michael: Hey. You alright?

Michael asks in an altruistic and curious but yet, nurturing way.

Darcy :   No!

She exclamates.
Michael is silenced and astonished by her answer. He then gathers himself again.

Michael: What's the matter?

Darcy :   Its just because I'm here.

She throws her hands in the air in an exasperated manner. She begins to walk away, down the path she originally was on.

Michael: Darcy.

Michael stops her in her tracks. There is nothing to it now, he has to say what needs to be said.

Michael: I know what troubles you, and I am sorry.

Darcy :   Sorry for what?

Michael: For everything. I want you to know that I will always want the best for you. I will always be here for you.

Darcy :   What are you talking about?

Darcy's voice tremors, it seems that she knows where Michael's intentions lay. Darcy's apprehension reverberates through Michael. The look in her eyes is one that deeply shakes Michael's confidence. He knows that a part of him will regret this speech, but the truer part of him knows that as presently constituted, their lives cannot go on. He takes a deep breath, he wants peace for Darcy. He looks into Darcy's eyes intently.

Michael: You married him for a reason, don't let that reason die. If we go down this path, we will hurt many people. You have a beautiful family. You've worked hard for it. I do not want to ruin something so pristine. We are living separate lives that cannot come together. But I am truly grateful for being near you these past months. I will never forget you. I cannot deny that I wish for more, but strangely, I am fully content with the path we have taken. This is a happy day, it is a new beginning.

They embrace each other, no words needed to be uttered. For neither of them knew where they were headed.

In the immediate days that follow, Darcy's mannerisms are ambiguous to Michael. She is no longer a portrait of turmoil, rather, now she seems determined on a course known only to her.

A week passes, she leaves, never to be seen or heard from again. Nobody knows about her whereabouts. It is as if she had vanished into thin air. There were no indications to all her colleagues to suggest why she left so abruptly.

"What now?" Michael asks himself. He gave up the one thing that gave his life purpose. The lack of purpose is a notable cause of desolation and sadness. He fears where this road might lead to. Yet, Michael knows that the situation could not have lingered on without imposing many hardships upon the life of another. Be it her Husband, her Son, or her gestating Child. A part of him hatefully rues the day he ever naively decided to embark upon this chapter of his life. Is he a better Man for this experience? Michael tries to discern the reason behind him ever feeling the need to search out such a peculiar form of companionship to include in his life.

"Why can't things be like they once were? Like it was before any of this happened. It was such a great feeling. I was happy. I wish for nothing more." Michael laments.

He tells himself that he should have known from the start, that there was never going to be any assurances to be gained by any person involved in this affair. Whether they knew it or not, All will be left in doubt, uncertainty and regret.

This trio of a resolution makes out for a perfect storm of a disaster. Through bitterness and anguish, a part of Michael could have impulsively steered himself toward trying to selfishly seize what he wanted, no matter the cost. He defiantly wanted to be rid of these sentiments, discarding them as an unnecessary consequence of his actions. Michael inwardly thinks that theses fateful events should not have happened to him, and yearns for a more favorable resolution. However, a growing part of him accepts all that has happened as the nature of the World. He has received much happiness from this exchange and realizes the choice he made of avoiding a seizure, signifies another part of him that has developed. One that sees Others, One that knows Others and One that knows One's Self. Michael realizes Now that the most conscientious way to live in this World is to go on while knowing what is taking place in and within his surroundings, lest, wandering into harm's way. Through a cautious deliberation of the Unfolding of events, Michael realizes that there are no regrets to be dwelled upon. He does not resent or feel great prideful joy in making the choices he has made. He just simply did not want to further impose a resolution upon Anyone, Michael did not want to bring pain to Anyone.

All the horrible deeds in his life flashes before him, all the pain he put himself through as a result of those deeds coalesce into logic and reason within his senses. He was and is the sole harbinger of pain and suffering in his own life. He commiserates with himself, apologizing sincerely and profusely to himself.

He confronts his recent fatalistic past calmly and absorbs the fact that he had lost friends, some of whom Michael formally attested to as brothers in arms. Brothers in arms who betrayed him and others through a slaughter of rage. He had let anger strangle and muscle out all sense and liberation of his mind. It prevails to him that his principles had severely leaden the nature of those friendships, robbing it of all compassion. Those bonds were deeply rooted in erroneous and immoral adherences. Those bonds were superficial and held no deep soulful connections. Michael's will of mind never gave himself a chance.

"I am so sorry to have caused you all this pain and suffering. I will never know what I could ever do to make it right for you." Michael sorrowfully moans to himself.

He just kept saying sorry to himself. He did not know what else to say. He is sorry for everything. The missteps of his past cannot be taken back. He was supposed to love, care for and nurture himself. He was supposed to be his own guardian and protector. And yet, he betrayed himself.

At this point, Michael is greatly diminished. He is riving in pain. Helplessly gasping for air through his narrowed windpipes that have contracted in acute distress.

After all that has transpired, Michael has nothing left to give.

He sees in himself true contrition, knowing that he is solely responsible for all that has passed in the time of his life. He wants no more remorse or sorrow to linger as punishment for himself. As quickly as it happened, Michael willingly pardons himself for all that has transpired. He made all the wrong choices in the past, the consequences that unfolded were natural and consequential. He stands firmly by for himself. He will help himself through the healing of himself. With that warmth that emanates from within, he examines the details of his previous ambition.

That Man he was, he lusted for commodities that represented power and validity in the minds of his cohorts. His whole existence centered upon being obsessed with the attainment of those desires. It was vital to him to appease and garner the approval of men and women who, in their own selfishness, had dark ambitions of treachery and deceit, which they used to hoard as much valuable means as possible for themselves. In doing so, Michael removed many essentials and indispensible intrinsic traits from his character, he forgot how to live in the comfort of contentment. He languished in dwelling upon a profane reality.

In an earnest moment of certainty, everything that was shrouded in the shadows became ever so clear to him. He sees that the hearts of his antagonists were always fraught with greed. Their hearts had always held the capacity for a deep betrayal against him. No matter how circumstances unfolded, this was always how their fellowship would have ended, he is sure of this. He no longer saw it as a shortcoming on his part, for it is the will of forces that he cannot control, such as Benjamin's vile thoughts.

Michael realizes, he no longer wants revenge on his antagonists. He is at peace with the situation. The reprehensible desires of their hearts would not be denied. He took a deep breath and recollected his thoughts and allowed it to come together with his mind. He then comforts himself. His mindful watchfulness of this day brought him clarity and peace of mind.

In his serene satisfaction, it gently dawns upon him that certain parallels can be drawn between his life and the life of those he had witnessed direct so much pain for him to endure, his antagonists. This draws his attention to the fact that if he were to ever lose sight of all that he has learned, he too could cause much grief in another's life. Michael realizes that he must never lose sight of this.

He will carry the thoughts and memories with him for the rest of his days. It will guide him through whatever may come.

Michael sees that in each moment that he spends being

open in mind, it brings him to a new place in life. Each new place feels warmer than the last.

In a normal conversation with his fellow volunteers, Michael learns about a gang-related gun shooting in the city. There is one fatality. This fellow volunteer goes on to seethe about how the streets are no longer safe, that something needs to change. All Michael can do is listen to her and engage in an empty conversation, for his part, on what the government should do to control the situation, there is no comforting her. She continually reads the news daily and is not pleased with what she discovers.

Michael takes a moment to have a seat. The social gathering is going as well as it can be. He picks up a glass of water to sip from and takes a look at the newspaper to read for a few moments. As he casually flips through the pages, his gaze centers upon the article articulating the events of the gang shooting. He decides to read further into the story. He sees that the deceased victim was identified as the Benjamin that he knew. He stares blankly at the paper for several minutes.

He sits back and soaks in this information. He is taken aback by it. He can feel himself losing control of his thoughts and feelings. Is he supposed to be happy or mournful? A few months ago, he would have wished for nothing more than to be the cause of this murder himself. Michael leaves that gathering.

On his way home, he wearily decides to visit the scene of the crime.

"So this is where he fell." Michael whispers to himself many times over in disbelief. Michael is rife with uncertainty. He knows his life will never be the same again. There is a special intangible significance transcending in the air. He cannot yet grasp his perception of the moment. But he knows he is witnessing a certain interval in Time. This connection with Benjamin had taken Michael on a journey through the kindliness of fellowship and kinship, to the bitterness of jealousy and vengefulness, and settling now at the partings of mortality. As the fellowship's finality, without them having spoken any words to each other, all appreciable attributes of their attachment comes to its end.

Michael just stands there staring at the bustling plaza that had strangers all around walking towards an objective that is solely their own. As his thoughts begin to gestate, he ponders the unfolding of events before him. He contemplates over how this must not be the first time that a human has felt the way he is feeling. At some point in history, some other Man must have felt the exact same way he is feeling right now. It is a sobering moment of orientation to reality.

Emotions and thoughts stirs within him. Michael sees every One in this World. Every single member of the human race is humbly a subject of the World, and the World always attains a form of congruency that is purely natural and foundational. This truth endures no rival. Changes in the World will come, and when it is made known for human understanding, it is up to that human to make his or her peace with that change. Michael never saw this coming. A part of him selfishly tries to steal away some satisfaction and pleasure in Benjamin's demise. But in allowing the moment to settle, he finds that he is neither happy nor joyous about the occasion. He does not know what he is feeling, it is just a feeling. This event is another chapter of the story that will continue to unfold until the end of time. Michael sees Now that all events, whether joyous or sorrowful, will pass into Forever.

Forever is the ceaseless body that is made up of the past, present and future. The past had already ended. Michael can see it now. It is happening in every moment of existence in perpetuity.

Through life's soaring heights and abysmal lows, Michael's desires and yearnings had changed along with it. Michael had shown great malevolence in some of his darkest moments. He decides to take a mental snapshot of this moment of immeasurable peace, committing to memory what tranquility feels like. Just remembering the balance experienced within the body and how it feels like is enough of a gauge to subdue his desires and keep its repugnance at bay. If he would ever need to, Michael would be able to hearken back to this point in his life for perspective.

Death is a point in Life. Benjamin is dead, never to come to life again. Michael knows that.

As each day passes by with Michael striding through it, along grows his fascination of the splendor that is Death. He has seen the other side and knows what awaits all who will come. Michael does not fear it, for it is no longer unknown to him. Michael feels a sincere ease for all who are at rest in Death.

Michael's attention now turns to the other side of Death, he looks to Life. In his many brushes with peace, Michael has grown a deep affection for the body he inhabits and how it feels in those moments of peace. Michael seeks neither abrasion nor harm for his body. Michael understands that the reason behind that peace is the complete relaxation and ease within the body and mind, which results in the expansion of a few many of his body's channels, enabling a harmonious flow of warmth and energy through his body and mind. In observing his body function in harmony, Michael knows now not to take it for granted. He knows it is a gift. Encased within the body is the mind, when the mind gives him no rest, Michael finds contentment in watching and remembering all that the body is, and what it in turn does for the mind. On a microscopic level, it is a sheer miracle how billions of factors coalesce to enable Life. He realizes that he needs to try his best to understand his own body through each and every moment, and in turn manage the necessary emotions and thus, corollary actions and decisions.

The body has within it many ways of corresponding within itself. Sending triggers to and comprehending indications from itself. Michael knows it will be prudent for him to recognize those triggers and indications in order to reconcile his conscious familiarity to his subconscious existence. These two segments of Michael are constantly fragmented away from each other as Time unfolds. Michael needs to focus in order to align his Body and his Mind.

Michael looks to his previous readings and experience with a calm and steady mind.

In working on his Body and Mind, Michael stimulates and initiates triggers, he also absorbs and observes indications that manifest themselves in times of either stress or bliss along with anything in between. In stimulating and initiating, Michael alters states of the Body and Mind in a yielding and comfortable manner. Michael realizes that all triggers of the Body affects the Mind, and vice versa. Michael tries to give himself the best chance to thrive physically. He cares for and trains his Body with great interest. He applies conducive magnitudes of stimulations so as to progress the Body's and Mind's abilities and thresholds. Michael nurtures any and all joints in his body, along with enhancing the muscles' potency and vigor through natural reparations, both allowing for a greatening of comfort within the body. Michael fortifies his system of veins and arteries through elevating its threshold and consistency with calculated challenges. These challenges within themselves initiated the appeasement and satisfaction within his Mind naturally. Allowing for a quiet and relaxed Mind and thus, amplifying Michael's appreciation of the Moment.

Within these moments, Time reveals its temporal nature

to Michael. Each moment can be a rekindling or relinquishing of a previous moment which has passed. He is able to hold on to cherished sentiments when it unfolds, just as easily as he can let go of anything that may occur within these Moments. Michael accomplishes both the cherishing and letting go without angst, greed or bitterness. Time allows for things to come forward. Whatever may come forth will have a course that is solely its own. And there is no denying that course. Michael coalesces with that sentiment.

Michael knows that there are many troubles in the World. He knows that Every event and occurrence has its own course to be taken. Some occurrences are iniquitous and malicious. There are also occurrences that are venerable and full of promise. Michael also knows that there is no reversing the wills of those who are in contemplation and adoration of cruelty, cruelty which is used it to satisfy greed. There are many violent and heinous acts committed in this World, One would commit it against another who he or she considers to be their enemy. When one considers another to be their enemy, there is a general sense of revulsion aimed towards this 'enemy'. That is how they are able to initiate the senselessness in their actions. Some of those targeted by hate try to equal, if not usurp the sentiment that had been sent their way. They do so through their actions. And in doing so, they create fresh new wounds to remember in both their mind and of the minds of their antagonists. There is some satisfaction to be drawn from both inwardly and outwardly exemplifying a stubborn resistance for all to see. It validates some form of strength. To tell those who wish ill upon you that they have failed, and that You are the stronger one. You are the victor.

However, Michael knows there are no winners in warfare, just two sides more broken then they were before. There is no victory. Life itself is strangled as vengeance thrives.

Each person's contemplation is their own. And to each, their own course they must take. Whatever course of iniquity or greed one may choose to take, it is separate from Michael's. Now, no burden is cast upon Michael.

Through the performance of cruelty, along with being enamored with greed, enemies can be locked in deadly battles of vengeful one-upmanship. All sides claim a facade to be their true face. They see their own venerations as paramount and discard those of others as worthless, all while treating those very others as such. They allow themselves to denigrate and desecrate the venerations of others, and in doing so, they contemplate and pronounce themselves as the victor. In proclamation of being victorious, they take great pride in those accomplishments. In that state of contemplation, there can be no perceiving relative facts as any other way. Their perspective's pride and satisfaction exalts them.

Such exaltation, while immobilizing their perspicacity, leaves some other frozen in Time. Frost that will continue to spread and dread a new course that is dark and rife with burden.

Michael sees a need to seek another path. He does not want to stake a position of opposition that would uphold such insight. Nothing can shake him away from his need for peace. He needs a life that accords with the coalescence, not inflamed estrangement. A path that is free of frost.

Michael moves on to the next moment with the acknowledgement of these facts. In Every moment for the rest of his life, he will carry these memories.

He comes across Annabelle, her mind is in a whirl, and Michael can see it from a distance. She is leaving the clinic after having just dropped off her husband at the therapy room. Nevertheless, Michael approaches her in the attempt to cultivate and nurture their bond.

Michael: How are things?

Annabelle sighs and frowns harder than Michael had ever seen her frown. Her eyebrows squeeze so tightly against one another that the crease in her skin nearly burrows to her hairline. Eventually, she does speak, after seemingly gathering herself from pondering whether or not she should say what is really on her mind.

Annabelle: I just can't see it. I don't. What is the point in me being here, taking care of him? Three hundred and sixty five days a year. Who's going to take care of me? Our kids are all living their own lives. I never see them. They don't care about this rut that we're in. Everybody needs to be taken care of. I have honestly passed my limit a long time ago. I don't even know how I've gone on for so long? I just need a break.

Michael knows a part of her wishes for all this to end, for her husband to die, and another part of her truly does not. She is torn. On a daily basis, she is enduring deep pains. Like many other kinds of pains, it inflicts damage. Most people who endure as such cannot let that pass. Annabelle is at a point of hopelessness and frustration. She seeks to find a way out. Time is of the essence in any solution within this mindset, all who endure such pains wish for it to end as soon as possible. The eventualities of the acts made under this rationalization is failure. Failing acts that are born out of the need to assuage the here and now. Michael remains resolute through Annabelle's vocalizations.

In these moments, Annabelle's mind is fragile. Michael knows it must be given the time needed to recover. She had already vocalized her anguish, the healing process had already begun. Michael is happy for her. He reaches over and clasps her cold clenched fists to signify his appreciation of her growth.

Her fists of rage discharge into its primal form and holds onto Michael's in acceptance.

Annabelle: I know I shouldn't feel what I'm feeling.

She is disappointed in herself.

Annabelle: But it's tough you know?

Michael nods. He is glad. Annabelle continues to grow. Michael does not debase her for any of what he had just seen or heard. All that matters to Michael is Annabelle's intentions. And her intentions were to be with her husband until the very end. She will endure what is to come.

The significance of bonds and fellowships instilled within a human life begins to take on a new meaning for Michael. Life is a natural course. And like all natural courses, there are similarities that can be drawn with others of their kind, other lives. The more Michael experiences, the more similarities he can recognize. Each life's natural course is significant and distinctly its own.

Michael goes on with his day. He had awakened portions of his psyche that had laid dormant all the long years of his life. Primarily, he feels the awareness of the mind and body of not just himself, but also that of others. He feels the need to be considerate of that awareness. His consideration stems from a general sentiment he feels for humanity that was until now, restrained by his greed and the contemplation of his past affiliates. He is feeling the confluence of the pieces of Life within him.

He accepts that One cannot truly understand One's self through external means of accreditation and acceptance. The external is of different and distinct properties within itself, therefore making it impossible for the external to truly empathize and understand One's true necessities in Life.

Michael sees the importance of being at peace in this world and not impinging upon the lives of others. Each person is responsible for each moment of their own ongoing existence. Each moment is significant and distinctly its own.

He constantly feels a necessity to take strides forward in life. Somehow, through all that has been thrown his way, he fatefully hearkens to that necessity, finding it within himself to prevent himself from decaying in the stagnancy of hate and vengeance. At many points, the yearnings to halt any and all forward progress in life, in order to alleviate immediate frustrations were sorely tempting and seemed pleasurable in his mind. However, in Time, as the need to move on began to exert itself, the tragic horrors of his past began to fade into a mundane wasteful occurrence.

Prideful traits of his unwillingness to give up ground to any opposition erode away from his existence. He calmly molds himself to the median of reality. He walks along this median in peace. Michael begins to live with the model of Time, living as a part of it.

Therapy ends abruptly due to budgetary cuts within the halls of legislation. In the immediate aftermath, Michael sees the ending of these sessions as a shame. Then, Michael looks to his experiences of pains, followed by the natural alleviation which initiated within himself. He sees this, he has felt its healing ways. He is grateful for being healed. Despite the shame, his mind and body are at rest.

8

Michael strolls into a neutrally lit café. There is a man dressed in a freshly starched suit sitting there, browsing through some magazine that fits the portrayal he meticulously crafted for himself. There is also a striking woman who sits nearby silently browsing through her novel with great interest. Somewhere in between these two individuals sits an unassuming man who evidently withholds a syndrome that lessens his ability to perceive and sense the world around him. His demeanor seems innocent and harmless. There is a sense of untainted decency that surrounds him. The kind that offsprings are born with, before somehow or other, it becomes lost in varying amounts.

The man reading the magazine shows a distinct and intentional attempt to avert and ignore all of the unassuming man's actions. In fact, his repugnance is shared by just about all who are visible in the room. All are silently judging his physical shortcomings on the surface. The man reading the magazine unwillingly yields his leg's positioning as the unassuming man arduously toggles through the limited space of the café. As the unassuming man takes the empty seat next to the lady with the book, she kindly smiles in consent of his presence. There is a space of a few seconds before the unassuming man breaks the silence with pleasant interjections. He is just happy to be in the company of another human being. The Lady responds in kind to all his interjections. There is warmth exuding from both parties as they conversed cheerfully and gleefully. Michael could not directly hear the conversation, but there stood before him a universal sign of camaraderie. It is pleasant.

As the pleasantries culminated, the unassuming man got on his two feet, the Lady does so as well simultaneously to acknowledge his leave and also to see if she could assist him in any way. This affair brings smiles to both their faces. They are both better people for having encountered one another. He bids the Lady farewell, she reciprocates. He then strides tenuously towards the door and tries to greet anyone who will meet his eyes with their own. His attempts are met with mild success.

The Lady smiles and returns her gaze to her book. Michael takes a moment to appreciate the warmth that had been fostered between two strangers.

Michael thinks of the man who browsed through the magazine. It brought back memories of those who prioritized themselves as the centerpiece of all needs and wants. Most of all, these slight hindrances revitalizes the memories of his former affiliates. When they were surrounded by entities which annoyed them, they churned in unrest, constantly stultifying the minds of all around at the time. Grinding and wearing upon the wills of others to the point of exasperation, simply because they failed to hold their composure. As much as it impinges upon lives, Michael cannot blame their nature or nurture. They were their own man. The responsibility to compose lays with the person and that person alone in that moment.

Michael returns to the facility and sees a grief-stricken Annabelle. With one look at her, Michael just knew that her husband had left her and this World. He approaches her with fear and doubt. But given Michael's placement in Life, and how the brush with mortality had spontaneously shifted him intrinsically, there is a nurturing acquaintance that Michael harbors with the situation. Nevertheless, Michael continuously steps forward.

As he paces toward her, he feels her gaze wearing upon him. Michael allows himself to absorb the deep sentiments that are being sent his way. The weight of Annabelle's ambition is a burden that Michael seeks to help her hold up. Even the subtlety of his silence and acceptance seems to somehow ease the passing of each fleeting moment.

And so Annabelle unveils to Michael what he had already deduced from her body language. Annabelle's loss leaves her in great tumult. Michael sees her weakened within this onslaught that is imposing upon her. Michael tries to search for a glint of hope. He tries to put forward the option of acknowledging the life of Andre, a life that was well lived, according to Michael's understandings from Annabelle's many accounts. And thus, embrace what is to come with a fair and free heart. Annabelle turns to Michael with a vitriolic gaze and utters,

Annabelle: No Michael.

So she proclaims with dreadful exhalation.

Time stands irrelevant and motionless in this moment. The frost spreads potently. In this trying moment, Annabelle makes it especially poignant that in her mind, she was left to grind out the latter stages of her marriage alone. She remembers clearly how her children were nowhere to be found when her need was great. They selfishly took pleasure in their own affluent existences.

They proved to be ungrateful and unappreciative of her and their father as parents. She means to right how she had been wronged over those long arduous years. She wants balance. She wants justice. She walks away from Michael with a heart full of those desires.

Michael feels a loss of promise and warmth in Annabelle. Michael knows it is saddening that it has come to this. The burden is heavy. Michael adjusts his focus to the present. He decides to take a walk to outside. He must clear his mind. As he walked and focused, his perception of the torment of Annabelle's predicament begins to reduce in severity.

Days pass, and so begins the memorial processions. Family and friends gather to pay their final respects to Andre and his loved ones. Annabelle stands strong for all to see, welcoming all visitors, alongside her is Andre laying at rest.

Adam, their son, walks into the hall. He is a man lamenting the loss of his father as he comes to grips with Andre's absence. At the sight of Adam, Annabelle cringes and blinks, while she consciously banishes the love she had nurtured for him throughout the course of their familial lives. His tears of sorrow meant nothing to her. Her sorrow for Andre has accursedly mutated into anger and hate. She beholds Adam with a sustained sense of disdain. Not only did Annabelle want to exact some form of retribution, but she also hopes to prolong and deepen the sufferings of Adam, her son, so that he could sample a taste of the hardship his ill-bred treatment of his parents had put her through all those long years while his father ailed.

Adam walks up the aisle of the hall towards his Mother. He hopes to cast away all past occurrences of discord. She turns away from her grief-stricken son who is in need of her acceptance. She forcefully strides away from him.

Adam silently turns inwardly in a hall full of people who witnessed the entire occurrence unfold. Adam knew every one of them, and they all knew Adam. His grief was too intense for him to feel shame. Adam knew exactly why his Mother did what she did.

Family and friends mingle in the hall, hoping to find and offer support as the situations deem.

Michael sees a man that must be a close friend of the family. Michael recognizes his face in some of the pictures that Annabelle had showed him at the rehabilitative facility. Michael walks up to the friend and introduces himself. The man introduces himself right back.

Michael: I've seen you in some of the pictures that Annabelle showed me.

Friend: Yes, those must be the pictures you saw of our families back in our little hometown, living near the lake. A lot of good times there, all those summers spent playing in the water, fishing, kayaking.

Michael: Nice.

Friend: You name it, we've done it. It's a shame though. Once the kids grew up and moved away, we never came home. Heck, I can't even remember when was the last time I've even seen a body of water, let alone swim in it.

He takes time to reflect on those good memories that have lasted in his mind all this time.

Friend: I don't even fish anymore, and it was my favorite thing to do. It's strange how we change as we grow and we don't even realize it until we look back.

The nostalgia experienced is overwhelming, it is mixed with a hint of regret over this given probability. Michael finds this meeting of people who had brought happiness to Andre's life very fulfilling. It widens the perspective of a life that was.

Old friends greet this Friend with joyful exuberance in their reunion. Their conversations begin to steer towards the direction of their present circumstances and situations. For they have not seen each other in decades.

Michael sees that Adam is kind and genuine to all he comes across, tirelessly welcoming and stimulating each interaction he shares with others. Through a series of social interchanges, Adam and Michael eventually come across one another.

Michael: Your Mother and Father are wonderful people. You are lucky to have them as parents.

Adam: Thank you.

Michael: They are both strong and kind.

Adam: I believe so.

Michael, having witnessed the unfortunate event, treaded

carefully through their conversation. He did not want to delve into any topic that deeply surrounded Adam's Mother.

Adam: My Mother especially. She is amazing. Pulling Dad through all those years of rehab. She's amazing. You wouldn't believe it if I told you so,

Adam says these things as his tone of voice morphs to one that trembles, is evidently restrained and is full of shame. Then he continues,

Adam: But I haven't seen any of these people for many years.

Michael: Is that right?

Adam: Yes

Michael: But you all seem so closely knit.

Adam: I guess, it's just because my Dad isn't around anymore. And the fact that Mom is here,

Adam sighs. Michael sees that Adam is discombobulated and knows not to press Adam to elaborate any further on his utterances.

Adam: I guess I just feel the need to be around everyone, and I guess, they've been there for my parents all these years. This is what I should do, as a person you know?

Adam looks to Michael for a response. Michael nods

back. Adam finds himself to be thoughtless and faint as he tries to gather his senses.

Michael however, can see right through this listlessness, Michael sees in Adam the conviction and will to perpetuate a sentiment that Adam currently carries in this very moment. It is a determination to do so for as long as he, Adam, can. A resoluteness to regard and take to Another for many days from here on out.

In the procession that followed, Annabelle recounts Andre's life, subtly remembering and justifying his mistakes. Poignantly emphasizing the loves he shared with others. She reminisces back on their marriage. Her eulogy however, is full of regret over the shortcomings of themselves as spouses and people. That their lives had lacked an aspect of self-awareness, that if they had not given into certain impulses, they would not have been put through certain sufferings. It seems like she is not content with the bitterness of this end. Michael had been there for the trifles of the latter stages. He knew Annabelle begrudged her children for their distance and inaction towards her dreadful situation. In this period of grief, she will not let that go. It took all of her internal will not to publicly admonish her children. However, the underlying intentions of her subtle messages gnawed Michael's mind to shreds. He closes his eyes in capitulation. He seeks nothing.

Adam shows true feelings of lament and regret of his Father's passing. Annabelle is noticeably distant from all her children throughout the ceremony. Adam vigilantly wants to keep in touch with every person he forged a bond with on this significant day. He is determined to do so.

Adam goes to his Mother in the hope to heal the deep wounds that were slashed through these events of distance and inaction. He stands before his Mother, before he can muster the breath to talk, Annabelle asseverates,

Annabelle: Your father died without getting this off his chest. Not for me. Your distance, your neglect saddened him. He is gone now, never to be at peace with you. You might as well have killed him. His blood is on your hands.

Adam's courage fades. His mother walks away from him. He wants to send forth a reply but is frozen over with ineptitude and despair. His mother's vitriol is paralyzing to his thoughts. His actions are indicative of that. He had hoped for so much more for this day with his Mother. Adam rests, for it is not to be.

Time passes, Adam lives a life that is imprinted with many struggles. This unrest was born out of what his Mother last imparted towards him amidst the trying grief he had and still has for his Father. This erratic mix of shame and despair greatly convolutes the outlook that Adam has on life. He has feelings of abandonment projected towards his Mother, at the same time he feels remorse for the folly which he exemplified while his Father still lived. He put his priorities before anything his parents ever called upon him for. This multiplicity of empowerment and despondency caused great precariousness in Adam's will to act. But in his actions, Adam uses his regret and angst to drive his resolve and vigilance to take on tasks in life. He did not let the haplessness of the situation further deepen the chasm between him and his mother. Adam diverts his progressively explosive resolution toward his professional career. He realizes that he has made a grave mistake in his past as an irresponsible son. He channels this ruefulness into a singular hope to make for a better future.

Adam often visits his Father's grave. In his visits, he

often tries to resolve situations that grab a hold of the Here and Now.

Adam: It hasn't been the same without you Dad. I know I have to move on. I've been trying, it's tough. I'm so close, I'm getting there. I can almost see it. I sure wish you were here to give me some guidance and make things better.

Adam thinks of his life and how he feels like something is missing. His gaze never deviates from his Father's insignia upon the tombstone.

Adam: Maybe I just have to learn to let go of the past. Maybe some part of my life isn't what it's supposed to be. Mom still won't talk to me.

He loses the will to converse. Rather, he feels that what is in his heart need not be verbalized. He places his palm on the tombstone as if it were his Father's flesh. He takes a moment to cherish what his Father means to him, then walks away.

A few months to the day of Andre's death, Michael decides to pay Andre a visit. As he arrives at Andre's resting place, from a distance he sees a lone figure standing where Andre lays. As Michael closes in on the figure, he begins to recognize that nebulous figure as Adam.

Michael hesitates for a split second as his recognition takes grasp of his cognition. Nevertheless, he decides to walk up and ingratiate both Andre and Adam.

Michael: Hey,

Adam silently acknowledges Michael. Adam's gaze is

firmly focused on the ground where his Father lays. Adam's body gently shudders all over as he gingerly runs his fingers over his beard repeatedly.

Michael: A life well lived.

Adam: Yes. A life well lived.

There is a brief pause among the two men.

Michael: How've you been?

Adam: I've been managing. Up and down you know? Taking each day as it comes.

Michael nods his head in agreement. Michael then goes on to assert,

Michael: That's the best way to live.

Adam: No other way to do it.

Michael: How has the family been?

Adam: We talk more often. Although, things with my Mom are still, um

Adam is at a loss for words. From Adam's expression, Michael knows that the bond is still weary from its past. Adam searches for a way to clarify the silence that endures. But there is nothing for that cause. A dreary silence mocks the moment. Michael diverts the conversation,

Michael: How are things at work?

Adam grabs a hold of his capabilities and replies

Adam: Work is work. You do what you have to do.

Michael: Absolutely.

Adam resolves to address the issue of his Mother to Michael.

Adam: I guess she is doing what she has to. All of us have to. She is no different.

Michael: She knows what she wants. It's rare. Not everyone does.

Adam: I know. No matter the dispute, I guess we just want different things for our future. I have no objections or absolutions, this is my life.

Adam shows an unbiased state of mind in the face of adversity. Adam understands the needs of another, his Mother. Michael lauds that ability. It is a gift.

Michael thinks of all that he has experienced in life.

Michael: I've lost much in my life.

Both men are weakened by that statement.

Michael: What we lose, we may lament and regret. Sometimes, moments take hold of us and won't let go. But these memories, they belong to us, not us to these memories.

Adam hearkens diligently. Adam's facade furrows and twitches as his pupils sway aimlessly in the sole objective to avoid the slightest glimpse at Michael, Adam subtly fidgets away from Michael with an expression of great discomfort. Adam begins to grasp hold of where he is in Life, in this moment, his life changes. His resolve is impregnable. His silence bellows in a void. He feels faint as vocalizations continue.

Michael: It takes a hold of us and tests our spirits. Sometimes we fall short of our ideals. In our desperation and stubbornness, we commit acts that are both heinous and intractable. Through Time, we may not even bear to recollect about the depths of which we sink to. It is up to us, our minds and our hearts, as to how we are attached to these memories through Time. Situations will undoubtedly leave its impression upon us. If we let it, it can integrate seamlessly into our lives. The shackles we feel as imposed upon us loses its invincibility once we know the nature of these Attachments. These memories are frozen in Time, we however, move through Time at a natural pace, the pace we've always moved at. It cannot catch us. It's not even chasing us.

Adam's eyes spontaneously begin to glisten and well up. His pupils and irises begin to settle at Michael's feet. Adam begins to ponder how unfavorable his circumstances are, how his amicable intentions became obscured in his pursuit of Life. Resulting in those whom he loves, having nothing but disdain for him. Michael continues,

Michael: There's nothing in the past we can't let go of, nothing we can't get past. This pace that we move through Time with is not influenced by sorrow or pleasure. It's all just a feeling.

Is this all just a feeling? Is this real?
Adam echoes silently in his mind.

Michael: Everything we feel, everything we experience is a product of our stroll through Time in Life. All that is frozen in Time is meant for our viewing pleasure. We behold it and appreciate it for what it is. All we have left to do is to learn from our own lessons, whatever they may be, and be conscious of how Others may perceive Us.

Michael catches himself, he realizes he is iterating what he has gestated in his mind through his experiences. Adam continues to process his thoughts.

Adam considers if it is even possible to embody such a focus.

Adam: I know what you're saying and I know what you're trying to do. But no one can lead me anywhere. I just have to figure it out for myself. Everyone has their own path to take in life. I know now it is not meant to be with my Mother. I have to let it go, I have to let her go. Thinking of her only brings me pain. I have to remove her from my thoughts.

Michael sees that Adam is so focused on the future that he is missing out on all that has brought him to this point and to be at peace with it. Adam is trying to discard something that means much to him as a final attempt to ascertain a solution. To act in desperation. It is no solution. There will be no surety. Michael had fell through a bottomless pit because of such acts. A mind that is in a state of desperation is strangled of reason. Michael wants Adam to abstain from doing so. But there is no reverting Adam's mind at this moment. There is only the option of relinquishing all imposition upon Adam.

Michael: Just know this, you're never alone.

Adam: Thanks,

     Adam smiles at Michael's warmth.

Adam: I just don't know how I will ever make it right?

     Adam bemoans as he runs his finger down his Father's tombstone. Michael sees this,

Michael: He knows where your heart is. He always knew.

     This sentiment frees Adam's mind, all the constraints in Adam's expression loosens completely. Adam stands before his Father's resting place silently for a while to ratify the past, present and future. Adam breathes freely as he soaks in the moment.

     Both men walk away with light hearts.

     Michael thinks of the art of parenting. It is a grand undertaking when minutely evaluated. A parent's actions may be rightfully or wrongfully perceived as lies and or scrutiny. A parent may have to pass judgment on or justifiably debase their child to empower reason over malfeasance. A parent must make instantaneous decisions that will potentially reverberate through the course of a life, maybe even several lives.

Michael finds comfort in this trove of thoughts. Michael finds that these feelings are engrained within his thoughts now. It reverberates within him as he had found them in Time, the kind of reverberation that will last through a course of a life. These thoughts have the ability to lift his state of mind when its state is in decline, providing Michael with intrinsic counsel when in need.

Michael hopes that the future would bring about a resolution for Adam and his family. Through his personal experiences, Michael knows that each act that passes presents the mind with new perspectives and possibilities. The hindsight within the mind reveals details that were previously obscured in moments passed. A person's perception of matters evolves as Time progresses. And so changes one's understandings regarding the severities of situations. Significance of matters amalgamate into a form of reality in regards to a Life lived. With all that is known, One propels the self on a course of life until death. One makes choices and sacrifices. Every One lives their Life with their individual inspirations as the main basis. Michael knows that.

Michael takes a walk one day through an old familiar park, one that he visited frequently in the past. He sits on a bench that he had sat upon many times. In his many visits, Michael never used to notice the openness of the air in the park or how tranquilly the trees swayed in the afternoon breeze. This moment brings Michael calming repose. He closes his eyes and just continues to breathe. He soaks in the memories that he had created here in his younger days. His reminiscence engenders a sense of nostalgia, an unfiltered form of genuine contentment. He allows himself to be enveloped in the fresh and light air. Michael hears footsteps upon the pavement approaching him. It dawns upon him that he is not alone. The sounds of the bustling city that revolves around the park begin to penetrate his awareness. Michael turns his head, he sees a face that he had seen many times before.

As Ashley approaches, questions and thoughts begin to percolate in Michael's mind. Images of their past begins to flash within his mind. Although their past was that of a devoted relationship, most of the flashing images which arises are that of instances blistering with anger and abuse that they have committed upon each other. Michael feels a temptation to fall back into those old habits. His mind feels the need to project a visceral anger unto Ashley. He wants to strangle her for deserting him in a time of great need. A part of him knows that strangling her will satiate an unyielding anger inside of him, that he will have never felt better if he would but yield his will to those indulgences. Another part of him knows that he will utterly regret such an engagement, that there will be nothing to be gained from those indulgences. It would all just be a feeling. He gathers himself with a deep breath.

By the time Michael recollects himself, Ashley is in front of him, standing over him. Even as she stands over him, Michael remains seated. He cannot muster the will to stand and greet her.

Ashley: I knew you would return one day.

Michael: Return?

Ashley: I come here every day, hoping that you would return to this place.

Michael searches his memory and he finds that in days past, Ashley and he used to take strolls and relish picnics together under the afternoon sun in this very park. The two of them have many amorous memories that have endured until this day. Michael's hateful antipathy waivers in the warmth of those memories. Ashley appears to have hung on to those memories for many days. And so here they are, Man and Woman standing before each other, neither with the slightest clue of what to do with those memories. Jovialness from nostalgia yields to silence, as the elated sentiment of their reunion dissipates under the oppressive weight of the reality of events that have transpired since those days of ignorant blissfulness. The current state of their affairs drags them down with its lifelessness.

A part of Michael knows that it does not matter what path the following conversation would proceed along. For he knows that nothing could possibly happen Here henceforth that would be able to erase the hardships suffered from events which have taken place, but nevertheless, he stares at Ashley and asks,

Michael: Where were you?

He looks at Ashley with sheer disappointment. Ashley cannot answer. Michael's disappointment deepens.

Michael: Ash?

Ashley's expression flails and waivers. She can hardly bear to look at Michael. She sits down on the opposite side of bench from Michael. She slouches over in weakness.

Michael: I needed you.

Ashley: I know baby, I know.

She crumbles and begins to weep.

Michael: I have so many questions about that day. But
                 no one can answer them. What happened?
                 How did I live? Why didn't I die?

Ashley realizes that there is a place of devotion for her
to reclaim in Michael's life, for she had the answers to all
those questions.

Ashley: You're going to hate me when I tell you this.

Michael remains silent. All he does is gaze at Ashley with
bated breath and subdued anticipation.

Ashley: I don't know how to say this. I guess I'll just
                 tell you.

Michael begins to get an ominous feeling about this
exchange.

Ashley: You deserve to know this.

Ashley's voice shrinks to mutters. It is as if her windpipe
had contracted completely, she barely draws enough air to
articulate anything.

Ashley: I've put this off for too long.

Michael continues to await Ashley's revelation.

Ashley: I actually knew they were coming for you.

Ashley schleps both of them through the events of that night

Ashley: I realized immediately that I made a mistake, so I came back for you. But I was already too late. All I saw was blood and bodies. The only thing that mattered was that I find you and save you.

Michael: Save me?

Michael is stunned. He is absolutely convinced that Ashley has lost her mind.

Ashley: I brought you to the nearest hospital and handed you off to the doctors.

Astonishment and bewilderment turns to outrage and animosity. A part of him is livid at Ashley for having meddled in the affairs of his mortality. Michael feels as though he had been robbed of a permanent escape from all his hardships and sufferings. Many a times in his recent memory, he recalls being no longer able to bear the weight of his memories. She had interrupted a chain of events that was natural and proper. This part of him asseverates that not only did she cause him a horrendous calamity, but she also compounded the situation by ensuring that his sufferings would be prolonged to its optimal capacity of strife.

Michael remains seated in disbelief. He could not believe that this was the reason how his broken body was salvaged.

Ashley: It was Benjamin, he tricked me. He made me believe that all this was for the best. I don't even know why I believed him?

The both of them knew who was truly at fault for the matter.

Ashley begins to console herself.

Ashley: Where we were, where we were heading? I saw only betrayal and pain for us. I never wanted us to go on,

He could not believe such heinous intentions had mulled within her without him knowing. This was a woman who he thought he knew inside and out. Much had slipped through Michael's awareness in days past. His world had completely fallen apart and it was witlessly unbeknownst to him. Michael felt weakened and sorrowful about the past. It dawns on Michael that on that fateful day, the life as he knew it to be had already crumbled before that night, and that for all intents and purposes, he should have absolutely died that night.

Ashley: We were destroying each other. You've got to admit that.

Michael stares at her blankly, his mind is racing with an infinite amount of thoughts. All that Ashley utters is just plain words to Michael. He is neither in disbelief nor in any form of anguish. Michael just stares at the sky that is behind Ashley. He relaxes the muscles of his lips and begins to breathe shallowly. It does not matter that the woman he had professed to love in days past had betrayed him. He is and always had been in a place that could not be sullied by any force of nature. And that includes any act by Ashley. All these thoughts run through Michael's head while Ashley continues,

Ashley: After I brought you to the hospital, I couldn't bear to face you if you awoke. I didn't even know if you were going to make it. I didn't want to face the cops or answer any questions. I had to go.

The silence and heedlessness on Michael's part is not the response that Ashley was expecting. It led her to search for answers to her own statements. And thus, she falls into folly.

Ashley: I didn't know who else was watching, if anyone else was following me. I don't know why I did what I did. I just did it. I could've done it differently, but I didn't.

She tries to embolden herself.

Ashley: This wasn't my fight. I wanted no part in it. I thought you were happy. Why did you even still want to be with me?

She is evidently panic-stricken. Her logic is incoherent and no longer makes any sense. Michael sees that she is somehow trying to pass the blame of all that happened onto him, and he has no qualms with such a sentiment.

Michael finally breaks his silence.

Michael: They hid their intentions well. They worked hard to do so.

He vacillates whether or not to utter his next words,

Michael: And you helped them do it. You empowered them. I guess I have realized that and come to terms with that. Now, you have to come to terms with your own deeds.

She sinks deeper than ever before, Michael takes no pleasure in compounding and amplifying her misery with this infirmed realization.

Michael decides to help her bear this burden through sharing the blame.

Michael: You and I, we created this monster, we fraternized with it, and we even loved this monster. We were just trying to sustain our livelihood, so we didn't see its wickedness. We saw and took part in countless damning deeds. We saw it committed and just stood idly by. We even saw it as fruitful labor. We were empowering a force that continuously grew in might and strength until eventually, it consumed us whole.

Ashley is taken aback at what she is hearing. Not only did it reduce the burden off her chest, but it is a refreshing perspective on a long-standing issue in her mind.

Ashley: You've changed.

Michael has no reply for her.

Ashley: Baby, remember what we used to be like? I want us to be like that again.

There is a sense of lightness to her will and tone. There is almost a sense of rebirth.

Michael stares directly at her,

Michael: There is no going back.

Ashley's heart sinks.

Ashley: Please don't do this. Don't lose hope. Can
                you hope again?

Ashley implores Michael. This question grabs a hold
of Michael.

Ashley: Come back to the world that we made for
                ourselves. I am so sorry,

She emphasizes her remorse.

Ashley: It was all my fault baby.

Michael calms his mind and gathers himself. Michael
realizes that if he chastises her for her fallen ways, he will
fall into his old cycle of petulance and need for immediate
gratification. He would be continuing further upon an endless
pursuit of self-applied satisfaction, one that has yielded much
anguish and frustration along the way. If he chooses to go
along with that petulance, he would never see the serenity that
is the direct alternative. These thoughts bring him ease. Some
in the world never overcome inner strife and the anguish
that ensues. They remain torn within. Through this awry,
they will not let go.

Michael turns and stares reassuringly into Ashley's gut-
wrenched expression.

Michael: No Ash. It's nobody's fault.

Ashley is lost and confused. She is dazed and disillusioned.

Michael doubts himself for a moment. A part of him prioritizes the need to tell Ashley the truths of the matter.

Michael sees Ashley for what she truly is. She is a void, numb even, and ravaged with much uncertainty. She seeks some form of finality from this chapter in her life. Michael is Here and watches. She desires holism to fill this void, some embodiment of totality so as to move on in life. Her expressions and mannerisms exemplify fatigue and feebleness from a prolonged pursuit that had not bore any fruit. She is sinking in an endless cycle of turmoil. Michael reckons forgiving her would greatly neutralize and reverse all the erosion of Ashley which had already unfolded. In his mind, he contemplates abrasively lashing out at her verbally, perhaps even physically tormenting her. But he is held back by a sympathy for her misery. She is a prisoner in her own life. In this life, she made all the wrong choices. A part of her genuinely hates herself. As his need to abuse her gently declines, it is reborn as a purpose to comfort her. He wants for her what Time in this World had granted him, to let go of that part of life that is holding her back. Everything that she comes in contact with in life will undoubtedly break upon that injurious part of her. Eventually, it will obscure her entire being. All which she needed to move on is within her. She did not need anyone or anything, no matter what was offered to her.

Michael remains silent as he examines the moment.

Ashley's confusion swiftly turns into anger, anger at Michael for being almost comatose in a time of heightened passion and emotion. This is a seminal turning point in their lives from Ashley's perspective. Her frustration led her to screech.

Ashley: Can you even show that you care??!!

There is a pause.

Michael thinks back about the beginning, their first meeting.

Michael: You were the most beautiful thing I had ever seen. I loved you from the first moment I had ever seen you.

Ashley: What do you mean?

Ashley still shows traces of untamed anger.
Michael refocuses to elaborate.

Michael: They took everything from me, and you helped them. They even took you away from me. Every day that I came home, you were my second chance at life, my great love.

A hint of a smile comes to Michael's face.

Michael: Whenever I needed to escape from all the horrible things that I did and saw, you were there for me, you were my redemption. You meant the world to me.

Michael searches for the same strength that had helped him overcome Ashley's previous departure from his life.

Michael: When you left, along with everything that happened, my world fell apart. You were nowhere to be found. Now, to know that you had a hand in all this, how can you expect me to take all this? How do you expect me not to lose any hope? You've cut me too deep. Where do you expect me to go from here?

Michael immediately comes into himself and ponders the path he had trodden since that night, and whether or not this revelation has truthfully changed any circumstances. And through his examination of matters, this divulgement only changes nothing. It shows the operation of Ashley's mind at the time. It does not strip away any of what Michael had experienced.

His thoughts land once again on Darcy. Michael knows that Darcy is somewhere content with her family. He knows that. He holds no vitriol toward these understandings. He is truly happy for her.

He emerges from his inner monologue and turns outwardly to see Ashley again.

Michael: I know you're sorry. But when you think about it, it was always meant to happen. You should've just let things be. You went beyond yourself. You did what you thought was right, who can blame you?

Ashley's anger reverts back to confusion.

Ashley: What are you talking about?

Michael: You took matters into your own hands. You chose my fate for me.

There is a hint of dissension which grows in Michael's tone.

Ashley: So now I'm wrong for saving you?

Ashley is incredulous.

Michael strives to stay calm in the face of Ashley's outrage.

Michael: You did what you thought was right. I don't hate you for it. I just wish you didn't do what you did.

Ashley repeatedly tries to subtly interject, but her subtle indecisiveness is due to her need to satiate her curiosity of the current state of affairs, she sees a moment of weakness materializing in Michael.

Ashley's curiosity seems to have drawn out an unfiltered opinion from Michael.

Michael: You just further knotted an already tangled bondage that I needed to escape from. As my life has turned out, it has become all about this second chance that I don't even know what to do with. There is no real reason that I can relate to for my continued existence, no redeeming motive. Sometimes, I think that I am in pain, but the truth is, I can't even feel pain, I don't feel anything. All this, it doesn't matter, it's not real. All this should've ended that day. I don't need redemption.

Ashley anticipates the conclusion to Michael's statement. Michael holds no regard for the present, he is lost in the pain of the past that has somehow clenched its grip on him again. In his memory, it manifested as his reality, not an aberration. His rant is hopelessly fixated on a past that he cannot change.

Michael: Ever since that day, I've been continuously
                 toiling, I don't even know how I got here.

Ashley sees that all hope is lost. Michael is no longer
capable of love or joy.

Michael: I have already met my End. I was One with
                 that End. You took that away from me. I
                 didn't want any of this.

Michael is drowning in this sorrow. Ashley is hanging
on to the ledge of a stable mind. Ashley's silence consoles
Michael.

There were things that Ashley could have chosen to say
to justify the moment and her past actions, but it is nullified
by the sentiment that has gestated in Michael's mind. There
is no going back from what has unfolded. There is now only
a sense to move forward on a path that was up until now,
unhinged by that dreadful night.

They both seem willing to do what is necessary move
on past this.

Both of them wander aimlessly back into a relationship.
They hope to rekindle a former flame with the ashes that
have dwindled and now rest upon the ground. They remain
determined to make it work. It is an arduous task.

Michael is reinvigorated at another chance of being in a
devoted relationship with Ashley. His every effort is dedicated
to trying to prove to her that they are right for each other.
That the love they share is a gift. One that the whole world
over craves for.

Ashley subconsciously engages Michael with applied
caution, her intuition leads her hand. She cannot help it.
She is an instinctual creature whose surety of circumstances

fluctuates boundlessly. This outward projection of instability on Ashley's part adversely churns Michael's decisiveness.

One afternoon, Michael and Ashley finish the task that they have at hand. They decide to take a rest. Michael puts down the glass of water in his hand and takes a deep thoughtful breath and looks at Ashley,

Michael: You may doubt me. I have no power over that. But this is all I am. I'm not here to hurt you. I am here to be with you. I want to be with you. Nothing else.

Ashley stares at Michael. Michael continues to gather breath to muster courage.

Michael: Don't be sad.

Ashley: I'm not sad.

Michael truly doubts her words. He can see the melancholy in her eyes, he sees the somber way with which she talks and carries herself. It also does not go unnoticed by Michael in the spurious way with which her laughter braves any conversation. She performs it in such an unwaveringly firm manner that she herself is convinced. Michael's intentions crumble to a ghastly form each time he hears it.

Michael: I just wanted you to know that I'm here for you.

Through the days, Michael finds himself constantly having to convince himself that they belonged together. He had to exhort himself repetitively of this sentiment to get himself through the bewilderment that Ashley drags him through each day. Some days, he feels she can help him find a way, a path to be taken so to speak, maybe even a life to live and to share. Some days were better than others. There were moments where the couple recaptured a former gravitation they both had towards each other. But for the majority of the time, they were overwhelmed at how much they themselves and the other have changed. Neither could get a grasp of their own or the other's mind. They remain clueless in fulfilling each other's desires. Some antagonism always prevailed that barred the confluence of their aspirations. This sometimes led to an unfortunate miscomprehension of the other's true intentions. There was always a hint of doubt in the corner of each of their minds. The trust that they once shared implicitly had dissipated. The mistrust engenders much unfounded derision and thus, aggravation. This persistent contention attenuated much of their minds. The erosion gradually began to spread throughout their entire beings, taking its toll in all facades of their existence. Michael uses many of his coping techniques learned through his rehabilitative processes. Ashley tries her best, but is beginning to wilt underneath the weight of their lives. More and more in increasing regularity, Michael begins to doubt and question them being together. And in so doing, needlessly begins to yearn for death again, it is sluggishly reminiscent of the descent he undertook in the immediate aftermath during the rekindling of his life. Where is this all leading to? Where does this all end? Those questions weigh heavily on Michael's mind.

He finds no repose in sleep and seclusion, the darkness and chill of night affects his thoughts. He wanders into murky corners of his consciousness. Seeing and imagining cynical and sadistic things that his fragile mind only yearns for, but in his heart, he knows it would take another mind for any of these deeds come to fruition by his hand. This much he knows, especially when he has transitions of serenity during the day. This further divides his intrinsic unison and identity.

In these transitions of serenity, Michael quiets his mind and just lays there. In this juncture of quiet stillness, his sense of hearing and touch gradually feels and hears the thumping of his heart. One assertive beat at a time. The repetitiveness of this melody lulls him into latency on some nights.

One night, in a slumber, Michael unwittingly slips into a dream hinged upon the past. He is reminded of all its former splendor. In this grandiose reminiscence, absoluteness fades away from the present, he is who he was. His friends are who they were. All of them brothers in arms lavishly consecrating a murderous victory, soaking in the spoils of blood-drenching war. Michael can taste the elation and satisfaction. Michael immediately senses a disquieting discord in what he sees and feels. He catches his Mind through this grand illusion's exaltation and rudely awakens himself. As Michael stares at the ceiling of the room, he can recognize how much these sentiments once meant to him, and in all possibility, it still would if Time had not unfolded the way it had. He is ultimately ashamed of the moment that just occurred. Michael is humiliated that this greed of what was and what could have been still lies within his Mind. However, Michael sees his very aversion to it, and he is sure the past is in the past and that he is ready to move through Forever. With that, he is content. They were once his brothers, and therefore a part of his history.

He slips back into his slumber and the dream continues. There is an image that is frozen in Michael's cognition, standing preeminent. The image is that of Patrick hunting him down to consolidate a greed for the entire share that is the spoils of war.

Michael was struck down from Patrick's attack. As Michael lays, a malicious retaliation from Benjamin begins to unfold against Patrick. Patrick falls to the floor within Michael's sight, battered, and defeated. Patrick agonizingly begs for Michael's help. Somehow, this beg for help resurfaces in Michael's mind. All these days it had remained hidden. Until this moment of slumbering physical inactivity, Michael had never recollected it. It is in this remembrance that Michael realizes a truth. That it was not infirmity which made him ineffectual through that horrid exchange. Rather, he was paralyzed by fear, laying still and motionless like a coward. Unknowingly to Michael's mind, a parting with reality occurs through this deep slumber, Patrick is now his friend. And in this different point of view, Michael senses real pain for not being able to help Patrick combat Benjamin, Michael knew he had some strength in himself, but failed to muster any of its potency due to a fear of the moment. Great terror and fright crept into Michael's mind at the sight of his own blood, and for fear of his own life, his innate need for self- preservation overwhelmed his yearning to be Patrick's friend. Michael feels a great disdain for himself, this revulsion sends shivers through his entire body.

The abhorrent guilt and shame violently awakens him once more. This violence is of no physical force, it is purely of a psychological nature. The mind bludgeons itself.

This mind's assault on the self makes Michael realize that the care and despair he felt for Patrick is and was real. At one point in history, all his past friends, they meant the world to him. In some ways, that former part of him will always cherish those friendships. And that indulgence is perfectly attuned with nature. It is in his past always.

The facts will not yield to any other objection. Michael did cherish them in those moments. However, they did not reciprocate his appreciation of them. Michael knows this and is almost ashamed to admit that to himself. This shame is compounded by the image and memory of Patrick's remorseless crusade that left him for dead. Up until this moment, his true appreciation of them had been hidden from himself, buried by his unwillingness to accept the truth, his denial and his self-flagellation.

It is a fresh perspective on his past. The potential for this perspective had laid in his mind ever since that fateful day, it had always been there. These thoughts feel weightless and without burden. It now comforts Michael. This perspective's clarity further unshackles Michael from his past. Now, he chooses to allow what little favor that is left of this transition in his life to stand alone, free of the malice that surrounds it. He knows that the malice is there, but it is the hope in this series of events that he will remember and cherish.

The state of affairs are as such. Patrick is dead. Michael himself, had been going in endless circles of self-perpetuated torment. It is so clear to him now that in punishing himself, he had covered and buried a pure feeling that he had always needed to feel. Peace with past events, that no matter what, it is all just a feeling in Time.

This revelation brings Michael away from reality for a moment. Michael goes back to sleep.

During the day, Michael takes a walk without Ashley. In this walk, Michael finds that he no longer needs Ashley in the current capacity with which she occupies right now in his life. Even more so, he begins to believe that their relationship does not need to be the way it is. He finds himself reviling the simple act of daily existence alongside her. All occurrences they share manifest as cues and triggers of the horrid past. Michael begrudges that. For it is a past that he is desperately trying to leave behind. A part of him wants redemption for him and her, but as Time unfolds, he sees that in being with her, he is constantly revisiting loathsome thoughts and concepts. Michael thinks of the triggers for these thoughts and concepts as strong. Even though this relationship may bring joy, it is greatly outweighed by the angst it brings.

The doubt and anger that he experiences frequently, it is cyclical in its visitation unto his life. He cannot escape it despite his very best efforts. Perhaps this exemplifies a life lived that is going against its very own nature. Michael can glean no other conclusion.

Michael: As long as I'm with her, I will be in this vicious cycle which I must escape.

Michael thinks to himself.

Michael's thoughts then move to Ashley. She is not capable of love right now. She is drowning in agony, love has alienated her and she has turned away from it as well. She cannot feel. She is numb. The contention takes an abrasive toll on her body. Her body weakens and begins to break down. Numerous health ailments continuously arise. Michael empathizes with her descent, for he too was once in a similar predicament. It is in seeing Ashley's pain, Michael resolves inwardly to be a part of averting the attrition that has already taken place. To recover what is left, not scourge a desolate surface. He will try to nourish it. To be there for her.

One night, Ashley awakes from her restless sleep to see Michael at rest. He seems temporarily free of all the world's troubles. Michael is a peaceful sight to behold. She wishes Michael could be as such for always, he had been through much that has made him weary. All whom he came to know had no idea of his current state, and what he had gone through. Ashley feels pity for him. Yet strangely, she is hopeful for him. She feels shame and revulsion upon herself for having betrayed him. At one point, she was his redemption and his home. He was maliciously defrauded in his own Home, the one place he expected to be safe. She had violated her own hallowedness. It was of her own doing. She regrets her exploits deeply.

Michael inches toward consciousness. He opens his eyes and glances at Ashley's face. Although he is barely awake, he recognizes the sentiments of ruefulness that stirs within Ashley. Her expression bore the same significance that he felt and wore through his encounters of inner strife. At this very crossing, Michael knows what this means for their relationship. Right now, it is not what it is meant to be, the radiance of an amorous relationship will not be appreciated holistically by the skewered perspective of angst which Ashley Now beholds it with.

He just stares at her. His love. The love that he thinks he needs. He instinctively fears what will become of him if he were to ever be without this attachment. He sought inwardly for the courage to do what is needed.

He concentrates with a stinging trepidation on where he is in this moment.

Their bond does not hold the capacity to withstand all the sentiments that currently churn inside of Ashley's being. She must balance the weighted strife within herself before being able to enter the world. A part of Michael wants to hold firm to their bond as presently constituted for the sake of his own pride and dignity. But a look to his past advised him against that persistence. He realizes that the relationship they share must evolve to reflect its surrounding circumstances. This means he must be completely forthright with her about the lives they live and share. The truth may help them both. The folly of his past Now gives him perspective Here.

Michael lays there staring at the ceiling.

He senses the doubt mounting in his body and mind. His mind grows petulant and his body chimes with a quiet combativeness. His entire existence teeters with uncertainty in this crisis. He knows he needs a calming approach to life.

The necessity of the moment flows through him. If he is to do what he needs to do, this relationship is never going to be amorous ever again. He sees the past, present and future as a holistic and natural part of the unfolding of events. He accepts this maturation. He does not feel deep sorrow for what he is about to undertake. Rather, he feels an overwhelming sense of Need. Their bond needs this change for both their sakes. They both need to grow.

He ponders his relinquishment of Ashley that comes with such willingness without bitterness. The mystery burns as to why is he able to be separate himself from something that he treasures? Why is he not more gallant in obstinate protection of this prideful attachment?

As he considers this bitterness that was seemingly nonexistent, Michael reminisces over all the horrors of his past. It is in this moment where Michael recognizes a familiar feeling creeping over him again. It is the harrowing one that usually preludes and triggers despondency and torment. However, this time, the feeling takes on a new meaning for him within his new place in Life. The horrors triggered have seemingly comes to grind him, the bitterness looks to be in position to besiege him. Both, in days past, would have been more than he could have ever imagined to be being able to withstand. All this gathers around him and yet, all that comes to Michael's mind is that he feels like he is living on time that is stolen, that he is not meant to be here to withstand these events. There is a sense of impropriety in this retrospect, an absence of logic in Time, and therefore, an indefinable thrill. A thrill that Michael knows will leave him soon and may very well never ever come back. It is inconspicuous to the mind. Time has parodied all forms of siege and grinding for Michael. Each moment is unpredictable and unexpected. This thrill leaves Michael in hallowed anticipation, an unspeakable breathlessness.

He looks inwardly and realizes he wants to be the force that stems the tides of perceived deterioration in both he and Ashley's lives. Through Time, he realizes that things were always meant to change, for better or for worse, not deteriorate, as he so laughably thought. The changes, he sees Now, is a Thrill and is natural. There were many times that he wanted to turn away from this bond, but he retracted and stayed for some belief of ardency and steadfastness. His inner sense of abdication through retracting was always right. He knows it now. There once was a part of him that is obstinate against what is needed to be done. There once was a part of him that was unwilling to let go of possessions that he treasured. He once saw the World as a limited and finite source of indulgence, and to impede any of these channels of these indulgences would be sacrilegious.

That part of him no longer stakes a stronghold in his being. In fact, within his journey through Time, it never came back to the present. Michael appreciates the World as it is. He does not lust for sumptuousness of any sort. All actions and events are all a part of the progression of Time that is right in front of him to see. Through it all, he is calmly content.

He slips into a peaceful slumber once more.

When he and Ashley awake, Michael feels a slight angst built up in his mind again. He is shaking in fear of the future, he is cold. He is staring at Ashley, but also at a great Uncertainty of what he will become at the end of this exchange, if he should so choose to do so. He knows he should not, but he fears to lose everything that he is. But for some reason, he finds it in himself to push forward into the unknown, knowing full well that a total loss of many dear things is at stake. He selflessly steers their conversation toward his objective.

Michael: I've reached the end of my will for this. I

have gone through this many times in my
head. I owe it to you to tell you this.

He does not breathe as he treads lightly with disquiet
in the moment.

Ashley is a picture of trepidation. Michael is a picture
of bland occupation of existence.

Michael: A part of me felt real hatred and venom
                  towards you

There is no animation or expression in his face as he
utters,

Michael: I hated you.

Ashley is on edge.

The surface of Michael's skin draws sweat profusely as he
holds back many terrible words for her. These terrible words
remained restrained deep in his mind. Michael then says,

Michael: We are both triggers of angst in each other's
                  mind. So much pain, so much tragedy. We've
                  committed so much iniquitous crimes for
                  the other to see. Deep at our inherent and
                  instinctive selves, we repel each other. But
                  due to the respect of what we could be in an
                  ideal situation, we force ourselves to prop up
                  our relationship. Let's be honest, we make
                  each other's world a cold world with no one
                  to trust and no smiles to flash.

Michael: I can't be there for you all the time. I can't
                  answer all your needs, I…

Michael draws a speechless moment of thought.

Michael: We are chasing something. We're holding
               on to the past. Trying desperately not to let
               go of something. But there's nothing to let
               go of.

Michael is short of breath.

Michael: We've lost a lot, you and I. We've watched
               friends die for nothing.

Ashley sees his pain. Her pain is borne concurrently.

Michael: I used to blame you for my pain. Then I
               wanted to kill you, I wanted to kill you all.

Michael is divulging to Ashley the darkest, and most
monotonous corners of his psyche.

Michael: But if I had,

Michael pauses yet again,

Michael: if I had killed you, I would've continued this
               torment that I have wished away for myself.
               I won't do it,

Michael is exasperated. But yet, he finds the strength to
exhale the words that follow.

Michael: I will not.

A bottomless disquiet brews. Michael has a look of

desperate determination as he squeezes out those words from his mouth.

He decides to continue,

Michael: I don't hate you anymore. How could I? We are exactly what is meant to be. This is where we are reborn again. We've been given a second chance. It is neither joyous nor saddening. I am neither happy nor sad. We are both Here.

Ashley attacks Michael's integrity and altruism by referencing his violence committed in the past. A past that he has left behind. She lays claim that he was and still is that scheming sly creature that has evil in his every plan and move. Michael knows he is no longer that man. That being said, Michael holds his tongue, he holds it despite of knowing the fact that she had betrayed him deeply in the past and that she too, had committed pain upon others. However, Michael does not want to burden her with the weight of the rueful past. He does not want her to feel the pain of belittlement and flagellation that he is currently enduring.

Michael recollects and warms himself, he surveys the moment. The silence that he exudes in not addressing Ashley's woeful claims steers the conversation in a different direction. Ashley's offence withers in aggression due to the lack of retaliation from Michael. There is Now, as it was always supposed to be, serenity between them both. Michael sees the calm and civility that both Woman and Man exude, and he is glad.

Ashley is bewildered but yet, accepting of this end and beginning.

It is in this moment where Michael thinks of Darcy. He realizes that within that short period of time where they were around each other, they experienced the beginning, middle and end of something beautiful in all its jovial delight. Michael realizes that it is not very often where people get the chance to witness exceptional experiences through to a favorable culmination and end. It is in itself, as beautiful as it could ever be. Michael knows that they had both felt deeply for one another despite being in two very distinctly polar opposite places in life. For having experienced each other's presence, they were changed forever. Michael is content. He truly hopes for her to be happy in life. Just the simple thought of her brings him peace. It is Here, from a distance, where Michael wishes the same peace for Darcy.

Michael takes a walk to give Ashley a moment for herself. And also some time for himself to digest the event that is unfolding.

He sees that through all the doubt and uncertainty, ultimately, he has removed his ability to inflict pain. Something his past self would have never relinquished or appreciated, never in his wildest dreams. Not in that existence that he chose to live. Through all that has transpired, Michael feels absolutely no discord with the moment.

Michael is now taken away from his former place in Life. By looking back, he finally sees his path taken for what it truly is. In the past actions, he thought he was gaining advantages while treading a way forward through many vast plains. It may have seemed so to Michael in the miniscule vantage point of being caught up in the desperation of the Here and Now, where he, like so many others have always withheld the desire for newer and higher quests. A desire that is made further more potent by their need to make their mark upon Others and this World through power and ambition. They seek to gaze upon all their conquests and accomplishments one day and proclaim that they have surpassed Any and All in memory. But in the unobstructed view from up high, Michael knows that it is to be seen that this desire gradually wears and burdens One, leading One to tread, alas, in hopeless circles. It is a burden that can last a lifetime.

Michael is glad that he has been freed of that burden. He no longer endures Forever in torment.

Michael looks to the skies, his face lifts. A gentle breeze grazes his face and streams over the rest of his body. That is when a thought comes to him.

> *"Throughout all my days, anything I go through. Pain, fear, doubt. It is all in the passing. Trying to persuade it or fashion designs of it is like grasping at the wind. It is needless. It will all be in vain. Air is all around me. I breathe it, I feel it, but there is no grasping or retaining it within this World. It just slips through my palms. Be at ease with the air around me. Breathe it, feel it. Let it all pass. Let it all go."*

9

Michael browses through a newspaper and it is illuminated to him that Adam has attained a prized position to become a prominent leader in the political arena.

Michael rejoices in the fact that Adam has regained his footing in the World.

Michael and Adam run into each other one day while each is jogging in the park. They are glad to be in each other's presence. They embrace each other as old friends. They have shared in the ebbs and flows of each other's turmoil. And they are both better for it.

Michael: So, I've heard that there have been some developments in your life.

Adam: Yes. Word sure does travel fast.

Adam humbly shrugs at the accolades.

Michael: Well, congratulations my friend. All is well.

Those words, 'all is well', Adam hearkens to them gingerly. It is as if he opposes that sentiment in silent protest. Adam subtly swallows his words as they are about to vocalize, so as not to objectify Michael. Eventually, he does muster some words.

Adam: I wouldn't say so my friend.

He says this with a hint of a smile.

Adam: In this line of work, you see things. Things you don't usually want to see. It's a different world, this political arena. It changes people.

They are both silent.

Adam: There are many agendas and motives that changes and moulds people. Many people don't notice what they become. The progression of change is camouflaged within the pigmentations of everyday living, and is obscured by one's general intentions. I am myself guilty of selfish acts which I would have not done in days past. I'll be the first to admit it. The change in me was slow and was almost unnoticed.

Adam finds relief in Michael as he speaks of his own guilt.

Adam: I do these things out of necessity. I have no choice.

Adam finds further relief through this admission. This

relief brings to Adam's mind the need to prevent all future misdeeds from occurring again. But more so than that, Adam feels the need absolve himself as he currently stands.

Adam: In order to be steered away from greed within a person's mind, a forceful impetus must be imposed on a person's trifling ways. I've seen these forces at work, imposing its will upon its victims. These could be forces of nature, or of Man. Forces that could have held within it, a greed that is of an even greater potency than its victim or predecessor.

Adam speaks frankly about his desire for the World.

Adam: We dream of the existence of an altruistic and forceful impetus, One that is of great virtue and focused on an objective of betterment. An Impetus that witnesses all acts of malfeasance and will not hesitate to seize an opportunity to develop the Offender's aversion to his or her current course, recognizing the voracious actions of the Offender as a product of circumstance, and thus, look within this person and their preceding events for answers. In the hope to find out why the Offender breached the wills of Others. And eventually, mending the wills of us all, bringing about convalescence. Not civilization's punishments through enactments of penalizations. It is rare for any Person to embody these traits with the intent for convalescence. These cycles of impositions and defeats, it is quite terrible.

That is a dream indeed. Michael sees in Adam a will to strive for governance in this land. However, Michael thinks to himself,

"More victims, that's all that these Forces will create. There should not be a need for forceful impetuses to bring about change in the minds of those who have greed. We should have no need for a change to be brought upon in this manner. This is all due to the fact that Greed exists. It has brought much detriment to this World. We need a World where there is no Greed that exists."

These thoughts bring Michael to reminisce about his conversation shared with George. And more importantly, the statement of George.

"there is always hope. It is up to everyone to want to hope."

Michael wants both of these hopes and dreams to come true.

Adam continues,

Adam: I've seen how the splendor of our entire world has been built. The expansive cities, the pristine, the marvel. It is all linked. Many fall in love with the grandeur. It is everywhere, the megalopolises and their citizens bustling about within them. They all have a dream. A dream which I myself, along with all my hesitations and reservations, have empowered admittedly.

Adam's guilt is present and palpable.

Adam: Fossil fuels burning and energy consumption in every waking moment. A life of excess lays much waste and decay to the world. We consume and expend relentlessly and needlessly. We don't see the waste because the gains we receive are the goals which we have worked towards for our entire life. Rather, we relish our accomplishments. We even gain personal peace from categorically ruinous techniques. Even organizations which are supposedly here to aid and rejuvenate the world are rife with individuals who are guilty of such greed.

A lesion of rue ripens in Adam's mind.

Adam: Where can we find something to believe in?

To Michael, Adam seems to speak poignantly from personal experiences.

Adam: Everywhere we look, we are mislead by Others who have their own schemes and plans. We all unknowingly inherit a livelihood geared towards a life of excess.

Michael feels the weight of the past.

Adam: We have worked toward an age of freedom. We have achieved it.

Michael doubts the future.

Adam: Freedom. It is where the wills of All are allowed to flourish, along with advancements of all types. Where all people are allowed to traverse in any direction as they so choose in their hopes to vitalize their independence and essence.

The greatness of the human race is on display for Michael to see and appreciate.

Adam: Freedom is a treasured gift. But when there are objects to be lusted over, people will expend inordinate amounts of energy to adjust things and situations against the needs of others for the sole purpose to satiate their own wills. Through their strenuous implementation of mental and physical strength, their entire beings are worn down, they are broken. What's left of their former selves is unrecognizable. Through this alteration, they fail to see what their actions mean or where it leads to. They lose sight of all meanings, deep or shallow, primary or secondary. The tertiary and all that follows is all but lost upon them. They do not have the capacity to save themselves. If and when One as such would meet his or her end, it would be agonizing and catastrophic to that person. All their life's work has been accomplished to avoid their essence's eradication. They treasure it beyond all fathomable ambition. And it has all been in vain.

Michael is shown the fear of the End in Others. Michael feels the need to dream.

Michael and Adam proceed to take a walk through the world.

Adam: There are many who succeed in life. Their success, whatever it may be, has always been a lifelong pursuit of theirs that has come to fruition. This inevitably leads to Others to seek them out for guidance. These conferences of tutelage are turning points in time. All mentors vary in their willingness to discern how and when past orthodoxies and more importantly, where and when their own ambitions no longer hold the capacity to lead and tread the way. To know when it actually stands in the way of relevancy. And finally, to have the courage to allow for the quests of Another to prevail.

Michael and Adam experience a group of extremely vocal anti-war activists through their walk. Michael and Adam surmise their cause from their signage. Their rallying cries exemplify disdain for the greed that prevails amongst the political leaders of their nation, a rejection of the conflicts that exists in the world as a direct result of that greed. Those amongst the rally want an end to all conflicts, an end to political greed. They want world peace. Michael and Adam hope that no violence will erupt from this congregation.

They continue to walk. They pass by a splendid ceremony honoring the soldiers that have fallen in service to their country. It is a magnificent observance. Its pageantry is not sullied by the rally cries from those that Michael and Adam had just passed. There are many heartfelt speeches.

The speeches highlight the many laudable attributes of the soldiers being remembered. The eulogies bring to mind how the soldiers who fought tyranny showed a single-minded valor and spared no expense to protect all that they held dear, and ultimately, died willingly for a cause in their very minds. That in itself, is a heart-warming sentiment. Michael thinks to himself that soldiers do receive some financial compensation for their function and duty. It is then utilized to feed their families, who would otherwise starve. For the soldiers, their services were always a means to an end. Every person in society has a function and responsibility. All persons strive to thrive in this World.

However, no matter the duty, there is no compensation for the payment of the ultimate price. The loss of life is irrevocable for those who come to meet the end of their mortality. Those soldiers and their families ultimately lost everything that they held dear. Michael feels within himself the willingness to give up everything. A sense of Completion comes over him. The time he had been given in life was ample and sufficient. No matter how he had chosen to spend it, this existence of his has been full and complete. He and the fallen soldiers share the same destination. Michael holds no fear because he covets nothing.

Adam, being a man of the government knows much about the changeful relationship between the government, its citizens and the armed forces. At every turn, governments execute orders that vary in popularity, geniality and potency. All of which are driven by many needs. Adam knows from experience that every decision the government makes draws its natural and inevitable retraction from some or all of the public. Those decisions sometimes involve soldiers and their livelihoods. Soldiers' actions can sometimes be a measure of a government's potency and will, the will and fortitude for the strength to survive and thrive. Sometimes, when one entity seeks to thrive, it impinges on another entity's ability and will to survive. Thinking of this leaves Adam to bemoan inwardly,

"It should not have come to this..."

Adam: It really shouldn't.

Adam mutters to himself.

Adam knows that governments are the brain trust of any autonomous land or people. Soldiers exist as one of many extensions of that very brain trust, an extension which in and of itself, has its very own needs while being a part of those autonomous people. The brain trust has retractors of its every decision. These retractors have varying levels of dissensions for the brain trust's every move. Sometimes, that dissension may stir with hate. Sometimes that hate is steered towards an extension. Sometimes, that extension is the soldiers. The soldiers who obey.

Michael knows that there is opposition from many sides against this military extension, as the soldiers have committed murder time after time while at war. Slayings were both initiated and reciprocated as acts by these soldiers. Michael feels sorrow for the soldiers who have to comprehensively devastate themselves in a vast amount of ways, both inwardly and outwardly, so as to protect a life that is precious to them. Michael knows that battles and wars are affairs instigated by expansive cruelty. Michael feels shame for those who are cruel and find enough hate and hostility in their lives to scheme and impose upon Others that are weaker than themselves. These cruel schemers have lost their way. Like he once did in the past.

Adam and Michael understand these protestors' perspective. These protestors' motives are put into motion because of their disdain for the government's lording policies. They believe that they have already witnessed the definitive moment where Man has allowed for the current cruelty to exist in great strength. To them, this defining moment is the worst chapter of the human history, where sovereign and independent nations consciously chose to hand the authority of government into the hands of those rulers who seek the expansion of their own and the colonization of Others. The colonizers' progressions were subtle, their tactics, silent and seemingly still. But the effects have been wearing upon Others in every passing moment. And there is no end in sight as to how the effects have worn upon Others. Protestors know this much, through this silent warfare, they and their future generations will have to bear all the heavy consequences moving forward. Their disdain causes them to ignore the formalities of dignifying the soldiers' life one last time. The governing Overlords instilled as the brain trusts, waste tax dollars of citizens with a specific agenda in mind. That being to put themselves in a position to eventually peculate more from what they continue to waste. It is all done while strong-arming their competition in the private sector into submission through the pursuit of their own personal endeavors. All this is seen and recognized by the protestors. The same protestors whose resolve grows in bitterness with each slight committed against their dignity.

These protestors see their future and they see their fate. They know that it is at the mercy of those they disdain. Those disdained by the protestors have the ability and resources to exploit an entire population's perceptions and needs through subtleties that are silent and still. And as the Overlords indulge in this power of circumstance, it drastically inflames the angst within the disenfranchised.

Michael lays witness to events that occur, there is aggression on all sides. This animosity lays waste to many minds and lives. Michael reflects on how he orchestrated many seminal events in the lives of Others in days past, all in the hope of engineering their collapses for his own benefit by strategically robbing and assaulting them in their weakest hour. Michael always had his motives and he always kept it hidden from the World and Others. Through this reflection, Michael sees many similarities between his past indulgences and the actions of those who are the object of vehement vitriol from the Disenfranchised. Michael recognizes the same conviction in their gaze, their mannerisms and ultimately, their elocutions as they supply rhetoric of deep persuasions for the viewing pleasure of admiring citizens and all audiences, including the Disenfranchised.

As Michael continues to survey the sights and sounds of the rally's many cries and dispositions, it is clear to Michael that the Disenfranchised have a knowledge that extends further and deeper, much deeper. The Disenfranchised know that funds and resources which belong to the public are recycled and utilized repeatedly in and around the social communities of those who hold sway to the baneful exploitation, Exploiters who ultimately consummate the betrayals in plain sight to flaunt their strength. Betrayers will act however they so please and they will shape things according to how they see fit. They hold sway of the power, and they see nothing wrong with their actions. Unfortunately, if they do not see anything wrong in their actions, there will be nothing peaceful that can be done in order to change their perspective to see that they are inflicting sufferings upon People. Some people think of it as a cursed and damned situation. The Disenfranchised know that these exploitations upon the public and themselves are carried out with the very funds and resources that they can rightfully claim as their own contributions to society. However, those betrayals cannot be justified as crimes in society, and therefore, there is no stopping or halting the Overlords' expansive campaign of conquest. Thus, the frustration and inflammation grows even more potent and afflictive as the Disenfranchised understand that at every corner, an Overlord's treachery and oppression lies in wait and preys upon All. To Michael, he cannot find a reason as to why these events occur the way they do. Michael knows these acts are disgraceful, but he feels a vague accordance with the events as he watches it all unfold, it does not gnaw at him. He cannot yet grasp onto a reason as to why this coalescence is occurring in his mind. Michael knows the reason could very well be a reason far greater than himself.

Michael feels this coalescence in his Mind. However, he questions if it is to be of a fair or foul nature. Michael wonders. Could it possibly be the residual effects that remained from the agony experienced from days past? Was it haunting him yet again, disillusioning him with wishful thinking this time? Michael is deep in doubt, and it is warranted. For he was there when pain and suffering struck him down hard. He watched as everything he knew to be his own was taken from him through brute force and verve. His life, his sanctuary was sacked, pilfered and snatched away right in front of him. Michael sees his past. It has happened and it is a pity in every sense. Michael has stood by and watched as the aftermath continuously unfolded. At times, Michael thought of the experiences to be stricken with far too much grief which he could no longer even hope to bear. At the nethermost depths of his descent through Life, Michael felt the weight of the past, he was ashamed, and when Michael looked to the future, he was afraid.

Michael sees that over Time, he had been exposed to quite a bit. Sometimes, he astutely observed it. Sometimes, it bypassed his attention. He made proclamations and drew conclusions through those passing moments. All of them were unquestionable absolutes in his mind at the time. And in being entirely certain in his will, Michael may have been convinced of a certain infallibility's complete truth. However, through Time, Michael has seen in certain encounters, and has finally accepted that the absolute truth does indeed lay somewhere beyond all that has had him convinced before. That aside, he sees one possibility. That he will get to where it does indeed lay eventually, and when he does, he will be anew in Time.

Michael knows there is much complexity to the course of events. Many Men have studied the unfolding of occurrences. Michael knows that this course and unfolding he has witnessed all his life is guarded by its undertakers of events. Undertakers who have a foretold motivation. This foretelling can be pored over in many texts in particular regions of the World. And All can refer to it as they gather and seek True perception and perspective in this Life. It is quite clear to see how this foretelling corresponds, relates and assimilates. Particularly when a clear understanding of historical actions and pertinent reactions have been attained and comprehended by One. An understanding that is unimpeded by Another. These foretold motivations are logical and natural occurrences due to preceding events, events which have as well, had its share of guardians and undertakers. Those roles have always had One or Another to be willing to step up to the task of guardianship and undertaking if necessary. Stewardships of those roles are endless in supply. One will in turn lead to Another. In History, these motivated Ones were placed in similar situations as Another that was to come, and Both always chose the Acts that was foretold. And when all their motives were and are uncovered, a pattern of predictability is distinct and recognizable. Any Man can see it and feel it. And so it is for the passing of occurrences.

However, through standing by and watching, Michael

feels that he has experienced much growth within himself. He is no longer the same Man he once was. All that has now passed is far more growth than he had ever experienced. All that he has seen has been an observation, this observation transcends any previous experience that Michael can recall in his life thus far. Through watching, he did not insert his will. This unprecedented growth is and was as it turns out, effortless. Moreover, understandings of the World allow him to finally see that his life was indeed, not a pity. He is privy to what the World is and was. And above all else, he is content with no regrets. Michael now knows that no matter whose hands actions ultimately occur through, an Act has a meaning known solely to the Actor alone. Actors are in the Here and Now of the actions, along with All else who exist in this World. Michael has been privy to this. He has watched this. And he knows this to be True. All he did was calmly survey what was in front of him to better understand Acts within Time. Now, he knows not to resent a cause of any conflict. And in doing so, he also knows not to participate in these Acts.

Michael's mind is at ease. He resolves to turn his attention back to the Here and Now.

Michael sees Adam, Adam has shown Michael some lapses within the lordships that preside over this World. The success of an Overlord ultimately relies heavily upon the Ones who assist and reinforce an Overlord's reign despite upholding a vigorous disdain for this dominion. Adam openly renounces the Overlords. And yet, Adam continues his employment and service to the government, that which is an organization of the Overlords. There are incentives offered to Adam that he desires, and in order to achieve these rewards, he must boost his performance and productivity. His enhanced service ultimately ensures the lordship's continued existence. Adam is One of Many. Adam knows if he does not perform his tasks, someone else will take his place, thus, removing his financial security. And that to Adam, would be a far greater travesty. Adam treasures his security. Michael sees Adam, Adam owns acts that he performed ritually, willing it to fruition all while holding the lordship and their rule in contempt. Ultimately, Adam greatly strengthened the government's ranks and processes to attain grand incentives. It all stirred a vibrant concoction of inner turmoil within Adam's own mind. He expended so much effort and created so much strife within himself. He raged against himself with infinite aggression. He gave in to temptation and he thought of his very own acts to be weak. He was and is pitiful in his own mind. Had he chosen not to take part, it would have been effortless. Michael remembers beholding what is effortless. The World and Adam could and should have been in a better place.

Michael knows the brain trust holds a position of privilege. Lying within this privilege is the potential to provide assistance and betterment. This position is similar to the very role that which the organ of the Brain will always hold within a Body. The Brain has control over every facet of function and deliberation within a Body, therefore, a Brain exercises complete and unchallengeable authority over an entire being's every flow of resources. If the Brain were to designedly choose to insatiably collect and hoard all of the Body's resources, that primarily being blood in a Body's case, then all other body parts would have no choice but to be amputated due to the deprivation of vital essences brought upon by the Brain. Eventually, the whole Being will wither and pass away from existence. And similarly, if a Brain were to be corrupted, it will decay in languor, and finally an entire being could and would ultimately collapse and so remain fallen.

Through the days that continue to pass, Michael passes

on a book centered on the human body to Adam. It is a similar book to the one Michael has read and appreciated. Michael hopes the book's content will intrigue Adam in the way as it has captivated Michael's mindfulness. And hopefully, great benefits to come for Adam's mind.

Michael has been shown that there are powers in place in this world, a system rather, a stratified system that is devoted to self-preservation. The brain trusts of the world are not the epitome of this system, they have their wills enslaved and constantly recalibrated by the Another.

Michael knows that One can blindly trust Hunters who betray One with every fiber of their being. Michael fell into this trap of friendship and companionship through many days. Michael miscomprehended the Hunters' characters and motives as his lens on life itself was obscured by his ravenous greed. He himself had yearned for self-preservation and rampaged with insatiable greed. He cared not about the consequences of his actions. Who so ever was in his way, bore no worth or sentiment in his mind. With these wayward beliefs, Michael's life had no friendship to hold true to, and even worse, he was ignorant to this scarcity.

Frailty within the Mind. That was Michael's life, it made him a wretched and cruel person. Michael looks to Adam, Michael sees a friend that comes with no underlying intentions. Adam is One who comes around at ease with no resignations and no whiff of subversion. This peace and ease brings about an amalgamation within Michael. Michael thinks of all the Hunters in the world and hopes that they too coalesce inwardly like he is right now. All this brings Michael to a watchful stillness. He finds himself feeling complete. With a unison within One's being, comes the ability to heal from within. Michael knows there is much need to heal from anything that Life or any Hunter can throw at One, fragmenting and often breaking One. Through healing from within, One can and might be the conferee and witness of being made Whole again and again. Throughout his Life, this unison has carried Michael many times. Michael looks to Himself now, and he feels at ease with Himself.

Michael hearkens back to the Dream which George spoke of, Michael is beginning to recognize the foundations of which that Dream is to be built upon. With the ease known in his mind, this recognition of that Dream and its attainability begins to seem real and within reach.

10

Michael looks at the World. The state of the World is as it is. All of Man live upon and populate this World. Most of Man feels the need to serve a higher cause, to believe in something to validate their time on this Earth, to find something that they can resonate with and ultimately, to steer and mold their inward and outward portrayals of themselves into that which can bring them the most gratification. Michael knows and remembers this aimless and tumultuous pursuit of validation and gratification. He had fought a good many battles to see and feel gratification and validation. However, in the midst of his fight, Time has clasped Michael, unfolding truthfully before him, and therefore ensuring that he appreciates in specificity the much desired brilliance which has already been entrusted as a gift within his very own nature and being. It is a state of consciousness that not only guides him, but also assures him even when he is unaware. Michael has experienced this continuously emerging comfort in the Unfolding. Michael knows there is faith and trust that cannot be denied in this gift. Michael must Now trust that this gift is all he needs, because It is. It always had been. Michael knows there is no Need to seek anything beyond the gift of his own existence.

One of the beacons of fervor that many Men have long resonated with is the banner of Passion. Michael has seen many Men rally to it. Many Men live and abide by that sentiment and what it means. Men have developed systems of leadership to proudly hoist up those banners to waive it high in the day's breeze. To have peace with and within these Systems have so far eluded Man. Throughout history, unrest and corruption have always crept from the shadows of these Systems. And as it always has been, at a favorable time of their choosing, the Agents of that Unrest will strategically opt to make a move. And in being caught off guard, the assault upon the general unsuspecting public will render the victims helpless in a desperate search for any resolution within that turmoil. Through Adam, Michael has seen that in history, these System's constituting Agents sometimes end up devouring each other through their own unrest, corruption and hopes of ascension. With that being said, Michael has also seen that Agents are getting more and more adept at molding and adapting their existing Systems to have it remain functional and efficient through corruption and failure from within. These practiced Acts have undoubtedly made all Agents and Systems infinitely more potent. Michael sees their might, it has tamed quite a few in this World. However, Michael is not swayed by any System or its distracting mechanisms. Michael's appreciation of his natural gift enables him to stand firm.

It is wretched calamity, when the Agents of Unrest assert themselves. Victims within the general public will lose much. If an Agent could do nothing else, they can obey. Their loyalty and treachery knows no bounds when it is adhering to a cause. Any act is readily and swiftly justified. Without their cause, they would be lost, for their cause is all that matters to them. In their minds, their causes have replaced the gift that is their own existence. Some of these Agents ascend through the ranks of this world. They accumulate power, foresight and knowledge to shape things as they see fit. They are calculating and precise in their ingenuity. They use their experience and lessons from past mistakes to calculate with discretion. Through an Agent's schemes, the desperate attempts of their prey to fend off an Agent's premeditated and erosive ways are nullified. For a prey's defense is immediate and bears no forethought or tedious planning. A prey's defenses are enacted through confusion and fear, and are therefore, unorganized with no sense or direction. It is outmatched in every way. Michael scarcely believes this, for he was once stricken with grief and panic. An Agent seeks victory in every inquisition he or she makes. Deception is one of their most coveted tools to victory. The agony and pain of Another is a conspicuous sign of their decisive victory.

An Agent that has devoured much is bold and resolute, and must remain so in the hopes to devour more. That way, his or her fortune will be favored. Like any efficient mechanism, with fluid responsibilities, Those seeking victory in expansion have and will amend their techniques as they come and go so as to better achieve victory. It is an aggressive trait to improve their own lives. She or he must not waiver in their pursuit of their goals. They have to remain focused with the task at hand. They have fears of losses of which they hide in the corner of their minds, for they covet what is theirs. If Another were to know of these fears, it would leave the Agent vulnerable. All who fear losing what they prize and value will do all they can to protect it. And as it turns out, all people fear to lose something.

Michael pensively thinks back on his days of such thievery and malice. What did he gain from claiming all those victories that he held so dear and close at the time of its occurrence and achievement? He sees that in each victory and success, he had created new cycles of pain.

Now in lies the question that arises in Michael's mind. Where had his victims gone as a result from his premeditated actions? Did he leave them with ill will to act unto others as he had unto to them? Did he cause the spread of rage?

Michael knows that in this World unfortunately, victims of rage themselves, may very well become entities of terror. The former victims are capable of anger as well as retribution. And they will call upon those capabilities to rectify the slight of being looked upon as worthless. Terror could come in any form. Nevertheless, it is dreadful. Through his own pain and doubt of the past, Michael has watchfully learnt that if One has intentions to hurt Another and thus, bring Another pain, that pain will come. And when it has come and gone, aiming the mind's attention towards stillness is important. It may help to distract fractions of contemplations away from the numerous upheavals, and thereby, easing the immediate moments of transition away from One's terror. This may allow Another to gradually heal from the pain.

Men have and will continue to have all these rules that try to instill order. When one Man decides to seek his own order, Many ultimately have disorder. The harder Men choose to fight disorder, the more it devises and mutates. Those who thirst for their own order, it is their passion that drives them. They use that passion to accomplish their will. And as that which has passion gets stronger and stronger, All who oppose are forced to evolve in order stem that tide of fury, All will lose much of what once was as the conflict lingers on. This World is too vast to be ruled. That much, Michael knows to be true.

However, Michael accepts that their Passion exists. A Passion for a feeling, many feelings. A search and chase for earnest preservation, to seek out a secure path to ensure One's future and existence.

Adam, as part of the government, oversees the management of various funds and resources. At all times, he is given various agendas by his constituents and superiors. He is expected to achieve all goals through versatility and hopefulness. He knows that the security and preservation of any one certain agency's reserves and resources hinges upon the brain trust's dictated stagnancy of taxpayers' reserves and resources. Adam has seen Men and Women honor and defame many other individuals in the hope to secure the agendas and future of either themselves or Another. Security in Adam's mind is a hope. Nothing is certain in life. When One or Many attempt to snatch a propitious share of what belongs to All, it destabilizes the distribution of reserves and resources. This drives inequality and many a times, inflation, which then churns a vicious cycle of unyielding economics. In a search for hopeful security, well-intentioned men band together to protect their fellow men against what they can foresee and withstand, thus, overcompensating for adversity which they cannot and will not deflect. They resolve hardships, but what Adam has seen in his years of civil service is that sometimes, the unity of these well-intentioned men will eventually become the hardships and bane for Others to suffer and endure. Others who hope to care and provide for Another, the hope of Another is exchanged for the security and personal gains of those that have banded together. This could result in disdain and vitriol from those living in baneful hardships, which might possibly give way to apathy. This could also result in times of anger and hate, where a vengeance would finally unveil itself. For all who engage in struggles have the perspective of reality which is centered completely inward, on themselves, and so is their conscience.

When Hunters try to change Another's circumstances to better their own, what a Hunter really ends up doing is taking Time from Another, because Time is known to All. In many portrayals, it is presented with an enhanced value. It can be taken from Another, Time spent in Life with Everything and Anything. However, Time is limitless. No matter how much a Hunted may lose, there will always be more in this World. Time cannot be stolen by any Other.

Michael knows this train of thought deeply from his past experiences. Adam has helped Michael yet again to shed some clarity upon a situation.

Michael knows of the pleasure experienced by a Hunter through attaining vengeance. However, had he not been brutalized, Michael would have never put any worth into the deliberate act of aversion. The aversion from bending everything to his will when there are Others that he sees. At all times, it remains as a whisper in the back of his mind that this aversion will impede his progress toward his luscious objectives, whatever it may be in life. However, he knows his ambition will never be deemed so significant as to resort to brutalizing Another the way he once was ravaged, what was once clarified to Michael is Now crystallized ever so much more. His ambition brought him and Others down a horrible path once. Whether he is to be the Punisher or the Punished, that path is not worth taking as a course. All his uncertainty and fears, the whispers that he hears, it is the yearnings of his past coming to him. Another memory, another Time in Life that is Now gone. Lost forever.

Michael goes to meet Adam one day. The conversation steers towards the days that have gone by. Adam thinks of his own plight, he detests its existence. He speaks to Michael,

Adam: I have lost a lot, I've been chopped down. I didn't think I was going to come back from

it all. I have many memories that come to
me. Good and painful. Not only are those
elements in the past. It is all a feeling. Life
is a sum of my many feelings, each one a
kin to the last. That is all I know.

After emerging from all that has transpired, both Michael
and Adam feel as though they have each been given clean
slates.

This emergence frees Michael's mind even more so to
draw upon its innate ability to appreciate the display that is
Life. He truly feels the verity of the definite and intangible
matters within and beyond the boundaries of himself. For
the mind, in Michael's opinion, now continues to expand in
how it recognizes and sustains much attunement to All in
the World. A bolstered perspective and understanding Now
reveals itself to him. Michael's senses within continue to surge
and flux with surety. He begins to recall the violent jostles
and subtle temptations that were always meant to be traversed
through in Life. He knows that it will come to him again.
Each rise and fall that comes with every feeling, releases an
outpouring rupture of obvious and underlying connotations
for him to perceive. He sees it Now, it is quite lovely to behold.
He gathers his thoughts and peers into his mind. He realizes
that he feels no burden in the face of this outpouring rupture
that is at hand, just an unshakable appreciation of what is,
that being alongside an undiminishable comfort within the
moment. He can see that due to his sense of inadequacy
towards Life in decades past, he had to endure a dreadful
angst that burned and seared him continuously from within.
It was upon him in every waking moment of his life. That very
retribution in Time that he suffered now fades to irrelevancy.
However, he knows exactly what his thoughts were in Time.
He knows now that his outlook of awaiting mounting highs

and even worse, being fearful within the hope of avoiding abysmal lows, had set him up for an unrelenting collapse into ruin. His intensifying angst that he had to stem at all times was a telling sign of what was to come. It is all faded away.

Michael feels a rush of pride and elation in accomplishment. He feels the scars that formed from the evident recovery. That very notion of recovery turns to a jovial delight which leads him to feel a sense of security in Time. He feels that nothing will ever burn or sear him again. Even if it does, he is untouchable. He is safe and secure. He is sure that Time will unfold in his favour. He feels beyond Anything that can ever happen. He loves to feel this way. It is all there in his mind.

Adam has a satisfying and successful career. And by all means, he stands to continue to benefit and prosper from it for the rest of his life. He is both accomplished and secure through his acumen and affiliations. However, Adam does not stand blind to the works that both he and his colleagues have ultimately fulfilled within the developing circumstances of the World. Adam feels that his course taken thus far is one which he kindly needs to circumvent. In his mind, there is a way for him to linger on in the political arena. And it is to resign from the long-established institution, and to continue on as an independent candidate, a candidate whose interests are free of coercion and control, unlike his present circumstances. That future offers him substantially less financial resources, and it would require him to leave his established life behind. To avert from the present course will require a firm nerve to stem the ineludible tide of reflexes that his mind will predictably impose upon him. He sees all this and yet, he continues to do what he must to sustain himself and his family, for they too have yearnings and cravings of their own which Adam will seek to answer or fulfill. Adam knows his current title and position is a highly coveted one, and whosoever should replace him would be in line to benefit and feast upon compensations and affluences that should have always been his.

Adam searches inwardly for strength. He knows he can change. He resolves inwardly to try his very best to amend his ways, to avert from his present course. He begins to envision the realities of the way of things are, and so he thinks to himself,

"I will, but it's not time. Not yet."

Through his procrastination, Adam's mind experiences splinters in each and every task of work that he performs. As his guilt grows, these splinters accumulate. And as follows, he remains divided from himself. It is because of the friendship that Michael has provided him with, that Adam often divulges to Michael the unfiltered opinions of events and occurrences. And as the dividing of his mind deepens, Adam's need for support heightens. And in that, these two friends have much to converse about whenever they meet.

Adam declares what he knows to Michael. Adam knows that People in and of prominence involve themselves in highly controversial issues to implant strong, resonating messages, which are then strategically developed into fateful causes that divides All. This in turn breeds conflict and contention within and between societies. A conflict that festers benefits those involved in this strategy of implanting and developing which Adam has witnessed. As he continues to watch and witness events unfold, Adam can see that conflicts are aplenty. Secretive but yet subversive struggles between countries, which are sovereign military and industrial stalwarts, are commissioned by many of the controlling Leaders of nations. It is a dangerous game of continuously standardizing new policies that aggravate and weaken rivals on the economic stage. The consequences of these campaigns are grave. History has shown this. Conflicts result in many calls to arms and weaponry. These Leaders who implement capitation and the weapon manufacturers are the Ones who stand to gain the most from the many transactions of weaponry. Through his affiliations and associations, Adam knows exactly who these Leaders and Manufacturers are. Adam is seeing more and more so that the same Leaders and Manufacturers that he and his fellow colleagues have backed for many years, through the favorable bending of policies, have further compounded this awful situation by ingeniously forging yet another facet to their schemes. These Leaders and Manufacturers have mastered and maneuvered ways to profit from the inevitable need of the Divided to search for repose and solace from their existential struggle by seeking out products, whatever it may be. These Leaders and Manufacturers have mastered ways to make much more than just weapons. Intricate and particularized studies of these inevitable needs have been launched to better understand and predict the patterns of mental states within the Divided who search for repose and solace. Results of these studies are then used to better formulate products. Products that will be manufactured in mass, produced with efficiency, prominently marketed and backed by the same beneficiaries of the bending of policies within society. It is a plan which has had an abundance of premeditation and forethought invested into it. This plan has been in the works since the dawn of society itself. For as a society, Adam knows that All that are divided have themselves let the Leaders, Manufacturers, Hunters, Agents and Overlords into the ranks where they have run rampant with impunity and authority. And as it stands, the Divided are just about bled dry.

Beyond the inward guilt that Adam sustains, there is the daily process of working with colleagues. There have been days where Adam is taken through a minefield of adversity. This current day is one of those days. He constantly encounters stinging objections which he strives to remain dignified through. He is seemingly inundated with difficult tasks to overcome, tasks in which appreciable progress is difficult to come by. Men and Women he calls colleagues constantly try to test his mettle to prove a point of their own. And in doing so, these characters pester his personal sense of identity, his physical appearance and the sentiments that bore deep within his conscience. Through it all, Adam slips and loses his focus on peace. He begins to rue the day. His mind is ripened to fall. Just as Adam cannot bear another second of scrutiny and boredom, a conversation he shares with his colleagues steers away from him. Adam can see that the subject which his colleagues are speaking of clearly brings them great joy.

Adam: Perfect,

Adam mutters to himself.

Adam decides to stay for a while. The need of social propriety is getting the best of him yet again. While listening somewhat attentively, he realizes that his colleagues pin much importance on many things. Just 'Things', and to them all somehow, their lives would be unbearably lessened without that tangible 'Thing' to hold on to dearly. Adam sees no sentiment in their pursuit. He does not resonate with their passions. He realizes that delight, for him, does not hinge upon such substances. He can only presume that it is his psychological state that makes him complete. It is a courteous endowment. He is indebted for it. He smiles as he recognizes what his mind has done for him. Through this conference, he ultimately depended on another person to pick him up freely as he was ready to fall. The additional and unexpected aid he was provided with only deepened the meaning of what he sees. His fellow human was there for him in a time of need. However, his need was not tangible or verbalized. It was only known to Adam himself. Adam sees that all occurrences in the world have a way of vitally lifting up the Ones in need. And as it so happens, this occurrence is fair and comely in essence. Adam sees that relief can be unveiled to the One in need from sources that One would not have expected it to be from. Adam can now see that chains of occurrences are conclusive and unmistakable. An event that may be maddening and nerve-racking to experience can really be revised to be naturally gladdening when placed alongside all that preceded and all that follows. Adam knows this now. Apart from the drear, Adam just has not seen many events from another perspective. Adam will see it all to be so one day. Adam has seen it to be so on this day.

Adam sees that he has found solace within the day. And by that, he is heartened. He sees his colleagues, he sees that through their search for the same joyance and repose, they have, through their own willfulness and resolve, indulged in the works and concoctions of these Manufacturers, Hunters, Agents and Overlords. His colleagues are willing to offer a lot of what they can give in order to attain this solace and repose. And as Adam has seen through his career, all the indulgences will consequently bolster and strengthen those that seek to divide All. This chain of actions and consequences remained undimmed in Adam's view. He is appreciative that he did not participate in this strengthening and bolstering. However, Adam knows that at one point in time, he was complicit in the bending of policies, which resulted in the consent of this indulging, strengthening and bolstering. And for that, he has played his part in the attempt to divide All. He sees his colleagues, he ponders sharing his beliefs with them. Adam does not know if they will conceive it the way he does. And in that, he fears to tell them and thus, further consigning All to the premeditated plan.

Adam feels a great sense of guilt for not being honest with his colleagues. In the heat of the moment, he was afraid that he might be shamed for his Aversion. To Adam, it is a sign of weakness to show fear. And he did. He resents this fear within himself. However, he knows that he has been honest with one Michael. And in that, Adam is able to rest at the fact that he has done something for Someone. Adam knows that all people are searching for something, seekers of life. And that sometimes, what One searches for is beyond One. At times, One ends up attaining it. Occasionally, One helps others find it. Intermittently, One causes Others to lose it, for better or for worse.

Meanwhile, Michael looks at the World. It was not the first time that he had looked upon the World as so, and it certainly will not be his last time. He is true to the nature of the World. He is deeply rooted in the ampleness of reality. He is not hindered by the stirring of emotions. Michael has seen that when growth is abounding, a being's response to an environment is that which would be intertwined and pertinent to what can or will trigger. Not to be overwhelmed by all perplexities or cheerless from disfavor. Michael has also watched trees vegetate in warmth, and wither in the cold. It is an accurate gauge of the environment. As long as beings are One and Whole, they will be at peace with the World.

The state of the World is as it should be.

Michael: I want nothing,

He feels free.

Michael: I need nothing.

He feels like One with the World.

Michael: Whatever may come, I will be content.

He pauses.

Michael: I believe I will.

He reassures himself. He stamps that sentiment into his mind. Michael sees that it is in what he does in every moment that shapes his life. He recognizes the effects of his actions. He sees it. He does not stand blind to it. He will not ignore it.

Michael knows that every person, through their deliberate ignorance and recognitions, will perceive events differently. That is the way the mind works. It is within this, that the course of Time is to be determined. No One can repress or oppress that.

Michael has seen that dark and cold intentions are always going to exist in Time. If One basks in warmth of the World, and surrounds One's self with it, then One will be free of frost. No matter where One is.

Michael: All we know is all we know

He thinks of George's dream. He ponders what it will take for that dream to live. After what Adam continues to tell him, Michael doubts if his fellow man can ever shed the weight and encumbrances of all that has happened. Michael knows that all the beliefs and inclinations that stir within, it will all pass us by.

Michael: Is it too much to ask for a steady calm will in the face of this uncertainty that is the future?

Michael cannot fathom an answer for his inward stammer.

Michael: Is the face of Forever not plain to see for All?

He remains silent.

He settles back into himself. He begins to accept that all a Person knows, is truly all a Person knows. He realizes that he knows Forever because he has watched how Time has Unfolded. Will anyone else in this World see Forever in the rest of Time? He knows that without a doubt, there will be. Nature is infinitely vast. So many paths are placed before every One of us. We are inevitably going to perceive nature differently from one Another. Each opinion is as true to its perceiver as the last and the next One.

He goes now to rest.

11

Michael revisits the book that once showed him how the body works through the rousing of its comprising systems. It reminds him of many things. And as he continues to meddle through the arising affairs in life, he can definitely see one thing exemplified. That an apt human body has the capacity to adjust to its surrounding environments by striking a balance within itself in the hopes to live and be. And through living, Michael sees an outlook that is obvious to gaze upon. The body can, and the body will.

Balance, he knows that it can be struck through the practicality of internal control. He also found renewal and stability in the releasing and inhibiting of flows and vigor that stand in regards to the inner balances and imbalances within the body's systems. Those systems are a part of Michael as that of the blood, hormonal, digestive, breathing, skin, brain, bone and muscle systems.

Proper care and conditioning over these systems is centered over Michael's preparation of his conscious mind with these systems' pertinent details. To Michael, concentration and introspection with the aid of those details were amplified by the unsealing of another component within his mind, that being his mind's amalgamation with nature.

Amalgamation, it required Michael to acquire ways to perceive the inner ebbs and flows of his body. That perception grew from the awareness of the convoluted processes of Life that are achieved seamlessly and autonomously by the body. It all allows his appreciation of the World to deepen, and thus, enabling him to intricately harness those flows of balances and imbalances. His grasp upon the Harnessing further augments the amalgamation in Michael's perception.

Michael thinks of Others who exist in this World without this Amalgamation. In talking to Adam, Michael knows that the rigors of Adam's life, along with the stamina and energy which it entails. Michael knows these elements will always cast its presences upon Adam's mind and adversely affect Adam's ability to harness and appreciate as Michael has. Adam's senses are hindered by circumstances of those rigors, and thus, appreciable occurrences of special significances will remain cloaked and concealed from the mind's grasp.

Michael knows that for himself, this Amalgamation cardinally came to him. He both upholds and withholds that inwardly through sheer familiarity. In a moment of jubilance, Michael is prideful and thinks he could have contrived a way to attain the Amalgamation, but in this instance, Michael realizes that it undeniably came to him. And as it just so happened, he received it with an open mind. There are Others who have mastered this knowledge through their own will and affinity. Certainly, if One has no interest in this knowledge, it cannot be taught or given to One. Michael knows if an affair or matter is of upmost relevance to him, that very same matter may very well fall meaningless and expendable to Another. Michael watches and conceptualizes himself. This appreciation he has of his gift, it truly stems from him delving deep within the perceptible material of the matter that is the schematics of the body, which ultimately, led him to find a semblance of how and why the body will act and react in certain ways at given times.

His mind is occupied with the flowing of thoughts. Michael completely rejoices in his failures' existence, his past missteps, knowing full well that it had served a purpose. He even grows enamored with the memory of his misfortunes. Sometimes he would even reminisce about the aforementioned negativity and find humor in it, for it is a parody of Life itself. These memories come to Michael as an alleviator of predicaments within the Mind during times of hardships. Michael is seeing first hand, that pain, any kind of pain, at a certain point can be transfigured in the mind. Preeminent on his thoughts within his thankful realization is that he did not consummate vengeance and thus, he did not churn the wheels of vicious cycles by becoming a different entity towards Others.

Atrocity and vengeance is passed around in cycles through All in this World. He cherishes the opportunity to absorb these odious deeds that will and have come to him at this particular juncture of Life. More of his mind begins to be occupied as he sees himself, the very last stop of this particular infliction upon the world. In fact, there is no pain, just a Memory in Time, an attachment, which is to be attached and detached to him as how the Mind decides and sees fit. He is glad to be at the End of these afflictions. He is One with being the Completion of events that were rife with contention. A series of blows and counter-blows rooted in tragedy and conflict. All has reached resolution. Michael realizes, he puts no value or worth in retribution and its perceived satiability. For there is no satiability, in days past within this cycle that is being passed around, feverish torment had arrived in Michael's Life, it came to him initially masquerading as ecstatic delight through several Acts, Attachments and Persons. Michael accepted all of it with open arms, for he coveted to be the Victor. Here and Now, Michael recognizes a pattern. The murdering of his inflictor would appear to come to Michael as victory, however, Michael has seen that it would eventually mean affliction, loss and Division for the Being that is Michael. The life of his inflictor means nothing to Michael, therefore, so does the Act of Murder. If another One were to see no value as Michael does, that Person would be able to halt all callings to arms or weaponry, and in turn, serve another aspiration. One that is free of contention and tragedy. Michael continues to watch.

Michael has experienced many persons who go through life with their needs often filling the semblance of many impetuses which lies behind their actions. Michael knows that there are an innumerable amount of people in the world who conduct themselves in such a manner. As needs are synthesized and then developed to be established within an individual's mind, based on the ever-growing external forces that even includes the individual's very own perceptions, it results in a savage pressure that reshapes the individual's mind, bringing about the individual to act based on those needs through a modified and compromised sense of identity. Michael understands that through Time, One could retain One's free reign to operate, achieve and succeed by those needs and standards within the Mind. By these understandings, Michael sees that the World's civilization does eventually take shape for All through the very occurrences and acts. In arriving in this present moment in Time, Michael can Now see clearly that there is no state-crafting ideology of promise which can effectively govern Man as currently constituted. There has never been one that has ever existed in the history of the world and Michael is beginning to see that one might never exist in the present or future of the human race. The human race, Ones who are Beings with Minds that search for all things different from One Another. There have been many attempts at crafting an ideology. The safeguarding of promises to a society, a civilization and All have always proven to be infinitely beyond the abilities of a Few and Others.

Michael remembers seeing George's discontent. Michael deduces that it is because George feels that elected officials have let him down while guiding the city and country of his residence astray. Maybe the officials did not mean to, maybe they did. However, Michael ponders a leader of a vibrant, strong and devoted family. A Leader lives a Life fully invested into the care of the family. A Leader gives it their all, their everything. Their job is on the periphery of their focal point, which is their family. An elected official has a duty. And the Masses have expectations that can only be met if an elected official's duty was the official's highest priority and focal point. But it is not. It is their job. An elected official cannot give the Masses their everything because this job is a peripheral duty. An elected official cannot give the Masses their all and the Masses cannot expect the official to invest themselves the way an ideal situation would entail. Not in this World. Not in this Time.

Michael has watched and heard about Systems that have through history, been initiated and founded by a Few and Others. Systems which have proven that through its constituents, a System willfully gathers and ends to serve the preservation of itself and only itself in kind. A System does so until the end of its term of warranted authority. Michael can see that the Masses have banded themselves to Others in the search for hope, strength and fulfillment. Michael has also seen that in their desperation, Some within the Masses have even handed over their entire lives into the hands of those Others. Through Adam's insight, Michael continues to see that these Others have calculatingly and premeditatively contrived a multitude of systems with the discreet designs to hoard and accumulate for themselves and only themselves. Michael knows the Few's plan truly contradicts and is completely antithetical to the Masses' hopes, thus, evoking a chain of events that have culminated in a continuously escalating angst between All who are within this climate of spiraling imbalance and strife consequent from the hoarding and snatching away of essential and vital resources. And Many can tell that this dearth of resources greatly destabilizes an already volatile and doubtful situation. A situational plight that belongs to the Minds of the Masses. Within the System that shapes All, the Few often disagree with or maintain disdain for Another's dedication due to the paranoid nature of their discreet and strategic dealings, all of which are rife with tension, stress and hassle. Michael knows that All just want to be free. Not in devastation. Adam, being well-informed, has also shown Michael that through the chronicles of world events, the resources of the Masses have always been misused and abused. Adam has also shown Michael that there has been and still is the relativity of currency as earnings and security, governing over the attainment of goods, and that All have left themselves vulnerable with these checks and balances, Michael can see that. In fact, All have seen it before. It is all a vain repetition. Michael also gathers that as long as needs can possibly be induced and synthesized within One's independent and conscious mind, the burden of external influence will continue, materializing as controlled popular expressions designed to entice and create lust to stir the proliferation of those needs. And thus, the Masses' malcontent will grow resulting from that influence and inducement, which causes many Acts to emerge. Regrettable Acts that impede, interfere and embarrass. The parameters of this system of influence, inducement, attainment and control impinges upon All with great discomfort, pressure and urgency. Bled absolutely dry, Michael finds All. He sees that All are betrayed in their vulnerability, he is a part of All. He renounces this bleeding. Michael resolves not to leave himself vulnerable from here on out. Michael now recognizes the true meanings behind that which initiates and empowers these products and influence. For him Now, to participate and indulge in these products and influence would only further strengthen a will that opposes All. A will that seeks to reverse the significant meanings of everything that is True. Our Great Adversary.

This is when Michel looks to his Gift, he can only muster praise within his Mind for having been given this Gift. It is in this praise and strength that he knows he has been given all he needs. This Gift is fulfillment. This Gift is promise. No Other or Few can possibly bring about the Completion of Michael. Nothing else is needed. He will not forsake this Gift.

In Michael's willful resolve, he sees that One can neither judge, accuse nor decree another individual. It is simply beyond One's mindful capabilities or capacity to do so as a Person. Absolutely everything and anything that flows within One's Body or Mind is impossible to be mastered by Another, Another who wills to judge, accuse and decree. If and when One chooses to act beyond One's skill deem, One's mind will either take flight or fight. And the prerequisite of Life is to be in the Here and Now, Here in moment, at peace, with no fighting or yearning to take flight.

That much Michael knows.

12

When Michael goes into the world with a sense of being whole, a sense that is brought upon by a steady heart, he knows it is because of the conscious efforts he put into his body, his mind and all their constituting parts. It is and was the mindful attention he asserted, an act that brought about a sense of fulfillment to his needs. It is all a gift.

His mind now listens to and absorbs the feats and exploits that surround him, both the slight and the august. In his past, within some of these similar feats, he did not even take notice of it all consciously, and when there were exploits, in his petulance, he may have invalidated and discarded it all as minor or frivolous issues when it all first occurred and unfolded. His Mind's focus was customarily and habitually elsewhere. Clans, Places or Things often took precedence over the Moment. In Time, this renouncement and condescension of relevant entities greatly influenced his mindset in momentous occasions of undertakings, and thus, disturbed his actions throughout the course of proceedings in Life. This all brought him many shudders that grew in disquiet.

A steady heart that is not violently shaken by circumstances and influences would have done Michael good during those turbulent times.

Forever once gave Michael an amicable and easeful rest. An experience Michael shall not soon forget. Michael wants this all to be known to as many people within the World as possible. However, he has seen that there will be Some that have a will instilled within their very beings that shall not accept this all as such. They thwart their minds, bodies and souls in their rally against causes such as this all. Their pride mocks every passing moment. it is known to Michael that All will search for everything different. And it is due to this thwarting, mocking and rallying that Michael Now accepts that this indeed, is also a part of Forever. The World continues to Unfold. Michael understands that the World continues to shift, as it always has and will. All he has to do is understand it and maintain his comprehensions with a steady heart. Forcibly, against his will, Michael has been brought to the amicable and easeful rest that awaits him. In the aftermath of being forced, Michael has learned quite a few many things as he continually gazed at the Unfolding, and through it all, his sound and reason remained balanced in outlook and firmly allegiant to that forceful moment. This allegiance is secured by the assurance that the future will be just fine, he need not be troubled Now.

A steady heart. Some live without it.

Michael knows provocation and exasperation are both frequent outcomes in Life when One has a heart that prescribes anger into Acts. In Time gone by, he truly perceived Life was that which was rife with hardships and encircled with slights. He reciprocated by placing the blame upon One after Another. And once having met with this bitterness, by his own discretion, he marched through Much to brave and endure additional hardships simply to acquire the means to equip himself with the weaponry and resources that would enable him to Act upon his exasperation and anger. To quell his heartfelt rage. To right the wrongful slights against himself. To judge Another.

His Mind and Heart both retained perceptions which consigned him to falter Life into doubt. Michael sees this World and thinks that there are many actual rigors that tests One in Life. Michael remembers himself perceiving slights and hardships that were actually fabrications within his Mind and Heart, which only impeded and perplexed the traversing of Life for himself. Michael thinks that it was not very sensible or reasonable on his part. There is much to endure in the Here and Now. So many sentiments and causes that people live and die for, as All have notions of an ideal Life, notions that are centered upon the very same perceptions that have faltered Michael in recent memory. If One were to somehow stand in Another's way, Another's bitterness might well turn into blood lust for One. Another or One, whose heart sanctions exasperation and anger, will always refuse to accept the perception of being imposed with hardships or slights by any One.

Michael knows this.

Michael looks in the news, there have been violent assassinations of several political leaders. All of the slain had significant power and influence within the chambers of leadership and have been at the forefront of passing bills of legislation to regulate all industries. The perpetrating slayers' acts were justified by the perceived inactions of the civil servants towards constituents in the times of steady economic decline. Even as slayings like these arise, the lives of All continue and does indeed, go on. Daily concerns are to be fulfilled. Routine tasks need to be accomplished. Michael sees the onward fulfillment and accomplishment of tasks, it leaves Michael knowing that the basis of the system continues and endures. All will hold steadfast to their own commitments and obligations.

And so Forever continues, Michael sees that.

Michael visits Adam sparingly throughout these passing days. Michael notices the rather consistent and rapid turnover in Adam's security staff. It is almost like a carousel. Every time Michael visited, the staffing personnel varied. As Michael looks, he can see that amongst the security personnel, there seemingly was a similar disposition being exemplified constantly. One that is intense and focused. A focus that is more vigilant than that which was needed for their job's duties. It seemed to Michael like they were on the watch for something more than just threats to Adam's safety and security. When addressed, they were all together dismissive and avoidant but yet, agreeable and complying. Their presence brought a sense of disquiet to Michael's mind. Michael should have recognized the true intentions behind those facial expressions, for he had seen it before plastered upon a few many Cohorts' guises, Cohorts that snatched his Life. But upon seeing those guises, he did not mindfully distinguish their disquieting inclinations. In watching, his very own discernment fails to jog an alert within his Mind's retention at the moment of occurrence. It all escaped his memory, he did not Act, he failed to truly watch with the mindfulness that he had learned. As the security staff turned around any corner at any given time, their demeanors unveiled their true emotions. This, of course was hidden from Adam, their employer. But Michael caught careless glimpses of this in his introduction to them. But as Michael's proximity to them accumulated, so increased their guard with their visages towards Michael, and so they managed to slip pass a potential detection of where their true loyalty does indeed lay. They take great pride in their progress within task after task as their objectives hone in closer on a goal that is solely their own.

The sun rises on another day, Michael stirringly sets himself on to offer his support to Adam. The destination is a news broadcast station, where a debate with Adam's political opponents will be held, where Adam is set to make proclamations of certain magnificence. Many eyes will be upon him.

Many threats have been issued and documented over the past several days through various sorts of media. The targets of these recent threats were the headlining debaters, Adam himself included. These threats cast a daunting shadow upon Adam's cabinet members and friends. Many of these cabinet members and friends have tried on numerous occasions to communicate the relevancy of these threats to Adam. However, Adam's mounting schedule consumed all of his availability and attention. The messages failed to reach him in the context of dignified urgency. It is now that he sits at the table where the debate is set to be held. There he sits, facing his political contemporaries.

Three opponents there are.

The First is an animalistic individual with an insatiable carnivorous appetite for wealth in his business ventures. He is creative in usurping and outsmarting his competition. The public and potential constituents have a great affinity towards him due to his personal successes. And why not? One would hope for Another's successes to be scattered, shared and circulated.

The Second is One who has a brilliant scholarly background and is scintillating in his accomplishments. However, his contemporaries and those who have had dealings with him know him for what he truly is. He has only himself preeminent in his mind, he will deceive when he stands to gain, leaving him with many personal detractors, all of whom he has betrayed on some level.

The Third is a man with a devoted following of supporters. There are masses that are in awe of him. He is eloquent and concise in speech. He galvanizes those who behold him. Many who have attended his rallies come away with great hope and promise that change will come to the Chambers of leadership if the Third will be elected.

A few of Adam's security members arrive slightly late and seemingly preoccupied. And so the debate begins. It is mundane with a noticeably cautious level of jabbing at one another. There is no engagement in conducive critical-thinking or practical problem-solving. About twenty minutes into the conversation, minor explosions reverberate through the halls of the building. At first, the transpiration is met with a quiet confusion. Then the surrounding walls of the broadcast area are smashed and torn down. Quiet confusion turns to frantic panic. The threat of a certain disruption is eminent and very real. From the smoke and dust of the intrusion, there emerge stout men armed and dressed for combat. Their thirst for destruction is plain to see.

The Intruders take control of the area and try to subdue all persons in the room. They do so by barking out orders along with threats of great harm. They cautiously and slowly disarm members of the security personnel. One of the security personnel members however, rises from his position of restraint and retaliates. A tussle ensues and blows are thrown. A waylay follows, there is no escaping it. Deadly blows are dealt at every turn. Numerous bodies begin to fall to the ground. It is then that Michael realizes, he has been Here before, and like it was in his first death, there it is, so much pain, so much death, all the passing moments drowning in unconscionable hate. Michael knows it is a willingness to possess malice. Michael looks around as chaos consumes the place, he looks inwardly and he finds that his acquaintance with this Unfolding is sincere and True in his Mind, Time for him, is Now saturated with familiarity and understanding. Through this saturation of familiarity, his Mind is not enveloped by the chagrin of the fray. Rather, his Mind settles upon the sight of these new Victims and new vicious cycles of pain that are being created. He knows what this all means. He understands that even in it all, the Unfolding is True. And in the End, All are witnesses. His and any Other's Acts that follow will also be a part of the course that he, Michael, shall not want. For he truly wants nothing. He knew this once before, but yet for another time, he realizes that he truly desires nothing from this World. He understands his peace in his experience with his End. Even though it was forced, it remained a feeling that was completely internal and intrinsic. From within, it was a complete psychological release from all that enticed him and all that he regretted. He is not saddened by it, he is not angered by it. He always thought to himself,

"it's all just a feeling",

A sentiment, really, he sees. It is all held within Time, Time is ever shifting and changing. It is in the Here and Now, it comes and goes, he sees the loss of life all over. The End of a Life, it is a step that he had taken. And he knows there is no despair there upon that Step. Here and Now, there is much to comprehend, so much that is changing and shifting. It is all coming and going, yet another transition in Time. And as it always was, Forever will endure. The Unfolding is True to the World. Nothing else can bring about its Completion. Michael knows this because he has felt Completion.

Michael Now sees clearly, his Mind subdues all ferocious distress fraught with rage within his sight. His Mind also galvanizes his past understandings and experiences to shape and fashion a scopious mental posture that can comfortably and adequately grasp what is perceptibly before him. His Mind sees through the encumbrances of external forces and doctrines.

He does so as he looks upon a certain affair. Adam valiantly fights off assailants, disregarding his own well being to help his opposing candidate get to safety. Adam calmly guides others to get as many of his friends to safety and out of this waylaid room. Just as Adam is about to navigate another group of individuals, the Intruders use powerful explosives to smash down the protective structures that have been shielding the victims on multiple occasions. Adam's resourcefulness in the moment is at an end. Adam jumps on an Intruder to help a fleeing victim break free from the Intruder's grasp. In this tussle, another Intruder decides to help his comrade by assailing Adam. It is too late. The fleeing victim has broken free of captivity. Adam falls to the ground with a significant wound, raising and turning his neck to ensure that his friends have gotten away to safety. In being assured of his friends' security, he turns onto his back, as his physical pain comes over him. Michael sees this through the crowd, he is troubled, his settled Mind is now disturbed. He struggles through the mayhem to get to Adam's aid. The sheer mass of bodies that are scuffling and tangled in panic stifles his desired path towards Adam. Michael does not want to see his friend executed right before his very eyes. Michael fears that these will be Adam's final moments. He truly does not want this Occurrence, there is a pervasive torment that begins to swirl within Michael's Mind once more. His utter surety of wanting Nothing begins to wilt, for his settled Mind continues to be disturbed by the desire for the safety of Adam. Michael sees himself to be disturbed easily, he disappoints himself. Michael sees that he is not

True to himself and therefore, he inwardly and insecurely supposes that this moment hence, is not True. He understands the need to find balance within this Unfolding.

Michael's struggle through the fray leaves him in great fatigue. In being under duress and distress, he continues to push forward with his limbs, while struggling to maintain a fractured line of sight with Adam's plight. His Body's joints bend and straighten with no conscious sense of exertion. The fray greatly hinders his path towards Adam. Vigorous and unyielding limbs of people flail at Michael with great force, for Those who flail, are themselves in a dire state of panic, trying to escape this ruckus. In Michael's exhaustion, he trips over a Victim's arm. Michael too falls to the ground. It is Here that he sees all the bodies laying upon a ground that is stained by battle. There are Victims of all ages. He can see all the petrified faces that lay still. There is no peace for Them. They are all dead.

For Michael, like it was in his first death, there he is, once again, surrounded by death. His Mind Now regains his composure, steadying his senses with a breath, he hears screams all about, his Mind takes it all in. In his continual steady breathing, Michael can hear that some of these screams are of those people who just want to go home, for they are not ready to die on this day. Some are the shrill cries of names. Michael gathers it is in the frantic hopes of being saved. Michael knows there is much that has to be mustered against a premeditated and well-executed Plan. A mustering made of preparedness and discernment to face a Plan like the one that is unfolding right now. Michael has no preparedness to put forth in any attempt at mustering, for he had no foreknowledge of this incident that is. No single person within this space can fathom or discern what can possibly repel this assault with a sustained vigor or potency. Michael also hears the screams of people who irrepressibly beg for death. Their begging cries screech with heartfelt desperation. Michael can scarcely watch or listen to what is unfolding, for there is nothing he can do to help. Michael looks around, the unfolding causes him to remember who the Divided are. All of them living lives being persecuted while also being utterly defenseless. Nevertheless, in Those that want to go home, Michael sees the fear of death, he sees it in the faces all around him. As Others quiver and tremble, Michael sees that his mortality may well be imminent once more.

He has been Here before. There was a Time where Michael had been struck down. To his Mind, this is familiar territory. He thinks about each transition that had hindered him through Time. It is all in the past. When the hindering occurred, Michael explicitly felt as though Time had pegged him in the Acts of Unfolding and punished him, striking him down. And Michael knows that in the minds of Those who currently surround him, they are all undoubtedly feeling that very same sentiment as he once did in the past, Time, pitilessly and viciously striking them down. It is Those who must surely think that the Unfolding of Time is and has been grotesque and hideous. Michael once again reflects upon the many things that he had deeply cherished. Particularly, the sense of pride he felt in just living his life in the past, the life-assuring loyalty with his cohorts that once emboldened him through every single social interaction. Feeling insured in knowing that if all were to be taken away from him, a Brother, a Comrade would be there for him. It all once brought him a certain peace, it made him feel untouchable. In the past, Michael chose to perceive Time in a certain way, he did so to empower himself and thus, take full control over Life itself. That Act failed, that Act broke him. It then dawns on him that Time had not punished him, it did not hunt him down. Time was neither cruel nor hideous. Rather, Time was flowing through him naturally at all times and instances. Through watching all that had arisen and befell, Michael sees the way Time resonates within him Now, it differs much from how it once resonated within him in the past, for his perception of Life is now different, but Michael senses that in both perceptions, the essences are quite the same. The similarities dawn upon Michael while he watches the Acts of an Intruder. The sounds and tones of the Intruder's voice and Acts, it is similar to the din and tonality with which Michael's inflection used to carry in days bygone. It was carried especially to embellish humor and parody. And it was sported within his Life in distinct manifold. This humor, it resonates harmoniously within Michael's memories. He did not recognize it in days past, but this humor, it was an Act that he indulged in. It too, was a Step, an indulgence he took within this search he has been in the midst of for many days. This humor brought him a much needed relief, no matter when or where it occurred. It was a resource freely shared among him and Others around him in his life. He did not have to snatch it from Another. There was no need to capture it, or lust after it. It flowed freely within his Mind. It was and is a part of this Gift. This relief softened arduous times of hardships, which allowed for a sense of merriment to arise. And arise it did, in great stature as Michael recalls. However, within this current fray, Michael is being reminded about the incomprehensible violence that can and will occur in this World. It is Now that he sees what had actually occurred in his past. This softening, and in truth, veiling of matters had barred and distracted him from truly watching and listening which thereby, left him with no opportunity to even attempt to comprehend and understand Time and the Unfolding. And there was a substantial amount of matters for him to contemplate and regard in Life. Thus, it did bring about his fall, breaking him in the process. For it did bring many matters to a premature and inconclusive reckoning, his Mind was commandeered by a feeling of great ease. This humor, it was the best part of his life. It masked a gestating betrayal that was to come in Time. He stops for a moment to agonize over what humor had truly brought him. Pain and torment, like what Those around him begging for death are currently experiencing. This humor contributed in pulling Michael away from Life. Desecrating many Moments. He no longer wants to indulge in humor. While this humor did improve the quality of his life, this surge in quality however, came with too great of a consequence. Consequences, he has lived through them in the Unfolding. And he withstood it all due to a balance within the Mind. This need for balance makes Michael realize that he will always have room for comicality in his life. And he will enjoy it when it arises again. He will balance the Humor and the Distractions. He does not let his past missteps ruin his future mirth. The Mind can only endure so much, and there will come a Time where Michael's Mind will need relief.

Michael feels a palpable and expansive thrill in the Moment. No thought is expended upon any existential ill or wayward fate. It is Now that Michael conceives a belief within himself. A belief that never before has he felt a thrill as such. The last time his memory can recall retaining such a thrill was in the days gone by, where he inadvertently sank into a life of secrecy, a life where he concealed ambitions of mighty plunders. Through the Unfolding, that thrill was used to mask what brought Michael many torments. The thrill itself however, it was and is the Promise of Time. He sees Now that he had felt this way all his life. It is something so basic, as Michael's memory Now recalls, it was something he knew even as a child before his choices inescapably shaped his path taken. At all times, he was connected to that which was and is expansive and palpable. It was always on his Mind.

This worthwhile recognition is interrupted by the task at hand, Adam's plight. And so Michael gets back up to his feet, he continues to tread a way to aid Adam. Condemners will preside over a persecution that will leave victims laying all around blood-drenched, limbless and lifeless. Michael is seeing a live demonstration of this tenet unfolding right in front of him. Michael sees their condemning Acts, for him to participate and retaliate would mean for him to attempt to empower himself, to try to right a wrong against himself, to defend his pride, to hunt Another, which is to painstakingly and laboriously attempt to control that which already flows freely, expansively and palpably within and through himself. Michael does not want to kill Another. He really does not want to. He has already consummated more than enough infliction and affliction than his memory can bear to remember. He has done far too much in the past to taint Time. There is blood on Michael's hands. His Mind is disheartened by what he has done in Time, fatigue comes over his Body once more. He is almost there to aid Adam, when an Act catches his eye. An Intruder is directing a weapon towards Michael himself. In his Mind's first contemplation of this Act, Michael visualizes a pride in retaliation, a need for empowerment through righting a wrong. What his Mind visualizes, he can see unmistakably in all the Intruders' Acts within this fray. Michael has been through many hostile encounters in his life of pillaging and plundering which was a celebration and consecration of deep camaraderie. Through all his encounters, Michael has taken a few many paths in life, and he has learnt that if he continually treads his way through dissension and discord like the one his Mind currently visualizes, eventually a path will be taken by him where he will wander blindly into struggles in which he will surely lose, for he does not know all that there is to know. And there are Foes that will be ready to oppose his foreseeable

Acts with a Great preparedness. It is not possible to know all that there is to know. Michael will lose. And in losing, he will resent Time even more, as he will perceive himself as being pegged and punished with defeat, thus, further hastening his decline in Life. And in trying to force a conclusively satiable outcome, he will further Divide himself. He will fail. Michael knows this. And with this, Michael sees where he is once again. He is right where Another is taking aim at him to destroy him. His life's course was once altered, stripping him of all balance and stability in Life. He found some balance in Time. Time that is in Forever. His findings in Forever gave him, and still continue to give him the balanced perspective needed in Life. Balance, he has found it. And in this Balance, Michael stays by and watches. He sees Now that at any point in his Life, this World will take a hold of him and clutch on, and that in Time, he is definitely not untouchable. He can also see Now that They will never stop. These Intruders, they continue to shake their spears and mercilessly pierce their victims' flesh. Victims that Intuders view as their enemies. They will never stop. Michael knows he is no Master of Another. And Now, peace is upon Michael. Peace is with Michael. In being surrounded by death, he knows exactly where he is in Life, he is in the Here and Now. And it is Here where he presently and sustainably has no regrets.

Being Here and having no regrets, Michael's Mind instantaneously grabs a hold of him and his senses, and in doing so, it causes him to perceive and be aware of the realities that had previously dawned upon him at the End, Michael remembers that there was no strife that was endured upon that Step. It was a Step that he took. He was there. He Now knows that from this day forth, because of the contentment within that experience, his Mind does not bear or feel any discomfort or regret. In the Here and Now, this contentment has given him vigor and security within himself. He sees what is occurring and Unfolding Now. Now and the End, his Mind has been to both. He has lived through both. This has therefore, given him the familiarity and intimacy with this duality to expand and exist within both. Michael can acknowledge Anything that may come, with both the Now and the End within his perspective. Michael has both within sight. He exists in contemplation of both spaces. This manner of existence expands his familiarity and intimacy even more so. Both places offer Michael favor and comfort. His Mind is comfortably in touch with both places at all times, drawing upon one or the other to bring about restfulness and poise within himself, wherever he may be in Life, within a Body which at this very moment, is Here and Now. Now and the End, both are a part of Time. In his treading through Time, Michael understands both Here and the End are a part of him.

The Intruders too, are in the Here and Now. Michael can see that, they are with him. They have come to him with a will of their own. A will of contention, and They have many deeds planned forth in their preparedness. Deeds that Michael shall not want. And so he will not participate in their deeds. He will not betray this Gift he has. For all that has arisen and befallen, he will go on to watching and listening. And so Michael continues to make strides towards Adam.

Michael almost makes it to Adam, and Now, this is where Michael himself is ultimately taken down. Michael feels his wound. There is great pain. Michael then looks in the direction of which he feels the infliction came from, he realizes that it is the same Intruder that he had within his sights earlier. This Intruder attacked Michael to ensure his team's tactical superiority. Michael falls. This might indeed be his End, but he agonizingly looks towards Adam's predicament.

The anger of wounded Intruders continually plummets upon a devastatingly wounded Adam. The Intruders gradually gain the upper hand over the fray. Michael continues to watch, as the Intruders continue to stalk their prey, Michael can see that they take great pleasure in this endeavor. This situation, their Acts within it, it all seems therapeutic to them. Being engaged in the fray, it seems to have a restorative and remedial effect on their Minds' welfare. Michael can hear it in the inflection and resonance of their shouts that bellow, Michael can see it in the jubilant grins that beam across each and every one of their demeanors. Their stalking of prey leads to a miserable drubbing and capturing of victims. One by one, the preys are all corralled. The Intruders begin to secure the area. Michael's wounds keep him grounded. Michael begins to make it to his feet for one last stand, but one Intruder ensures that Michael can do no harm by kicking Michael back down to the ground. Indeed, Michael is not untouchable. This World has taken a hold of him once more and is clutching on. Michael has no regrets.

The assault is all but complete. Many victims are made to kneel. Out of the kneeling masses of captives, emerges the Second. He takes his place alongside the Intruders, his comrades, who are in front of an idle and battered Adam. The Second then looks at the faces of confusion before him. He locates the First and the Third. Each of them were pulled out of their kneeling places and dragged along where they were finally put at the feet of the Second, right next to Adam. Michael lays on his side. He watches and listens as this vicious cycle churns.

The Second takes a moment to bask in his success of his plan's fruition. Then he remembers why he is where he is. It is because of his will to dominate. He must secure his standing in this world.

A woman among the captives screams,

Woman: Murderer!

The Second is utterly flabbergasted by the truth.

Second: Why can't anyone see what I'm doing here? These three! They are not decent men! They are the real murderers!

There is a great sense of desperation in the Second's voice.

Second: Can't anyone see the warnings? They are surrounding us all, slowly tightening the grips. I have spent my whole life trying to guide you all. I've tried educating you all, to warn you all. But they have complete control over the entire voting process. And no one dares to do what's right. I can't win this election. I can't be the leader everyone needs me to be. I'm done with being the nice guy, now I have to destroy them once and for all.

His glare turns from the crowd towards his three captives. Most of his anger is directed toward Adam, the candidate who is favored to take office.

Second: This is the only way. All they've done is bring us pain, and abuse their power. We will brutalize you and those in power until you stop. You think you are the light, but you are not. You are the darkness, you are evil. We will never stop. When will you get it? We don't need you. And we sure as hell don't want you.

Michael knows Adam. Michael knows the Divided.

Michael fathoms that the Intruders do not know what he knows. That is why he and Others are currently held captive. Michael also understands that he is not familiar with the Second's mind. Michael continues to watch.

The Second pauses for a moment.

Second: This is the only way.

He repeats this with a shallow breath. Michael sees doubt in the Second's stance.

Second: I have to end you. Or you're going to continue to destroy more lives.

The Second seemingly consumes his mind's doubt in the moment, fighting it off almost. He came here prepared to do something. He holds onto his goal, he is steadfast in his ambition. He walks authoritatively towards Adam, killing weapon in hand, and looks Adam in the eye.

Adam, who at this point is being forced into a kneeling position by one of the Intruders, looks to the ground, and in doing so, he drops his head in resignation. He is unsure of this moment, he is full of doubt. He stares blankly at the ground. He begins to tremble with disquiet and fear. His eyes close.

From where Michael lays, he can see Adam's face. Michael is watching another Unfolding.

Adam's acceptance and resignation is now bringing the disquiet and doubt within Adam's mind to an outright halt. This disquiet and doubt had utterly inundated the moments of the fray until now. Adam's thoughts begin to swirl. It swirls over his entire life and all that had occurred within it. Adam looks up at his executioner. The withdrawal of disquiet and terror from his mind allows Adam to break free from his current mental posturing. His mind and its posture seem to be strengthened by an acceptance of this occurrence. This new posture causes the subtle tremors of doubt to dissipate as the mind now begins to be enthralled with a new focus, a steady focus. This steady focus calms Adam, for this experience is an aberration compared to what he has tangibly encountered in life. It draws Adam's engrossment, for he has never been Here before. This is his first encounter with death, and he wishes to fully understand each of the entailing circumstances to better assimilate himself to the occurring theme, thereby, making his mind able to fully grasp on to what his life is actually turning out to be. Michael sees that Adam is at an incredible sense of ease in this very moment. The occupation of Adam's mind is complete, in his life and career, this is how he is most comfortable, being assiduously engaged. Michael sees that Adam feels no burden at the many thoughts of Life. Whether it be the past, present or future, Michael sees that it is a calm that Adam has never known. Michael looks at Adam. He sees that Adam's understanding of Life's existence and unfolding has come to peace. The panic has run away from Adam's face. It is malleable adaptability that has come to him. The trembling visage is Now transfigured. It is Now a much more quieted and composed version of its previous self. This transformation is enforced by his steady, repetitive breaths. Michael deduces that Adam Now has the similar feeling of Completion that Michael himself, has continuously treasured and experienced for quite a few many days. Michael knows that Adam Now heads toward a Step that All will get to know one day. Michael turns to lay flat on his back, facing the ceiling as the anguish too, runs away from his face.

Now, it all seems so clear. Then, in an instant, a deluge of smoke bombs hail through the windows. Stifling gas from the smoke bombs spread through the room in a hurry. Asphyxiated airways of Intruders and Victims alike all choke as they struggle to grasp for air. Through the hail of smoke, it is clear that the Intruders' time of oppression is at an end. An agency of armed individuals begins to file into this space, searching out and securing the First immediately. They then overpower and subdue the Intruders. The Second, who in realizing that all is lost, makes a swift escape. As the will and presence of the Intruders wane, the armed individuals conscientiously scan the area to make safe and secure this place. All holds still. Michael and Adam are then tended to and watched over by anxious friends as the chaos declines gradually to a gracious banter.

Many have fallen. The witnesses are starting to realize this outcome through seeing it in plain sight. Terror and disbelief smeared upon the faces of every person in the room. None can believe they had failed to see that there was a murderer within their midst. This moment's security is lingering in great uncertainty, for trust is now absent. All try to grasp onto something, anything really, for stability. Many, who lay on the ground, still need care and assistance. Some commiserate with Those who need to be consoled, holding Them close so as to offer some relief from Their grief. A grief suffered from realizing that a life is indeed lost, a life that was close to Them. Some curatively tend to those that need aid. They band battered body parts and wrap open wounds with available articles of clothing. For Some, this disbelief gives birth to an anger, and in Their anger, They instantaneously desire revenge, They want to be heard within this disturbed and disoriented crowd, They find Their message urgent because They realize that a real threat is Here. Now, They attempt to wittingly formulate a plan of attack, They do so by acknowledging and recognizing Their resources and its capabilities that can be pertinently integrated into the attack plan. Some try to keep a cool and calm composure, in the hopes to find a firm footing in this World for Themselves. It is a composure that exudes a supple oratory. Those that desire vengeance see this calm civility as blatant ignorance and are then, aggravated and thus, grow even more anxious in Their need to act and avenge. They assert Their rightful justifications regarding a vengeful pursuit of this foe. And that this foe's death would mean the peace and security for All. And in this justification, Their voices grow more and more exasperated in the face of a lingering calm civility. They seek to find an immediate and forceful rectification with which to combat this assault, and even more so than that, They fear what this threat may become if it is not dealt with or destroyed. And above all else, They fear for Their own safety. Those that are calm and civil try to assuage this anger, but the anger will not relent. In Michael's Mind, the logical opinions from both sides reverberate and ascend to relevancy. He however, decides to not interject his opinion, electing to watch and listen, for this debate of heightened exasperation will not draw a compromising agreement in this hour or any hour near it. Weary eyes are sullen at the disagreement of People.

The forces that came filing in and secured the area moments ago are now disarmed. They address one another with familiarity and candor, it is also seen Now that those very individuals are actually the private security of the First.

In the immediate aftermath of this event, a hint of guilt comes over Adam. He cannot help but think that he had somehow played a role in this travesty coming to fruition. In fact, he knows for certain that it was his controlled accomplishments within his arena of employment that had led directly to this event occurring. The Second had made that point of aggravation very clear. Adam looks around at the survivors and lost ones. He feels burdened by this guilt which he carries onerously. And he is somehow envious of the fallen. For they are not burdened with guilt and regret the way he is. Adam would not mind switching places with them.

In the days that follow, the media feasts upon this incident. The Second's attempts had been foiled. His hands are stained with crime. Cursed is he in the minds of the survivors, ever is he to be condemned and damned by many tongues. He flees prosecution and is presently nowhere to be found. A manhunt is initiated by authorities. Also, the Second's affairs are made public. At the time of his plan's fruition, he was going through difficult and bleak financial straits. Although his business ventures had been reaping decent returns, his prodigal ways have racked up exorbitant costs and expenses. Much is now made public.

Candle light vigils are held at that building in the days and nights that follow, it is done so to remember those that were slain. As some survivors in attendance hold their candles, the waves of heat emanating from the flames of those candles then radiate upon their skin. This triggers and awakens scores of senses. This awakening brings them back to a time where they felt smoke rising upon that very same skin. The rising smoke which they felt upon their skins was a commencement. It signaled the sweet release from a kneeling captivity upon floors that were stained with blood. It was a similar sensation that the radiating heat now offers. This offering is now accepted willingly. The survivors all share an unspoken bond for having escaped that episode with their lives, an episode which could have meant certain death. Solemn tears and embraces are shared this day. Mutual admiration is exemplified at every turn. For Michael, he holds and embraces many of those who have lost someone significant, he tries to comfort them. He stares at these candles. It is almost as if the hopes and dreams of those who mourn are set aflame. For the orange glow now flickers upon all the people's faces and bodies. Michael looks all around. All he finds is a hue that is of a great fire and flame. To Michael, he sees it, everything burns.

Michael hopes the emanating warmth rekindles the essences of all who are Here. Their grieving hearts are so very heavy with dismay. Where do they go from Here? Michael senses much uncertainty for the future. He knows that this remains as an event in the course of Forever. He will for the rest of his days behold the Unfolding. For his part, he knows he will be the End of this cycle of pain. Michael does not want to be any One's Adversary.

Michael ponders this accursed and infernal case of the Second.

It is so clear to see that the Second had condemnably attempted to bring about the End of Others. Wrecking their livelihoods was to be the immediate consequence, no matter what he had asserted his intentions to be. Based on the proclamations he so boldly claimed that murderous day, it can deduced that he did so to satisfy an indignation that had grew deep within himself. What grew from within appeared to be an obsession. This obsession was geared solely towards intensifying the morally detestable and hateful nature of his outwardly undisclosed fascination. From the looks of it, there was something in the Second's existence that had brought about this strife. He seemingly could not resolve it to bring about a peace of mind. One could venture a guess that his troubles were beyond him. And so he incorrigibly chose the only option available in his panic-stricken mind, and that was to lash out against an unsuspecting and defenseless crowd. He did this so as to encounter as little resistance as possible. Somehow, their pain and agony brought about a sense of accomplishment and a notion of success to his mind. This time, thankfully, a scheme was foiled.

Michael can perceive the acts of the Second and its meanings which the Second might have regarded them as, for Michael had once trodden down a similar path that the Second is currently marching down.

13

On go the days. Michael and Adam both have wounds that begin to heal. The two friends help and support each other through the lingering ailments and memories.

As for Michael, he has been through these vicious battles far too many times. He sees all these tribulations. These memories, if it all continues to linger within his mind, it will grind his existence into one that will break him before his time is done.

As Michael and Adam talk, the book which Michael gave Adam is mentioned. Adam reveals to Michael what was to be regarded and appreciated from that gift. Adam reveals that within that book was illustrated knowledge that was basic, overlooked even. This collapse of observance was indubitably evident at the time where this illustrated knowledge was first glanced at. However, Adam makes it known that this necessary information has Now secured a certain foundation within his cognition. This basic knowledge was amplified after the fact of the tragedy.

Adam: I guess it brought a few things to light. One of those things being the nature of the body. I never paid it any mind.

Adam looks at his own physical being, he runs his hands over parts of his arms. Then he gazes away from them.

Adam: Reasons of how and why things fail.

Michael realizes that as harrowing as it sounds, these fundamentals awaited triggers to be made conspicuous for Adam to detect or regard. In other words, this physical assault was and is completely essential and therefore, irrevocably natural. Through their conversation, it is also revealed that Adam's Comprehensions from these readings about the Body were released in an extensively enhanced effect upon his Mind, consequently, reconciling a reality to his Mind with an abundance of effectuality right before he arrived at the moment where he was ready to die. Adam had gained a certain measure of control and understanding over the manifestly notable way a Body and a Mind is and will be.

Adam: I guess it just crept into my mind, you know, what the *inability to go on* is. I guess in a sense,

For a moment Here, Adam doubts himself. He doubts his surety relative to these sentiments. And more so than that, he doubts his surety in respect to what he intends to utter within those sentiments. He reassures himself. He forcibly swallows this doubt whole.

Adam: I am no longer haunted by death. It will be my end when I meet it.

Adam's relief is clear to see. In his Mind, Michael reflects over the comfort and relief that he too was once offered and given when he was at his End. Michael can see that Adam comprehended and Now understands what Michael was once offered and given in Time.

However, through swallowing it, Adam's renunciation of this doubt was not natural. Time is a natural course, and Time always Unfolds in this verifiable manner. Michael can see the forced nature of Adam's swallowing of his doubt. One day, Adam will have to revisit this doubt again. Adam will have to do this time after time. The Mind will find ways to renew itself until a balance is achieved. It will be renewed. It will be redeemed. And once redeemed, a Life will be given to Adam anew. Michael knows this. Michael has been through these revisitations many times. He has since left the revisiting, his Mind has found another way.

Through encountering, comprehending and by the best of his abilities, understanding the needlessness of being haunted upon a blood-stained floor, Adam's mind recognizes this hideously bloodied encounter and naturally associates that encounter with any other relative situation. That association and recognition stretches through the past and present of his life. The many relative situations' corresponding alikeness to the blood-stained one leads Adam to realize a determination doubtlessly. That he can always achieve an eventuality which would have been and still can be similar to the way he has Now transcended the Haunting. In fact, he also realizes that he could have always achieved that eventuality, most particularly within those relative situations. This transcendence shows Adam something, it shows Adam that peace and the ability to fare well was something he was always capable of. The only maneuver which he truly had to carry out is and always was a reasonable belief in himself. Adam Now understands that this belief was always plausible and feasible to expect from himself. Belief, it laid quiet, untapped and untouched for many days. And there lying with it, is and always was a willingness to accept all parts of himself. His Courage. His Compassion. His Determination.

It brings Michael great joy to see Adam achieve peace within. Adam's Life as is, triggers a joyful reminiscence in Michael's mind. Adam's growth has given Michael another perspective in Life. All the past occurrences have all led to this. Having a natural reason to Live. Michael then looks inward once more.

He looks at the path he once took. He ponders all the failures that had befallen him and had thus, stood firmly in his way. It had all at one point, drew his derision and pain. Inwardly in silence, his Mind swirls mightily.

"I got bolder and more deceitful with my lies and betrayals in criminality. There were many chances for me to turn back. I should've turned back. But I didn't."

Michael rues how he did not turn back, for it would have saved him from so much pain. However, he remains calm and objective through this ruefulness. It does not despond or immobilize him.

"I made a choice not to. I was a Man who made a choice."

Michael rues the choice he once made even more. There is a sense of despair that comes to him.

Michael searches his Mind to calm that which despairs him in Time. In his search, what seemingly comes to his acknowledgment is the sorrow and throe he had witnessed from many days gone by. He saw this sorrow and throe casted upon the innumerable faces of Others. He remembers seeing all this. Incidentally, he noticed all this while being deeply engrossed with the enactment of his many crimes. These sorrows were all recognizable visual signs that had occurred around him repeatedly and consistently. In hindsight, each manifestation has prevailed in Time. Michael's Mind recognizes this prevalence Now. At the time of those many occurrences, his Mind should have been triggered to surge and escalate in its perceptiveness within, thereby allowing him to be acutely aware of the Unfolding. An awareness of where he was in Life. An awareness that he was indeed, on a scorned path. But, he consciously chose to brush off any insight, ignoring it all with the aid of his inward reasoning and persuasion. And so there he was in Life, entangled by his own resolve.

He willfully blocked out all thoughts of sympathy, sorrow and kindness. He thought that those traits made him weak. He could not bear to show a weakness outwardly, not to those cohorts that he recognized as friends. Within the days of his life, he would not even show it to himself. He would try with all his fortitude to hide it from himself. An arduous task it was, to be a prey of his own thoughts. A prey that was unceasingly watchful, ever he lived in fear and doubt. His perceptions of devotedness did not extend much beyond what was said and done in plain sight. He did not know how to comprehend the layered profoundness that needful human interactions offered. When Michael came across any Act of Another, he did not see the reasons behind those Acts. Even if he were aware of a reason, he would not perceive it as a valid basis. He never used to watch or notice the way Another would develop and emerge as they Act. He never wanted or even desired to consider or understand the reason for those Acts of Another. There were broader meanings in Another's realizations. He did not want to know these things for himself. He could care less. And as these broader meanings fell away from him, he began to esteem the loss of meaning in his own Acts as adequate and delightful. There were important achievements he wanted for himself in life. And he feared that if he had veered any of his time and efforts towards another person, he would waste much of his very own limited vigor. Everything to him, anything that sustained him, was limited and scarce. He would never have enough of what he coveted and attained. He always and ever was in a struggle against his inward anticipations of what the future might hold. This diverse and copious combination of disdain and ignorance bled his Life dry of meaning and conception, which tragically submitted him to the mercy of Others. For he had no inward conceptualization to lean upon when there came a need for adaptation in Time. And so the numerous chances to turn back fell away from him time after time. In this falling away, he chose to do many Acts that caused many sorrows, he willfully saw his Acts as growth and progress. Every statement and claim he made, held within it deceit and anger. His being was continuously ripped and shredded, it came to grow incomplete. He went down a path he should not have gone. He always had to turn back.

As his Being grew ever so much more incomplete with every passing moment, it was clear that his greed would not be tamed. For in those passing moments, he did not view any potential taming as desirable or safe. In being incomplete, he viewed those voids he withheld as many emptinesses which were to be possibly filled by what his greed coveted. In the aftermath of procuring those desires, it ultimately did not overcome the emptinesses' unease. As the unease failed to cease, he remained stubborn in his entangling resolve. So there Michael was, entangled by this stubborn resolve. Added to that entanglement was the crucible of having to fight off the disquieting emptinesses which bore within him. Consequently, Michael's mind was overwhelmingly occupied with many moments of inward oppression, moments where his hopes for the future were in terrible doubt.

This loss of hope and lurking of doubt gave Michael in to despair. In order to relieve his mind of this hopelessness and despair, he desperately attempted to tread a way forward in life. In fact, Michael was so desperate that he paid no mind to what losses had mounted around him, or even how those losses had occurred for that matter. Michael treaded so as to achieve some semblance of progress or advancement upon this path he had chosen to cling on to so desperately. It was a way forward at least from his previous vantage point, a vantage point which was in hindsight, miniscule. This ultimately resulted in the prolonging of a Cycle which had within it, much treachery.

That being said, the chance to better things will always be there. Michael clearly remembers this presence. In hindsight, Michael also remembers that on far too many occasions, he passed it by. Those chances, they were all a single reality. He recalls seeing and passing them by over and over again because he treaded in hopeless circles. Circles of missteps and exploits. There were many times where someone or other came close to discovering his true motivations. This might have forced him to confess, come clean or even start afresh. Thus, causing him to show his true face to Others. But in order to conceal the truth of his malice and greed, he lied and deceived, further avoiding the taming. It was his choice to strangle all truth within in order to maintain this concealment. He continuously searched for ways to thrive and connive in his surroundings. However, he saw no depravity in his ways. He was doing what he knew to be fair and right for himself. And so he withheld his guiltlessness. He continuously chose the path of perceived ease and repeatedly gave in to temptations and impulses, for he grew enamored with the way it made him feel. He could not look past the potential of his incoming gains. The satisfaction of fruition ultimately nullified any guilt Michael might have felt in those Acts.

> *"I couldn't help it. I'm no longer a proponent*
> *of that. I have let that go."*

He comforts and forgives himself once again.

Through Time, many pains and derisions could end up showing a particular purpose. And as Michael can clearly see Now, all he witnessed had all been put before him to inspire him to steer clear of any future travesties.

He lifts his chin and breathes in the free air. The moment saturates Michael with appreciation. An appreciation for what is and what was. The ponderous weight of his past is leaving him again. Michael is very thankful for this saturation. Adam turns to Michael,

Adam: I guess these attacks will continue.

Michael: Yes. There are troubling circumstances out there. The baneful masses have evolved in Time and have grown to be bolder in their actions. Their atrocities are unkind and cruel. They bring forth a resolve that is motivated by the very pursuit of vindication. And not just vindication alone, but they seek retribution as well. Retribution with a vengeance. Their past failures stand preeminent in their waking thoughts and actions. You can see it in everything they do. It is also clear to see that there is a sense of reckless abandon with their prolonged existence and continued success. However, look around, this World has already seen much reconciliation occur, Many have been appreciative and content for many days. Life and the World offer much more situations of decency that are in need of examination and appreciation. It flourishes and adorns the Mind. We have to delve within this appreciation and allow it to be a part of ourselves, that way, we can make amends and reparations in Time. Hope is eternal, may you and I remain steadfast and hopeful. Let us begin with that.

Michael says this with a smile coming to him. As he talks, he hears himself. As Michael hears himself, he begins to remember George in this pact with Adam.

Michael: Those Few and Others, they do what they can to influence Another's way of thinking with subtle approaches. They wish to instil and impress a concept upon Another, a conceptualization that is sympathetic to the Few's cause. They do what they can so that Another will come to interpret the Few and Others as being deprived of numerous certainties in Life. Thus, forming an eagerness within Another to help the Few, whose need is thought to be great. The Few's offerings of influence subtly inundate our daily lives. There are offerings of products and options to consummate this manufactured eagerness everywhere. This however, can all be abstained and refused, but only if One were to so choose that outcome as a preference. We need not be Divided or bled dry. Many who have chosen to oppose the Few and Others have been deposed from their posts of services. These acts of deposing and influencing Another are all part of a plan that has been fashioned since the Few's last shameful collapse in days past. This plan will continue to unfold so as to consolidate their power to ensure that another Collapse will never happen again. The Few dare to take from Another what they themselves dread to live without. Their current path is justified in their Minds by fear. Those Few and Others, it is not for nothing that they Act the way they Act. Their folk and kin that remain dearest to them live far away from the Few. And over there, their kin and folk live a life where invulnerability is not certain. The Few and Others are now trying to gather all strength and power within this house of their own by bleeding Another absolutely dry. Historically, it has been proven that there is no escape from the clutches of the Overlords. Subversion or overthrowing their rule would only leave a vacuum of power which will be quickly occupied by Those with a great motivation. You can put your hopes and faith in other men if you so choose, but for all you long for, Another cannot live your life for you, it is literally impossible, only you can do as such. Another may have intentions that are altruistic, but they simply cannot navigate

through unfamiliar territory, no matter how
resourceful they are. Another does not have
the Mind or Time to live for any other One,
there is no need to find an escape within
Them, You are all you need. Casting your
hopes and faith upon Another will only be
a temporary solution to a problem that has
plagued Man since the dawn everything
we have known. We, who are bled dry,
the Few truly pay no mind to us, the Few
are not threatened by us or what we have
within as capabilities, and they definitely
do not worry about the consequences of
slandering or shaming us. And why would
they? We are bled absolutely dry, and the
Few control the flows of might and power
in our lives. These Overlords do worry
however, about Those who have a great
motivation. Those Few and Others, they
are trying to protect themselves against that
Foe which is furious, a Foe who is quickly
becoming one, whose arsenal, is that which
no amount of strength or resources can
harbour the Few and Others safely away
from, a Foe that has always been against
the Few's cause in this World, a Foe who
has assiduously and constantly attempted
to duplicate the feats of the Few and Others,
but to no avail. The Foes want and gravely
desire what the Few have been in possession
of for many days. All are matters that can
be pored over as facts within Time. It is
and was subservience that has left and
will leave these Foes indignant. However,

the Foes have attained a great might in this world once more. And this has been achieved through their many endeavours. They crave to be preeminent in the World. This craving has driven their every act and has landed the adversarial Foe in a position to threaten All. If there should ever be a vacuum of power left behind by the current Few and Others. These Foes will be strong enough to challenge for supremacy. The Foe will crave for the submission of All. It is a strong yearning that would result in a great torment for All.

Michael can see and hear all around that there is a verbalized and actualized form of desperation within Many, a desperation for a sense of direction in Life. And they will seek out this direction, no matter the cost. And so he continues his conversation with Adam.

Michael: We have seen it, haven't we? Those who seek submission will force the shame of All to come to past. The World will see much fury and throe before all things will be said and done. We have no choice, no matter how much we dominate over Others. No matter how many means and techniques we accumulate. All deeds are creations of Man's will. Nothing we can ever do will ever change the finality of where this World will eventually arrive. This nature of the Unfolding has always been True. Through their frustration at Life, the truths of the Foes' intent have been unveiled and shown.

For their minds have a finite ability, and they have unknowingly let their guard down in Time. Their minds have misplaced the memories of just how arduous and meticulous of a task it was when and where they seized control over many things. They have eventually taken those many controls as a given in life.

Michael then recalls the day of protest and animosity.

Michael: We are disenfranchised with the Overlords. Overlords have hacked and sawed their way to power. Along the way they have accumulated many enemies. They are firmly opposed by Foes that hate these Few Overlords and despise us, the ones who are bled dry. This contempt and animosity is real, for as we are bled dry, the Few grow stronger.

Michael knows he must be at one with himself, through and through. However, Michael decides to further consider what is Unfolding before Adam and himself.

Michael: They have a shared history together you know? This struggle can be traced back through the aged ancestries of both the Few and the Foe. And it is a far way back indeed. The works and acts of these kinfolks within this struggle have extensively determined this conflict's present course and consequences. All of their countless deeds have been set in Time and is the story of

this World. Some deeds had unfolded upon
All as a Gift, other deeds were achieved
through the works of a man or many men.
Plain and simple. In my own Life, I look at
what I've done, and it is clear for me to see
what was a Gift and what I have snatched
through my very works.

And Michael knows that he has snatched much from
Many. He thinks of the Few and the Foe. He knows that he
must not and he will never participate in any of their deeds
and acts. No matter the prosperity that it could and might
offer for his participation, Michael knows that he has all he
will ever need in this Gift.

Michael: The adversarial Foe is and has been gingerly
                  consummating a progress into a form that
                  is eminently capable of challenging the
                  Overlords' supremacy in this world. The
                  Foes have had enough and they will fight
                  the Few to the death. And not the slightest
                  concern will be given to the matter of how
                  many lives it will cost to achieve victory.
                  The loss of life will be accepted as the
                  necessary sacrifice that is to be given up
                  in order to attain the advantageous spoils
                  that this world has to offer. Through the
                  days that have gone by, the Foes' powers
                  have grown, and so too have their numbers.
                  They begin to surround that which the Few
                  prize most to have and to possess. It is this
                  Foe that has threatened the Few many
                  times over through intimidation and brute
                  force. The Foe covets that which the Few

are in possession of by way of legitimate inheritance. On the world stage, the Foe continues to inflame disagreements and conflicts within situations that the Few remain engaged in. It is clear to see, the Foes' strides are purposeful. They use deception as a potent tool to sway Another's inclination. They appropriate acts of betrayal against Another to impose their will. They strike arrangements with Another in this World. The angles that they enter into these accords with are highly suspect. In the minds of a Few and Another, the doubt and suspicion stirring rampantly with regards to the Foes are warranted, for All can now see on the global stage that there is an amassment of weaponry and allotment of forces that have been achieved through the gingerly carried out steps of the Foes. All suspicion is Now validated, this amassment and allotment, which is threatening the center of all the Overlord's assurance, possessions and priorities, factually shows which direction the true objectives of the Foes had always been steering toward, no matter what they would like us to believe. And like we have once learned, they have a finite ability, and they have unknowingly let their guard down in Time. These are circumstances that can be concluded and can therefore, be seen by watching the World. A Foe is only waiting for the time to ripen. They wait patiently for the will of the Few to be that of a weakened state, which will make conditions favorable for a Foe's restless aggression to be unleashed. An aggression that the Foe conceals as they can. Over a lifetime, there will be turns where One or Another would be worn down. And so the Foe lies in wait. The Few have committed this exact same set of deeds against Another, Those who are Divided. And that is the aforementioned throe my friend. Only this time, it will not lead to untroubled protests and moderate disapproval. Moreover, it will unfold as a swift vengeance in enmity and slaughter. No force of object can save the Few from the Foe's intense rage. This rage will set occurrences in motion that will pass, just like this Few's kin and folk have done on far too many occasions in days past.

Through watching, Michael can interpret the Foe's cursed motives. These comprehensions have come to Michael in spite of the Foe's calculated outward portrayals of good willed intentions. Michael's thoughts then fall upon Rulers and Leaders. That segment within All, Michael knows Another will choose to follow that leadership and rule.

Michael: A person that is entrusted to rule has to be essentially infallible and flawless. However, there is no One that is. One simply cannot be. It is not that I lack faith in people, it is just that One cannot suffice in a Completion for Another through the matter of governance and rule. A Mind and Body does not coalesce as such. It is however, decent to learn and share with Another so as to grow and maturate a Completion that assimilates in the Mind by cause of a personal appreciation of what One has been through in Time. And not be indoctrinated by the pronouncements of Another. But, the decisions made by One will always be flawed from the perspective of Another. This ideological system of ruling and following, that will have All follow the Few, has always let All within the system down. The Few have accorded promises to One after Another. That there will be a coalescence for All through the Few's rule. Look around, there has been no coalescence. Rather, we are Now presently more Divided than we have ever been before. There is no beauty in these failures, there will be no recovery where One or Another will emerge stronger than ever. How can there be? Especially if generations upon generations of All have to endure the consequences that are brought on by the actions and choices of a Few. To be under this system of rule and leadership is not very sensible or reasonable. There is no clear resolution in this world. It will be precarious from here on out.

Michael then realizes the uncertainty that comes with the absence of a resolution.

Michael: In past times as such, Many have often hurried into comfortably leaning on Others as a resolution to all their uncertainties. A leaning that will throw both the lives of Many and the lives of Others off balance.

Instead of casting an accursed imbalance upon this World by depending and leaning on Others who are Few, Michael chooses to lean on a Completion Given in Time. This Completion gives him the assurance to say,

Michael: This World, Forever, it is all as true as can be.

With All in the World, Michael knows that there is no certainty in that statement. And so he continues,

Michael: Some are true, and Some are not. Some parts of Those that are true are subtly false. This further tilts an already imbalanced and volatile situation. And that is why Everything is incongruent in all directions of focuses and ideals. It is a constant and consistent veering away from all things that were already separate. It is reflective of this disparity of many Minds in the World. And it all gives way to Acts that sustain in Time. All these Acts will be completely diverse, when reflected upon in One's memory.

Michael sees this incongruence and divergence again. It does not change him, for he knows that he remains a part of Some. That is all there is to it. It is a sentiment. He sees it. He feels it. He knows it.

Michael: As true as some parts of All may be, it is the parts that are untrue which are the impetus for the pushing and tearing away from One

Another. The benevolence of many Acts are nullified and completely turned on its head by that which is an opposing Adversary. It is an Adversary that obscures Truth to strengthen the development of what is False. Sometimes, belief is entrusted into that which is False and seemingly great, for there are Some who need answers. They will search anywhere they can to obtain these answers. This search however, will be Futile.

An Adversary's charge will always harbor and bear opposition. And that hostile engagement against that Adversary will melt and destroy All involved. If Michael involves himself, and rallies to a cause, he knows that there will be a weakness within him that Another will use to throw him down. Before that will ever happen however, he might find a weakness within Another and cruelly exploit it. Michael knows that One or Another may make it worth his while to rally to their cause, in the hopes to form a common wealth. Michael knows that he may see friends of his that have a good will within Them who will be drawn to these causes. Those who have a good will might tempt him to feel for and resonate with these Offerings of many sentiments. It is Now that Michael's Mind is triggered to remember what these Offerings truly mean. It is a product of a Hunter who seeks to prey on the Divided. This Offering's true meaning may remain obscured behind any number of ranks and layers of individuals and or sentiments. Michael knows that even though this Offering may have come to him as being Offered by One or Another that he is familiar with, it remains simple to see that there can be nothing True that will come from this known establishing, promoting and upbearing of the very same Hunters, Agents, Leaders, Manufacturers and

Overlords. He has seen it, he has seen the consequences of the Offerings and the Acts that follow. Michael has seen these unfold in cycles. Michael had taken many Offerings in Life and Now has nothing to show for it. Michael can do nothing but watch. There is no contempt in his watchful stillness. All rallying cries trying to draw in forces do not reverberate through him, for he is still. Stillness is peace. If there were enough stillness, it would stagnate a rally. Eventually all will be still, Michael knows it.

He does not know how to turn Another's Mind from those cyclical issues. Michael knows that if he can gaze through the obscurity of what is False, he just might stand a chance at becoming True. He knows that becoming True, for himself, can quite possibly happen in Time. Michael knows there is another way where he can turn aside from what is False, and it is the way of the path that lays inward. It is safe there, it is a Gift. Sometimes, the path outward might lead any One to be mislead by the sentiments or representations of Others or one too many products. This obscuring of what is True can and will challenge anything any One has to hold true to.

Michael says these words to Adam, but yet he himself wonders if the pact will be upheld. Michael and Adam part ways once again.

As Michael walks away, he sees that surety had seemingly fled from him yet again through Time. Why was that? He thinks of his former experiences, the ones that brought him joy in respite, his friends and companions. He looks back with a great nostalgia.

What was so special about those moments? Was it not just another set moment in Time as he had come to comprehend?

He begins to search his Mind.

"In those days, I found myself to be completely immersed

and lost within those moments. I was as free of care as I could possibly hope to be. I lived my life with a certain reckless abandon. For in being completely immersed and preoccupied, I abandoned and disregarded many Cares and many Things. I did so in the hopes of freeing myself of any existing or possible burdens. This buoyancy in Life was mine and mine alone. I thought of this buoyancy to be a thrill that brought me much gratification. I thought it to have given me strength to gain and maintain. No longer do I relish these passing moments the way I used to. How I used to welcome those moments, it felt to be priceless and inestimable. Now, experiences do not come to me silken or lustrous like they once were before."

He thinks back of his convalescence.

"Maybe it is because I lost a part of myself and it never really came back to me."

He realizes his Mind is changed. This Life, which has been revived in Forever, it is now not to be lived in the same manner.

"How do I go on in this same Place, expecting the same mesmerizing sentiments from Life, when my Body and my Mind is changed? Nothing's the same. In the past, while I adeptly twisted and altered many Things to satiate my many desires, in so many more ways than that, that which was in front of me was all I ever really knew. That is the unfortunate truth. It is unfortunate because all Acts have within it so many kinds of significances to it. And any given significance will be born out of any beholder's perspective. And that is mightily vital to understand. I deviated my Life's course so horribly by letting an unfortunate truth

bore within my Life and my perspective. So many deeds
have occurred before me, and there were so many times
where I could not make out the many meanings and
significances of the Unfolding. This was because I was
trapped by my own mind. Everything will Now take
on a different meaning. Everything will Now take on
a different sentiment. Everything is changed. Forever
will Unfold and be. I am but in the Here and Now. "

Not the same manner indeed. How can it be? The
Mind has been exposed anew to another lore. A lore that
was previously unknown to the Mind. Michael goes on as
he knows how to. After his convalescence from hostilities
involving fatal camaraderies with Cohorts, Michael had been
attempting to continue living with his Mind's preceding
disposition. He did so with the hopes to overcome barriers in
Time. He is however, a changed person, and he will continue
to change. So will his expectations for Life. And in all these
changes, he will adapt. Michael's expectations change with
his surroundings. In striving to continue living, Michael
felt worryingly adrift because all that continued to Unfold,
to him, were occurrences which he did not expect. And in
so being casted Adrift, the hostile turbulences brought a
tremendous disquiet to his Mind.

"What I once thought to be buoyancy, I now see is
actually so very much lacking, incomplete even."

In Michael's Mind, doubt is Now being cast aside by
several thoughts.

"Like how I Now erroneously think of myself as being
categorically grim or somehow lesser than what I once
was. This very concern here is yet another error that I

have unfortunately made in Time. For this Gift is all I'll
ever need. with this Gift, I am very much grateful."

Michael stands witness of his own recognition and Now realizes what he has just done.

"Ever so much Now, I appraise and regard Things in my
Mind. Do I really miss Things the way it used to be?"

Michael continues to appraise his prior days, days where he conceived himself to be pricelessly welcoming in moments as it all Unfolded. In the past, at every turn he had desired to avoid all toil or suffering by any means necessary. And so he over-emphasized, over-developed and over-compensated in certain compartments of his life. This resulted in him suffering and somehow surviving a few many consequences. And before the emphasizing, compensating and developing of life was even initiated, he was at the mercy and under the controls of others. Others, they are faceless entities who no longer bring Michael any misery. They embolden parts of Time in Forever. That has all washed away, far away from him. He is finally where he is. He has experienced Much. He is Now eager to let the Unfolding run its course in Time.

He has Now grown ever so enamored with the memory of his own misfortunes. Sometimes, he would even reminisce about it into parody and thus, find humor in it. Tragedy and sorrow at a certain point, can become natural in its own distinct way. Michael is Now witnessing this conversion.

That Humor, it was a relief. He remembers laughing, desperately grasping for air in that expressed amusement. That feeling in his Body, the euphoria was brought on by this grasping and convulsing within the tracts of his Body. It triggered flows of energy that invigorated him. He remembers this.

Everything fair or foul empowers his peace. Perceived hardships hold absolutely no shackle upon his Mind. Balance is appreciated with transcendent joy. All that has washed away has shown the World's nature to Michael. Michael finds no need to fear losing anything. He sees no sense in lamenting the past. He finds no reason in lamenting his earlier ignorances which had led to much loss. It is not possible for Michael to have known then what he knows Now. It is neither possible nor natural. He found all his previous desires to hold no worth in retrospect. It all means nothing, it is all Nothing.

In the days that continue to pass, Michael keeps up to date with current events. Over the years, there have been quite a few many unsolved missing person cases. As it turns out, detectives have finally come to the end of this conundrum. The news report which reveals this transpiration to Michael makes it known that all those missing persons mysteries have culminated in one gruesome conclusion. One man has been ending lives at an unnatural pace. And to conceal this frightfulness, this man has buried his many victims away in a large private field. The report goes on further to state that this discovery puts to rest over decades of disappearances. Some bodies were hidden away for so long that the remains had become a collection of completely unrecognizable bits of substances and apparent body parts. Most of the bodies' physical nuances have disintegrated and seemingly disappeared. The organs and its means were all contorted and distorted in decomposition. Michael volunteers to be a part of an investigatory team on the constabulary. He sees all these deformities lay before him, and it is hideous to behold.

In his findings, Michael can see much. As his Mind gets around the hideousness of the crime scene, Michael decides to take a closer look. In his closer look, he can tell that all which has seemingly disappeared has actually changed into another form and has already coalesced with the earth. Michael sees that this process of coalescing is indeed, natural. Michael has seen on many occasions in the wilderness that all sizes and forms of greenery, when collapsed, have disintegrated as well, and in Time, had also returned to the earth. Just like these contorted and distorted bodily deformities which Now lay before him. Michael thinks of his personal experience. Michael remembers an existence without the aid of his organs and its functions, an existence that was adjusted and sustained through medical and surgical mechanisms. If not for the application of surgery and usage of mechanisms, he would now be undergoing a natural decomposition himself.

A return to the earth.

It is and was an existence that was at his End. That Step brought him through a moment which was a singular, boundless and vast harmony. In the aftermath of this harmony, he awoke. And as he returned to consciousness within a naturally sustained existence, he was left feeling lesser, hindered even, with a sense of longing. He longed for a return to that Step, as it was without strife, and that ebbing of strife gave way to the saturation of contentment. It was Completion.

There, he was free of discomfort. There, he was free of regret. He was free in so many ways because he was given vigor and security within himself. Michael remembers that familiarity and intimacy which had allowed him to expand and exist from having both the Now and the End within his perspective and sight. In this remembrance, Michael's thoughts Now settle upon that very contemplation of both spaces. He remembers what it felt like to be comfortably in touch with both places at all times. He also remembers being able to draw upon both to provide the Mind with a fair interpretation, no matter how perilous the Unfolding became. That Completion, it gave Michael favor and comfort. It all felt harmonious, boundless and vast, for it was and is Forever.

Everything of this World is and always will be a part of this World, no matter what Step it is to take. This and much more is exhibited for Michael to Watch through his taking of a closer look. All those victims that were murdered, they are Now returned to the earth. Michael Watches. It all keeps him aware and conscious of the nature of this World and Forever.

In being a volunteer on the investigatory team, Michael is given access to many pieces of evidence. One of those many pieces of evidence that drew Michael's attention was a logbook which the murderer had kept through his many days of concealing the frightfulness. In reading this man's memories, Michael can see that this man had no sense of excitement through life. No source of satisfaction whatsoever. He was just seemingly going through the motions of each and every day. He had reviled many peoples' existence for many years. He hid this revulsion away to secure and maintain a life of considerable pride and prominence. Michael continues to pore over the journal. He sees that even before the killings began, this man had often wondered what it would be like to kill. This man often pondered over this. He did so by inscribing this in extensive detail when the subject was on his mind. The act of taking life away, he had always been fascinated with the act of murder. He struggled at times with the intrigue which pulled him towards the deed of murder. For he feared many consequences that would have come with committing murder in this society, thus, he ably concealed those deeds and thoughts, especially in the latter days of this journal. The contention within this man's thoughts was evidenced by his very struggles against this intrigue, he would often note about this inner struggle whenever he experienced it. The notes of it were recurrent and numerous. In the early stages of this man's fascination, it seemed to Michael that this man maintained and harbored personal precepts that he still tried to hold on to with conviction. For it was at that early period, where this man still recognized murder as a form of defilement, as he was not completely enthusiastic about the act of murder.

This man wished and hoped day and night for certain outcomes. Much, in his view, has been taken away from him. Much of what this man wanted, he did not attain. Some of what he wanted to attain was menial, some of it extravagant. In times that he was alone, he plead and begged in whispers and screams. And those screams were blared out at the top of his voice. Michael can tell that this man had surrendered to what had perpetuated and preceded those whispers and screams. But in his own written words, those yearnings burned him most in the privacy of his own thoughts. It was in that very silence of his private thoughts and reflections, where he would absolutely bellow for what he had not attained. That is what Michael perceives from this man's written words.

In this man's scarcity of attainments, he grew bitter. Much gloom fell upon him. He felt miserable. He wanted all his sufferings to end. He resorted to take it upon himself to search for the answers he needed. And so he began to read many pieces of literature. Through his interpretations and bitterness, he adopted many beliefs. He came across doctrines of depopulation and race murder for certain portions of society, and it all seemingly appealed to him. He saw the need to cut down the world's population. He thought the world had become too populated. He saw the current population of the world as not sustainable. He also saw this over-population of the world as a major contributing factor towards his many hardships. Those doctrines somehow assuaged all the disquiet that he felt within. As his views of the world changed, this man wished for others to experience no success, he wanted everyone to be miserably poor or in pain. He wanted everyone to be worse off than he was. This man found pleasure at just the thought of another person's misery. When this man wrote about major events that happened in the world, especially events where the destruction of life was prominent, Michael had always felt that there was a discernable sense of delight that this man adopted in receiving and broaching upon those subjects.

This man continued to liken those readings of killings and death more and more. In that likening, he proceeded to search for even more literatures of that similar expression. As he searched, many suggestions were put forth to this man by the designed algorithms of Another. It was within those designed algorithms, where this man eventually came across the many ideas which encircled around the catastrophic death and destruction of the world in the hindmost hours of all existence. The anticipation, expectation and promise of complete ruin to come for the entire world within those literatures brought this man a hint of comfort.

As Michael decided to read over all those compositions which this man had cited as sources, Michael found that all those literatures of calamities were written by Many who were Disenfranchised and Divided. They yearned to be released from this life for they have come to feel tormented by what Life had become. They yearned to see this world destroyed, for they have come to begrudge many things about it. Today, the Many who uphold those very same literatures are Disenfranchised and Divided as well, and continue to be genuinely exhausted by the broken promises unendingly issued by their Leaders in government. Leaders who would only do what the Few want, and not what All need, Leaders who have championed the chief ideology in this World. The very same World where no state-crafting ideology of promise has either existed or will ever exist in the history, present or future of the human race to effectively govern Man as currently constituted. Michael sees this. Michael knows this. It is an absolute abuse of power and authority, which ultimately, places the assurances of All in the way of the fire that will burn in conflicts between whosoever the Few have decided to provoke and weaken through political acts and deeds. Those many provocative acts and deeds which the Few obscurely commit in secrecy is clear for All to see. The Provoked and the Foe therefore, have many reasons to hate the Few. And in many ways, the Provoked have an enmity which far exceeds that of the Foe's.

As Michael continues to read, Michael begins to behold a larger perspective. It can be seen that this man felt of this hint of comfort, along with all its underlying sentiments, to be very much necessary to his mental stability, vital even. It was similar to what this man would find within his many documented flights of imagination, but yet, this comfort remained fundamentally more meaningful than those flights. He wrote that he was inspired by those underlying sentiments, that he even needed those readings of underlying sentiments to go to sleep at night. He took delight in those readings. This man did not know why he experienced a hint of comfort from those literatures, but Michael had an idea as to why. For Michael too, once had his Mind preyed upon by his own thoughts. That hint of comfort came from this man's comprehensions. This man was certain that all which was anticipated, expected and promised in those literatures was going to happen within his lifetime. It was an anticipated, expected and promised time where many troubles and sufferings would be no more. For this man, the expected onset of many catastrophes in the hindmost hours of all life, promised a release from all that haunted him. This man has grown tired and weary of the Here and Now. Those literatures, it appealed to him, it comforted him. This man desperately wanted those catastrophes to occur. He welcomed those many anticipations and expectations with open arms.

However, the comfort and joy that this man felt did not

last or reverberate. It always left and deserted him without fail. It was always gone too soon. And it was always without fail, that this man would be left feeling hollow and empty. In feeling as such, this man's writings circled back and forth between lucid coherence and disjointed brooding, all backed with a theme of desperation. Michael knew this desperation all too well. In this man's weakness, he began to see no point in pleading or begging with exasperation, for it too, brought him nothing. It got him nowhere. As this man continued to search for answers, he spent his days meticulously meditating over words, phrases and symbols from scripts and scrolls which were rigorously followed by many adherents in many places. This man did so in order to initiate and sustain a hypnotic state to cleanse his spirit, for he thought of his body to be vile and in need of purification. His many trances, which this man had meditatively brought about, numbed his mind and sent him through sacred dimensions and heightened realms. It gave him what he thought to be a supernatural focus in life to influence and nurture the disposition of his fate. He utilized this focus to plan realistic steps to fulfill hateful daydreams that he would spend visualizing. These visions were brought about by people who wronged him, at least from his perspective. The anger that he grappled with was only exacerbated in his meditative sessions. He is drawn to the violence which he dreamt of enacting. He felt as though those acts were calling to him. Through the meditation which consisted of repetitive techniques, this man found a sacred and devout focus within many things. The ground underneath his feet at times, another person perhaps, historical accounts of significance, past memories of other people, his own body, even futuristic writings spanning both fiction and nonfiction. While within his many dazes, this man would compartmentalize himself to study and evaluate his time spent under that hypnosis and meditation. He would evaluate the way his body would act, how he perspires or how his eyes rolled perhaps. There were many ways in which this man would critique himself. This man needed to find out and create works that would render him as worthy of his life or this world. Michael knows of this pursuit. It was a pursuit that was proven to be needless upon the realization and acceptance of this Gift. The many works and literatures, all of it was never enough to assuage this man's strife and discontent. This man remained desperate for answers. He was at the end of his wits. All this man had was the many flights of imagination, further compounded by his longings, anticipations and expectations. And so this man continued to Imagine.

As days go by, he imagined killing most of the people he ever came into contact with. These people have slighted this man in one way or another. He saw no worth in these people's lives. Trains of coherent thoughts in his journal entries were often interrupted by poignant broodings. In many passages, he stopped to assert how he hated himself. He also routinely paused to make it known that one day, he will indeed kill himself. All the broodings seemed to energize him, its effects were there for Michael to read. In the immediate aftermath of his many broodings, the decisiveness of his expressiveness became considerably more lucid and even more coherent. This man recorded many of the daily conversations which he shared with the people he knew. All those conversations conceived a great amount of boredom within this man. He claimed to be bored to the point of immense frustration and aggravation, which further deepened his desire to kill. In speaking with the people he knew, this man felt that these peoples' comments trespassed and crossed the line against him both ethically and morally. This man chose neither to address those trespasses nor leave the matters to rest. This man could not stand the weight of those sufferings, he just wanted the disturbances to dwindle and diminish in the immediate aftermath of its multiple occurrences. When bothered by the disturbances, he would stew and brood over the ramifications resulting from these people crossing the line.

Michael thinks this man's expectations of dwindling and diminishing to be impractical and unreal.

Beneath this man's polite and respectable outward demeanor, he hid a keen affinity for violence and murder. In the many of his journal's passages, he celebrated the many acts and traits which upheld both violence and murder. His writings were strikingly similar to many Offerings that Michael had come across in the past. This man ruled over his own acts. He chose to embody those traits. And thus, the desperation continued to advance against him. This man was desperate because even as he celebrated, his very vitality and essence were both being cornered and surrounded. To counter this growing desperation which continuously gnawed at his existence, he began to acknowledge himself as his own master and lord, thus, empowering himself. He answered only to himself. Nothing else mattered. He wanted to serve and please himself only. He only committed to Acts that benefited himself.

This man refused to change, he refused to search for or find new ways to adapt, in order to reverse this desperation that had come to him. Instead, this man chose to find many new motivations to kill and spend more time within his flights of imagination, which he poignantly recorded. Those many flights had him inflicting bodily injuries which increased in severity. Michael sees how vulnerable the Mind can be to Offerings in this World.

At some point of this man's recorded history, he killed a person through a fit of rage. This man chronicled his thoughts after he finally brought his many flights of imagination to fruition and reality. The victim, on that very occasion, completely crossed the line and shamed this man. This man did not document what exactly it was that the victim did to him, this man just wrote about the particular aggravation being a terrible disruption in life, and that this disturbance would never be able to be dwindled or diminished, which to this man, justified the outcome. The violent actions all fell into place abruptly with great rapidity, a subjugation to anger it was. And before this man could fully grasp onto his wits, he was in position to lay down the killing stroke, as this man stood over the victim, this man's fear of legal prosecution and potential penalization determined that there was no turning back for both this man and the victim. And so this man laid down the killing stroke. He stood firm in words that the deed had to be done. To be imprisoned was not an option for this man. This man also wrote that if he was ever going to overcome a desperation that had now taken over his life, his many flights of imagination had to be fully realized. It was the only logical move to this man's knowledge and decisiveness.

The victim was a person that this man often came into contact with. The act of murder was something that intrigued this man. Murder was something that this man had greatly desired to enact. Those sentiments were stated as such in this man's own words. Yet, after the first time this man killed, this man claimed it had left no lingering sense of pleasure for him, and that nothing had changed within him. But still, he felt the mighty urge to kill again. This man could not explain it. He was just expressing how he felt.

Even days after having fully absorbed all the implications of the deed, this man resolutely emphasized to himself that it really had not mattered that he had finally achieved murder. Something he previously desired so strongly to do. He also stated that he could care less if that murder had never occurred. But with that being said, this man chose to do the deed again and again time after time. He carried out and enacted fantasies of past murder cases which he had studied through various crime reports.

This man saw the joy which lives of people brought to their children, parents, spouses, friends and all kin. And yet, he glossed right over that joy, and instead, he chose the idea of murder. He had gained the boldness to put all his thoughts into actions. He no longer wondered about the act. He did the deed and had no regrets or remorse in removing that joy from Others. He saw no repercussions to his acts. His acts carried no consequential meanings to him.

And in so doing, this man continually searched for many ways to murder, and he had indeed, found many ways. Michael read over the many ways this man had sourced. The written details of the murders were fierce. The precise language with which he used to describe his butcheries was highly detailed and it was evidently penned by a person who was supremely motivated to do the deed. Michael could see that this man was very resourceful through finding many ways to do the deed. This man's capacity for savvy and intellect was on full display. In being resourceful, this man turned back many possible occurrences and achievements of others, all of which would have been otherwise, natural. This man fully embraced this Turning back of occurrences and achievements as a real power that he prided in having. He was a man who wanted the world to go as he wanted it to go.

As the body count continued to pile on, he continually showed no regret or remorse. Each murder was an accomplishment to him. Every murder was a quest for him. For this man constantly looked for new ways to improve the kill.

From time to time, this man claimed to see the misery of many around him. And in so doing, this man referred back to those doctrines and literatures which he had been exposed to earlier. This man professed to love this world, and that every murder he committed was achieved to better this world.

This man continued to experience much through his days where he committed many murders and concealed it all as best he could. He chose to kill at every turn. He absolutely refused change, no matter what form it undertook. To adapt and harmonize himself to the changing realities that were constantly coming his way in life was not an option. This man would not yield. This was the path that he had chosen for himself, and as imperfect as it was, he was going to stick to it no matter what. He found that there were many imperfections in his life, much aggravation and frustration continued to come towards him. Wherever or whenever an aggravation or frustration came, this man refused the requisite patience crucially needed to let those arduous times reach an end. Unfailingly, to satiate a vexation, this man would handily contrive many acts to bring about those ends.

The End of Anything, Michael ponders the End. Michael's End was brought about in Time. And Now, being Here, having come through Life, Michael has watched and learned, all while standing true to this Gift. Michael also recognizes and sees Another's Gift. It is through Time that Michael has been delivered a convalescence through a coalescence.

Michael continues to read. Having strategically brought about many ends, this man built a successful life that had capitalized on the incidental absence and disintegration of Another. It may have seemed incidental to any casual onlooker. However, all absences and disintegrations were thoughtfully contrived by this man. In this man's final note, he stated that he would be gone for the time being, because he could sense that the law enforcement officials were beginning to piece together many logics and reasons, and were now getting too close for comfort. He also stated that the work he started on this very ground was not done yet, that it would be completed eventually, that he would continue to right the wrong, and that if other citizens would capitalize like he did, there would be greater success and happiness all around the world.

Michael looks inwardly again, he sees his own Completion, he feels the Saturation. While he is content, Michael knows that Others have been where he is in Life without having been through his path taken. The path that Others have taken is that which is Finished. Now, they need not add or work to complete it.

Michael thinks of this man, the steps this man took were short and tenuous. He could scarcely bear the weight of Life. Michael knows this tension. For once, Michael's every thought and act was constrained, stiff and ridged. He would come to exasperation often. In Time, he has untied that rigidness. His Mind and Body Now feel loose. Michael knows that there are only so many blows that a body can take. Many blows, Michael remembers being in control of numerous situations while delivering many blows to strike people down. Michael remembers those Acts and that path which he took in the delivering of those many blows. That path and those Acts lead to definitive and horrific falls of Others. Those blows which he delivered were subtle at times. At other times, they were severe or even worse, fatal. Then there were times where the many blows did not even exist to bring people down. The blows were simply tactics of lies and deceit. Lies and deceit which were used to engineer, manufacture and manipulate a fall of Another. For in those blows, Michael knew that there were gains to be had. That aside, the falls and losses of Others were substantial and real. And so is the pain. Michael knows this. If One bands with Others, it introduces a collective endurance against those many blows. But Michael has seen people band together and still fall. That much, Michael had witnessed. Michael can feel that he needs something else. And there, Forever is. Forever will always be Here. Michael knows this, Michael feels it.

Michael is strengthened yet again. In being reinvigorated, Michael finds the courage to further explore this journal. Michael tries to imagine living this man's life of ubiquitous contempt in the desire to kill in order to capitalize and satiate. Michael attempts to put his Mind in this man's place and life, to surround himself with this man's sentiments. To feel every insult as this man does. To be brought to rage so often and easily. Some things came to Michael as his Mind met this new place. It was a great deal of fatigue at first. Caustic thoughts against the Self and Others began to generate. These things that came to Michael in this new place were unwelcomed by Michael's Mind.

However, over the days, the undulation of the Mind continues to tilt between uncertainty and Completion. At times, Michael's Mind strays and forgets about the ease of which things are. During those times, Michael was easily engulfed in whole by the matters that laid before him. Now, Michael sees that his balance and his sanity can indeed be tipped and could very well be toppled over in Time. Michael needed the matters and unfortunate affairs of Others to cue his Mind's internal will. It was all there for Michael in a time of need. There are recollections within his Mind which uplifted him and kept his Balance from toppling and falling. All Michael had to do was remember. His retention of those memories was a gift within this Gift. And Michael knows that it is not to be taken for granted. Michael knows it is a gift, for he did not create it. And so Michael continues to watch.

Scattered and littered within All and the systems of the world, are folks who are just searching for decent ways to forge their many paths through life. Their presence is known to Michael, and as long as they remain Divided, Michael knows there will be more angst to be endured by All in Time.

Michael's path has had plenty of angst. Michael remembers his angst, he remembers being under its dominion every single day, it was something that was significantly preeminent in his life. But Now, it is all but faded. Michael wonders, if that dominance and preeminence could fade, how can anything that happens to him truly stay? Michael questions that in his Mind. Everything is faded.

Michael's thoughts stray yet again. Now, he remembers the many pages written by this man. From that journal, Michael remembers seeing that there were so many layers to single occurrences that continually change the reasons and motivations of the act that follows. If One were to absolutely understand what singular occurrences truly meant to Another in Time, it would be the answer to many questions and mysteries in this World.

Michael Now sees that One's Mind is truly not within the grasp of Another. Especially if One truly desired to protect it from Another.

Michael then aims his concentration back upon the remembrance of his angst that is Now faded. Michael knows that the angst of the Divided will fade as well. Everything is indeed faded. Michael knew a boundless, vast and harmonious peace at the End. But as his life was prolonged and continued, Michael made a conscious effort to remember how he felt in the hopes to remake and duplicate his life as it was at the End. Thereby, redeeming his Life in Time, where his Mind will become stronger than any Act's influence. Michael is quite certain that all this will come to him in the days that are to follow.

Through his days, there are many distractions that reside within his Life, peace and joy periodically flees from Michael's Mind. In fact, there is much that comes to Michael and causes him to stray. In experiencing events which stir countless legions of regret within him, Michael contemplates making amends for the past so as to compensate for what he regrets Now. This contemplation arises within his Mind from time to time. In profoundly pondering it, Michael realizes that these chances to make amends were and are indeed, within every passing moment. Michael can conceive what had happened before these chances had ever come forth. Even more so than that, Michael is able to grasp on to what had occurred after those chances had come about. It is all in the passing moments as well. In his many Acts, he has fought and struggled against the passing of both Life and Time, Time that passes and continually Unfolds. He fought it all ever so hard. The Fight is Now over. Michael sees it. Through both Life and Time, Michael has discovered that the Fight was never even Here.

Michael knows it is up to him to understand that the Fight should have never begun or occurred in the first place. The Unfolding is and always was Natural. Michael once realized that on a previous day, and in both moments, in all moments really, it is unequivocally True. In the aftermath of that Fight, there were plenty of consequences. Michael has lived through it all. It is Now, where he does not seek to redress or amend any Act he has ever carried forth. To amend or to correct would be to stray from the Here and Now. Moreover, it would be to continue that Fight which should have never occurred. Having lived through the consequences, Michael is not drawn to do as such. It is all Time that has gone by. It is not Here, it will never return. He has seen Life through being alive. And through being alive, Time has given him much, he wants no more. He is Here, he has all he needs.

As Michael sees his balance make yet another return, he begins to question one thing. When and where will this undulation end? In the face of all that has faded, Michael continues to question what he has to do in order to make the appreciation of this Gift truly stay forever. In being pelted with the questioning's uncertainty, he begins to remember the Completion he felt when he recognized events that were Natural to the Unfolding. It seems his Mind is there for him yet again. Michael feels safe and secure. In this calm state of Mind, Michael knows what has to be done. He knows he is One of All, and All are patrons of Time. All will always be needed, wherever they are. All move along with the Unfolding, even as All search to find many things. Michael knows this. Because wherever this Unfolding ends, the cause of the Unfolding will be justified and validated within Forever. Michael knows this as well. Mightily, all this had come to Michael's Mind before in the Unfolding.

14

Time continues to pass since that hospitalization of his. And so Michael continues to live. As he lives, Michael is able to not only identify, but also recognize when Another hopes and bids to project many blows upon someone else. It is a projection from Another, who is attempting and intending to engineer, manufacture and manipulate many baneful circumstances against another One. Michael is familiar with all this, for it is a parallel to the bygone personifications of Michael, who had himself personally engineered, manufactured and manipulated much detriment to Others. Through his identification and recognition of these many ramifications, Michael is neither shocked nor blindsided by the many perils that continue to stem from various circumstances which have Now come to him in Time. It does not leave him despondent or abjectly disheartened, for through Time, Michael is able to consider, distinguish and conclusively understand parallels and similarities. Thus, bringing about a coherence to Life. However, it does still provoke some form of strife within

Michael. All this strife Now causes Michael to remember what this man had previously stated through journalistic records.

As Michael recalls, those records illustrated a discord similar to that which he himself still encounters presently. Often, Michael would meticulously adjust the Mind in order to avoid going down the same path as that journalized discordancy. It Now dawns on Michael that all these memories were recollections of events which were and are an active and living series of matters that will continue to proceed relentlessly until the End. Michael knows he can adjust to it, Michael has done it before.

Michael remembers adjusting. As he reflects, the Mind also considers the lives of both him and his parents. Michael sees that given their knowledge, experiences, availabilities and abilities, they could only carry forth acts in a certain manner. It was all they could possibly hope to muster, both consciously and subconsciously. In their lives, they did not know certainty and did not recognize events or transpirations which unfolded right before them. Michael has seen them stumble over and over again because of this hindered perspective of theirs. Michael knows that their identification and recognition is obscured and perverted. And so much is blocked from their perception, they do not even see it. They cannot even hope to see it. Here and Now, Michael can scarcely dare to form a mental picture of what it must be like to wander down Life's path in that manner. Michael has also seen much desperation in this world. His parents fought many fights on many fronts. They too, were desperate. They defended what belonged to them. However, in their desperate fight, they would have always claimed everything they possessed, as insufficient for their needs. This was because the losses they had sustained were an amount they had never wished to bear. Besides the losses sustained, Michael knows that there are layers to every single juncture or experience in this world, and when those layers presented itself to his parents, Michael knows it must have only added to their desire to possess more. Thus, it could have only fastened desperation to their divided minds. Michael is at peace with that, he knows Now that there is absolutely no need to redress those previous issues of throe. He knows that no One can perform beyond their Mind's natural or acquired limitations. In the past, he chose to see his parents as antagonists of his. To comfort himself of that determination, he drew a line and embraced certain other individuals in friendship, fellowship and brotherhood. He forcibly poured more and more of himself, unjustifiably so, into those bonds which he chose to embrace. That very pouring made him and his existence very much assailable. Michael understands that Now. That act of forcibly pouring was not reciprocated, but then, Michael thought it would be. And so he falsely comforted and Divided Himself even more, just like his parents. All he wanted was the security of affluence in life, but yet, he likened Himself to the company of Those who would only snatch and hoard any form affluence for themselves, wherever they may find it. That being said, Michael also recalls those others who mirthfully meant him no harm in Life and came into contact with him with the best of intentions. But yet, they all had certain many parts of themselves decimated and shattered for having met Michael. Through many coarse interactions which had developed in Time due to a multitude of dynamic reasons, Michael remembers himself ultimately wearing down all those mirthful Ones. Michael also remembers training and measuring Himself to live under many different standards and ideals at one time. He unknowingly oppressed and Divided Himself. Some of those ideals he chose for Himself forbid the essentials which were at the very core of other standards that he favored, thus, Michael further conflicted a Mind and Being that was already suffering in discord.

Through suffering under those standards and ideals, Michael Now firmly and steadfastly allows himself to survey inwardly and make it known to himself that at those particular junctures in his life, he and his cohorts indulged in their very own personal selections of happiness and propriety. It was plain to see, they saw no errors in their ways. They justified their every intention. They had a fierce love for their own lives, and they loved to live it. It is a ferocity that has scorched Many. Michael has met with that ferocity many times. Michael too, was scorched. Their Acts and deeds against him were merciless and had no end in sight. The scorching aggrieved Michael. The fire burned. He could bear it no more. Even in those Moments, Michael could understand that Forever was in motion, Michael knows it is a motion that had always been actively and lively stirring.

Into Michael's sight Now comes the events of his birth, his life, his death and his recovery. All the memories of those events intersect and overlap one another in Michael's Mind. Here, it all forms new interpretations, interpretations which show that all events and memories were and are vitally and mutually dependent upon one another. Memories and events took on other forms of significance which Michael formerly chose to have his sight depart from. But Now, through Time, Michael sees that it was always going to be his very own Moments to cherish in Life and in Time.

Michael realizes that after the conclusive stages of his birth, by the slimmest of chances, it was yielded that his Life was to begin. Michael moved about and things began with no palpable or perceivable hindrances. Eventually, Life and the World revealed itself to Michael. He beheld the many affairs and concepts of this World as it Unfolded before him. He saw it all, Michael viewed all that was before him in a tragically absurd manner. During a more easeful phase of his Life's untold undulations, Michael recalls his

Mind uncovering this absurdity as being a parody first and foremost. It was truly pitiful and meaningless, but somehow, the Mind transformed the Unfolding into a Humor. A parody, with this understanding in his sight once more, Michael Now attempts to apply that understanding to Life. Michael's Mind and thoughts continue to be drawn to this parody which is absurd. In his hindsight, the utter irrationality of many predicaments' various causes and consequences, back when it occurred, Now brings about a lighter perspective of many situations. This relinquishes a view that was sullen. Leaving it to be rightfully deemed as senseless and thus, meaningless. This leaves no anguish within Michael.

Michael sees that his Mind has become quite imaginative and creative. He Now seeks to utilize this imagination which he so desperately lacked in the earlier stages of his Life. He paid a price for that very shortcoming. In seeing the chain of events take its course, in seeing causes and results materialize and come to Past, for both better and worse, it all adjusts Michael's perspective.

A Perspective Adjusted, with that, Michael can Now behold Life and not fall again into folly. Once before, Michael fell, he fell and lost everything that Life had bestowed upon him. As he fell, it all Unfolded and resulted in his Mind's new Perspective.

Before this Perspective, his sense of identity was still in formation. He mistook all the unsavory advances and initiations of Others for inspiration in his search for selfhood. He was drawn into them. These Others were attempting to sell Michael a dream. He bit the bait and bought it. He understands Now that he was not as weak as he had condemned himself to be. It dawns on him that he barely even stood a chance. He was just caught up in an overwhelming moment and did what he could. Michael grasps once again that indeed, no One can perform beyond their Mind's natural or acquired limitations.

Michael knows Now that he does not need any promises to be made or consolidated from any Other in order to better or advance any circumstance in Time. He has all he needs. Because he is and always will be One and Whole in Forever. Michael does not want anything. He really does not. From where he laid during his hospitalization, Michael never even dared to fathom that he would have ever come to this state of Mind. For seemingly to Michael, many parts of him never came back from where he was at his End. He thought it to be lost forever, Michael thought he had to let himself grieve over the loss of those very parts, he thought he had to let himself mourn and heal. For due to those losses, he was broken and incomplete. That was certainly how Michael felt, and it definitely weighed heavily upon Michael's Mind.

Through it all, Michael Now realizes that not only had those parts always been with him, but they had also been transfigured in Time. He sees Now that he was always Complete. What was once thought to be lost is Now found. He had been entrusted with a gift. And he will never turn his back on it as he had once done. To Michael Now, all is set.

Michael continues to grow. Even as he grows, a side of him misses the Past. For impressionably upon Michael, it was a simpler time which he remains significantly fond of. There is however, another side of him which knows that in this very simplicity, there is the availability to be overwhelmed, Michael will always remember being overwhelmed. Michael Now knows both sides. He also understands the Mind and the Body. Michael knows that with these many familiarities, he can weave though setups and events concordantly in Forever, he can also watch more Unfold and come to fruition in the comfort and assurance of both Mind and Body in this World.

Michael remembers the first murder he ever witnessed

and played a part of. His role was that which was depraved and sickening. The following strife within Life which he then suffered was justified as he sees presently. He is Now glad that he was able to withstand that strife. He knows however, not to be prideful about this survival. The strife he endured in the past taught him how pride could mock every passing moment, and hide many truths from any One's perception.

In being able to notice what could have possibly been hidden, Michael sees that there are external forces out there that have formed and banded in this World. They are all ready. They have been in place for a long time. They have creatively and subtly turned many Ones against Ones' Self. They used foresight and experience to premeditate their actions. Michael knows that he and his fellow Man have minds of certain attributes. Attributes such as needs for escapism and solace, needs to save and secure as well as needs to embellish and adorn.

These needs have Now been tampered with by Few to be used against many Ones' Self in a plethora of ways, Michael sees that. Michael has Watched Few Agents knowingly and wittingly establish a world of outlets and institutions. Few Agents do so to constantly and continuously draw in many Minds of Ones. The act of drawing in is accomplished by relentlessly satisfying, appeasing and exceedingly encouraging the intensification and escalation of those needs. Needs that have Now been tampered with. This tampering, it is undoubtedly a brutal process. It is the insidious and besetting art of temptation. In Time, Michael has Watched and witnessed various temptations' selective applications and onslaughts within the Unfolding. As it turns, these selective applications and onslaughts act to breed and persuade the embellishment and adornment of a good Few allurements to any One's optics. Michael can see this in far too many places. When these needs are encouraged and constantly escalated, Many put their trust in the unreal, but yet, readily accessible option of safety and security. A safety and security which is Offered to Many from those Few institutions and outlets. As Offers are procured, those Institutions continually grow. Agents benefit however so proportionately from an institution's expansion. Thus, also grows the licentious motivations of many Agents within ceaseless and untold premeditated plans.

These Agents have a greed within themselves. Agents use institutions, and vice versa, to synthesize artificial economic cycles which viciously impinge upon All. These Agents and institutions also finance and fabricate conflicts on a grand and global scale, conflicts which will expectantly service and assist the condition or haleness of any particular ideology in power. Agents choose to viciously impinge upon All to pursue, embellish and secure their very own places of solace. Agents use these places of solace to escape from their very own hardships. That is all they seek. And they have achieved it, Michael has heard Few's boastful brags in some places. It is clear for Michael to see that many Offerings are really only meant to help those Agents themselves. As for his Self, Michael knows he has this Gift. This Gift is all the solace he needs. With the vainglorious ingenuity of establishing institutions announced, publicized and Offered by the Agents, All, with their attributable needs, channel their wealth into those institutions so as to sooth their anticipatory needs to save and secure, which are made even more urgent and prevalent within their Minds though the influence of Few's Offerings. And so the wealth of the masses gets stored and collected, it is done so just to be kept away from All.

Within the Unfolding, Michael has Watched these institutions and outlets imagine and fashion considerable amounts of tentacular entities. These entities have burrowed far into vital societal organizations, persistently festering

Now deep within. This allows for the ability to command and hold sway of economic momentum. Those who control the institutions and outlets operate with this stored and collected wealth however they so desire and wish. They do so with a forbidden impunity. Ever and always do they aim to seize and misappropriate more. The controllers who are Few, have gone to these extents in order to continue the expansion of might held formidably so by these institutions and outlets. The Few also do these deeds to turn what One hopes to be safe and secure unforeseeably, unpredictably and ultimately, against One's Self. It is accomplished through subtle attrition which leads eventually, to the overwhelming subversion and perversion of One. That is where One becomes Divided.

Sometimes, the institution or outlet fails at an objective. Sometimes, the institution or outlet may outlast its beneficial practicality. Sometimes, the institution or outlet may even push a forbidden, but nevertheless retained impunity, recognizably too far. Michael has seen this occur before. In being exposed to the Unfolding, Michael has come to recognize that in Time, these Controllers have and will unknowingly and erroneously let their guards down. Their minds have finite abilities. Michael recognizes this as well. Besides letting their guards down, Controllers could also and have already grown careless by not adequately concealing their blatantly pilfering deeds and intentions. This carelessness is due to their innately prized perception of their much embellished might. This pompous inward representation of speculated vigor, extravagance and potency magnificently and delightfully inflates their innermost pride. As this pride grabs hold, they then indulge in lives of excess to embellish even more aspects of their lives. They do so in the hopes of furthering an already inflated delight. More than enough time and resources have been used to attain embellishments, Michael has seen this occur. As pride and indulgence overwhelms the mind, Michael knows that the deterioration in awareness is natural. Michael has witnessed this Unfold. As Michael has seen, in their diminished discernment, they carelessly leave trails of damning evidence wide in the open for All to see. Those trails are exposed in Time because in this unmindfulness and complacently, they failed to remember just how meticulous they had to be in order to succeed at the arduous task of seizing Control over many things. In doing so, they have also forgotten about the vigilance which had aided them where they finally did seize Control. Michael knows this. Michael also knows this lack of awareness has exposed Guardians and Undertakers, whose allegiances can Now be traced doubtlessly back to Few Overlords.

If and when those unmindful failures do Unfold and occur, a premeditated contingency plan is already in motion. Michael has seen and heard this purposeful premeditation within many Leaders' public portrayals and responses regarding vicious economic cycles. This is where Leaders falsely place reasoning and blame elsewhere. The dishonest placement of reasoning and blame is yet another expression which leaves a profound effect upon Michael.

There are many figures and individuals whose services have been enlisted to be held accountable as Guardians and Undertakers. Michael knows these figures and individuals are a distraction, rooted in the same principles as the Offerings. The Few Now have a complete grip over the situation, this Control arranged between Few and Agents is Now bruisingly sound. The Provoked see it. The Provoked have revealed this knowledge to Others. Now, even more in this World are Provoked and want to rip down the Few.

Michael knows that Provocation fractures the Mind. Michael Now recalls how time and again, his Mind had been savagely dismantled and overtaken by Others.

Also, Michael Now recollects his Mind's inattention and heedlessness. He had more than enough of what is being recollected within his Mind when encountering many depictions and representations of literatures. Literatures like that which brought this journalizing man a hint of comfort. The depictions and representations of literatures were not welcomed by Michael's inattention and heedlessness. All have witnessed these literatures captain bodies of lastingness, bringing together timely meanings of words within lawful essences. Michael also realizes that with a fractured, dismantled and overtaken Mind, it is downright possible for Some to be unaware of those many meanings and essences. In Time, miscommunication could also take place when messages or inscriptions within literatures are passed from One to Another. A Mind could likewise depart from arrangements and classifications which specifically name and set aside Times of when certain Occurrences are to take place. Once departed, the Mind will be blind to the signs. And when One is misinformed and Another is unfamiliar, these meanings and essences can sometimes even be circulated with suggestive and subtle traces of hatred and enmity which can be bound to One or Another.

This man, like Michael, was inattentive and did not heed many relevant and significant matters. Both individuals' inattention and heedlessness accomplished a dreadful dismantling of the Mind. Inattention and heedlessness barred this man from conceptualizing the material which was before him, which thus, did not allow this man carry his Mind forward within the Unfolding. Through inattention and heedlessness, this man had allowed his Mind to be undone, for this man did not let into his Mind the perceivable layers such as those underlying sentiments which were very much necessary to his mental stability, vital even. Within those perceivable layers of comprehensions, are full disclosures of clarifications coming to Alignment and coalescence in regards to any and all inconclusiveness which come to the Mind. For some particular reason which remains unknown to Michael, this man chose to part ways from his very own Mind within the Unfolding. Had he not parted ways, he might have discovered matters considerably more fundamental and meaningful than those understandings which he had already uncovered. He may have even ferreted out further recognition by piecing together scattered notions within the Unfolding. This would have accomplished much more for this man. Far more, so much more in actuality, would have been attained than just possessing the meager capability to be able to go to sleep at night. These accomplishments and attainments could have been carried out before he turned to desperation. If those accomplishments and attainments had come to past, that hint of comfort would not have deserted him. In fact, that hint of comfort could have been furthered upon momentously, Unfolding towards Now Completing an accompanying convalescence in Time.

The hatred and enmity within Some irreconcilably contradicts the unmistakable permeation of comfort characterized in specific portions of this man's journalistic accounts. While reading those specific portions, Michael recalls understanding and discerning this man's decided and unquestionable comfort. That contradictory hatred and enmity within Some has given rise to their many knowingly hateful deeds. Michael can see the spiteful and vicious qualities of their many deeds line up boastfully with their need to alleviate this circulated and burgeoning hatred. The potent cause, the trying consequences and the indeterminable effects in all, do not sway their many brutal intentions. Intentions and purposes which have and will Provoke even more knowingly hateful deeds.

Michael also sees that Many are searching for

Completion. Within Many, Michael knows there are Those who have given in to many Offerings, Those have done so in the hopes and efforts to fulfill many needs of solace, security and embellishment. Michael himself had similarly and despairingly gave up the same. In that, Michael knows what they gave up. If they took it all back, Michael's thinks in his Mind, they would in turn be even closer to achieving Completion than where they are Now. And above all else, if they took it all back, it will keep All in this World Truly safe. Michael knows the Few have nothing. Nothing to Offer, nothing to create and absolutely nothing which can be worth Offering as a Gift.

Michael knows not to participate in all that is Offered by Few and all which is Acted out by the Provoked. Michael knows to search for that which is absolutely True. Michael sees that Those who Offer and Act torment Others by their deeds. Michael continues to watch many deeds Unfold, many deeds align with what has been accomplished beforehand.

In many deeds aligning, it seemingly justifies, assures and affirms any current deed's existence. Michael has watched Few utilize those sentiments of justification, assurance and affirmation against All many times, especially when Some remain skeptical of any deceptive deed Unfolding or occurring. Aligning deeds with what has come before brings joy to Some, aligning also references or suggests Truth. That referencing or suggesting is employed methodically to strike back against doubt or skepticism. The alignment equips occurrences with apparent credibility and validity, even if the logic behind the occurrence is unsound, amiss or reasonless. For many poignant and True events that have occurred did align and have indeed mirrored past seminal events. With that being said, Michael has also seen those aligned Truths get mocked so that cynics could conform sentiments to an agenda. Michael knows it is difficult to find Truths, because it is surrounded by layers upon layers of mockeries. Mockeries which are established by Those who will defend their beliefs violently if they have to. They do so to secure their very ways. And thus, the difficulties that comes. Michael sees that many alignments in this World are yet another technique which is used by Few to Divide and Control All. Michael has experienced this methodical technique. He recalls the many techniques' impediments upon him. Michael recognizes it Now as not being able to hinder him in the Unfolding of Time.

Adam and George have shown Michael that governments are not obligated to tell the Truth. There is nothing in this World which can govern the wills or admissions of politicians who are Few Leaders. Like Some, the Agents, who are politicians within governments, will circulate propaganda as they deem necessary, they will advance plans to uphold agendas. They do what they can. They emphasize all available flair and techniques upon any benefits which may be reaped by whosoever maintains a specific place or position. This arena is theirs after all. This is their World. Michael sees it Now, this is their world indeed. Many concealed agendas are not too difficult to uncover. Michael has watched and witnessed Some uncover much in Time. Through all that has Unfolded, Michael has watched and witnessed that there is no agenda in this world which has been or will ever exist to remain beyond the prowess of any One to catch or come across. However, Michael knows One must have the Self of Mind in order to digest and receive the findings uncovered. Within this, Michael knows that it is imperative for One to have the determination and fortitude to withstand many exposed individuals' defenses and counterblows. For these exposed individuals Control the past and the present. And they are vigilantly placing, sustaining, fortifying and reinforcing mechanisms to secure their own future. They attempt to lord over every facet of every situation. The Truth of this world continues to come to Michael. In this Unfolding Truth, Michael remembers to not participate in all that is Offered by Few and all which is Acted out by the Provoked.

Michael Now also recalls George telling him all the facts. It all registered in the Mind without any drawbacks or throes. Michael did not seek out George's commentary, Michael just happened to run into George that day. And George, on any other day, would not have been so outspoken or transparent with any One, least of all to Michael. Days after their lucid conversation, Michael seems to recall that George recoiled himself both socially and outwardly as an aftermath to their conversation. This just brings a sense of Completion to Michael again.

Michael knows that each individual human being is what they are, One upon a claimable place or position, One in Forever's Unfolding. Michael knows that each and every separate and individual Body and Mind is completely capable and sufficient without the will of any Overlord's creed. There is great strength in every One's Body and Mind. To impinge upon any One's growth with obstructive, stunting or hampering directives would be to essentially, assail One. Michael knows that total and utter governance obstructively impinges upon the growths of many Ones with stunting directives. And with this form of governance, comes the precarious but yet, subjective and specified part of the world where corruptive deceit and prejudices could very well prevail.

It has always prevailed. Michael has seen it come to be as such in Time. Overlords and their political agendas shape this world to fit their own purposes and preferences through Few prohibitions and alterations. In Time, Many will witness this world's shape get systematically and shrewdly arranged. Michael has witnessed this. Michael has also witnessed that prejudices are inevitable when prohibitions and alterations are placed upon any situation. Prohibitions and alterations are both conceivable consequences when there is complete, total and utter governance. Overlords have to impose upon the will of Others, it is the nature of the process of Control. The abundance of persecutions and executions perpetrated by legislated bodies of nations over human history exemplifies this fact. Within conflicts, Overlords more often than not will gain the Control they so desire. In so doing, they will set Another aflame with the many hopes of weakening and staggering Another. In setting Another aflame, they will also hope for the chance or opportunity to amply warm and illuminate their own lives. They anticipate that these hopes and accomplishments would conclude in a complete avoidance of gloom. They hope that as the fire burns, they will see or feel many conceptions, ideas or interpretations which may serve as a form of illumination or enlightenment. To them, what they see or feel appears to be true. Michael knows that there is no Truth in what they believe. They will look upon all which has burned one day, and they will be astonished by the accomplishments and progressions which they have achieved. That and that alone, is what they will see and feel. It will bring about a sense of satisfaction within them. Michael remembers his very own impulsive reliance upon satisfaction.

This System and its Agents, as powerful, accomplished and insurmountable as it may seem, Michael knows that it feeds off the toiling backs of All. This System and its Agents, Michael knows that it gorges off the indulgences and impulsiveness of All. Michael has seen that if One were to simply no longer take part in the intensifying of All's needs, interestingly enough, the System will lose its potency, ability to inflict and seemingly Control. For Offerings of this world are Truly no Gift. In being familiar with this notion, Michael Now chooses to indulge in this Gift which All have. Michael knows that every One has and has always had everything One will ever need within this Trust. Michael is aware that All do not need any of the Offerings or temptations. And neither does their family nor their friends. It is plain to see. Michael has seen this. Leaving those Agents and Overlords, it should be effortless. Michael knows this.

As all of nature persists, Michael knows that there is a Warmth which resides within the Body. This warmth is doubtless. This warmth Gives Michael Trust. He has recognized this warmth within many Moments. On the other hand, there were also Moments of uncertainty where Michael did not maintain this recognition. However, he Now knows that he has all he needs. Often, Few will Offer warmth and hope to many Ones, heralding that the will of All can and shall be fulfilled by Few. An ideology, that is what comes to Michael's Mind. An ideology is what Few often Offer All. Historically, One such as Michael can see when Agents exercise Few wills, prized upholding and observance of laws cannot be guaranteed or served for the welfare and integration of All. Michael is aware of that. The many presentations of ideologies by Few are all sound in theory. Michael remembers those many presentations and Offerings. This memory comes to Michael's Mind because he was an onlooker at many of those presentations. While being sound in theory, the matters presented had not quite translated as brilliantly within the world. At least not as countless deductions and inferences had plotted it would have. For much in this world will Lead One away from legitimately carrying out the diverse and various theories of those ideologies. Through Time, every Mind eventually develops weaknesses which are not Given. Michael knows this. Many keep a firm hold upon these weaknesses so as to Control it and develop it further. It is an indulgence in the need to embellish as Many of All pursue the desired relief of solace.

Much in this world has already Lead One and a great number away, far away. There is no One who can Lead while resisting the world's many Offerings and temptations. The world has convinced Michael of this. Even if there was One, Michael has watched them fail when challenged by the mechanisms which were vigilantly placed, sustained, fortified and reinforced. All Leaders will not have the capacity to Lead while the Few maintain Control. Michael has seen that within this world.

Michael Truly knows One will always have all that One will ever need. Michael knows One will never need what Few have to Offer. And even though it should be effortless, resisting those Offers and Acts has been and will continue to be challenging for Michael. At all times, there is the availability to give up on the Self. Michael has watched many Ones give up on the Self. Michael Now thoughtfully decides to no longer participate in any Offers or Acts of Another. By his Mind's side is where he secures all he needs, he craves for no more. And by his Body's side is where no One can abuse for their own purposes what Michael has thoughtfully secured. His Mind and Body are One.

At present, Michael gathers yet another notion. At a future and different Time, he could very well be One who will stand either with or separate from a group or groups of Persons. Persons who all, while upholding innocence, will arrive regrettably in the wrong place and at the wrong time. As events have Unfolded in his life, and as issues continue to transpire in numerous public arenas, Michael sees what has irrefutably arrived Here in Time. Michael recognizes that there are prevalent similarities between the cohorts from his life's past and the Agents in public arenas. Michael identifies an execution of well thought out strikes. As much as it seems to be disgraceful and atrocious, Michael sorts out that there seems to be purposeful strides as to how All's wealth seems to be steered and utilized by Few. Michael grasps that he will behold this transpiration in an altered manner at yet another different Time.

Something is to come. Something always does. Michael acknowledges that a greater form of this current situation is to come. Every situation driven and Provoked by motive and incentive has always advanced and progressed as such. Michael knows that they are in the world Now, the constituents of this form which is to come. They will have bred within them a doctrine where abhorrence and detestation is arranged for everything and anything which is in opposition to their point of view. Nothing would please them more than to gain All's submission. They have been Provoked, they yearn for every One to submit to them. Michael watches their premeditated schemes strategically unfold. Michael knows they mean to submit if not, slaughter Another. The manners with which these traitorous schemes unfold are treacherous and corruptively vicious. Through deception, their Acts are justified. They have convinced Many that their way is one of necessity. They will try to make their ways last forever. Michael knows that this permanence may very well come to be in this world. Or it may not. However it may unfold, it does not hinder Michael's Peace.

This realization acts as a form of signage to Michael in his Mind. There is no doubt to him that Others will be able to acknowledge this foreshadowing as he has. Michael has seen the reactions of Others. There is a great desperation on all sides of Many. And in that desperation, Many will defy reason and conscience.

Many acts will follow from Here on out. The Unfolding of the future and Time is uncertain. Many will act in petulance in order to influence the outcome of this uncertainty. Many will seek, anticipate, demand and crave a violent end to this strife. The violence and the thought of ending their strife empowers them. Many need this empowerment, crave it even. It is the desire to rectify and amend what is thought to be amiss or mistaken. Michael does not want to be a part of those Many. Petulance, as Michael has seen, strips each and every One of his or her patience. Patience to allow Events to Unfold naturally. Michael does not want ill will to fester anywhere. He will attempt not to be presumptuous or prejudice. Michael will always be Here for any One. Even if One's anger is steered towards Michael himself. If he can, Michael will try and help any One turn back from a path that has brought Michael himself, more than enough unwelcomed pain and anguish.

Being Here for One, it may not always work. But as Michael was once told, there is always hope. Michael remembers being told that. Michael also remembers himself turning back from a desolate Mind. In living through that desolation, Michael's Mind comprehends what a reckless abandon it was which he once had. Every event has its Time and Place in Forever. Forever's Unfolding is promise. Forever's Unfolding is familiar. Forever's Unfolding is sincere and True. Michael sees no need to mislead Another or delude facts for his own biddings or purposes. Michael has seen all those persuasions and Now finds no need to misrepresent the Truth. It is the cunning and untruthful practice of lies. Michael has seen what deception's grasp can do. Whether or not it be subtle or severe, it obscures and twists much in this world. From his own experiences, Michael knows One deceives when One greatly desires something that is not theirs. And that is the inception of a cruel path. A path which One can and just might decidedly tread upon in order to attain their own desires. And upon this path, One regularly dismantles, consumes and impairs. Michael was once on this path, and it progressed to the point where he committed a multitude of chaotic crimes to attain coveted goods. Along that path, Michael was definitely not Here for One. Michael wants to lay down all utilities of deceit.

Michael is leaving this churning plot behind. He knows that he has participated in this System with his willingness and allegiance for far too long. He does not seek anything at all. However, there are moments where he feels weak. In those moments, he wishes to take back all his past actions. He hopes to remove a heavy regret from his Mind. That is why he wishes for this. He wishes as such so as to achieve another feeling. A feeling to Oppose those momentary feelings of weakness. That weakness comes to Michael as a feeling within the world.

Michael sees in the world over that Many bind within their Minds, more than enough reasonings which convey an agreeable and compatible impression of these Offered attachments. An agreeability and compatibility with Many's desires housed within the Mind. There is much influence placed and devised by the Few in the world. Influence which comes to Many both severely and subtly to introduce and necessitate the housing of desires. Michael Now Truly understands the significance of those reasonings. At the times of appertaining presentations, those reasonings all seemed logical and true. Those reasonings are presently binded to attachments Offered in this world. This has resulted in the placing, sustaining and fortifying of the attachments to the Mind. If and when attachments are lost in Time, the Mind's feeling of loss will be immeasurably intensified. For an Offering was accepted. Michael Now receives affirmation for his resolve to not participate in all that is Offered by Few and all which is Acted out by the Provoked. He clearly sees what the addition of reasoning can do to One. Michael does not want himself to be torn apart.

He also sees Some who commit violations against Another in this world. As Michael ponders over it, a certain stagnancy comes over his thoughts, for he has been troubled and torn apart in the past by the very deeds of Some. It is and was Some who love and desire a great fortune fiercely with all their hearts. Meanwhile, Michael knows that fortune will never favor a heart which treasures it. For the heart in essence treasures a feeling. The heart is within the Body. The Body and the heart are both of nature. Fortune is not. Michael knows that fortune was introduced and necessitated by Few to strengthen and empower an Adversary who Opposes and Divides All.

Michael knows that All were fine long before any of these treasurers ever came along, and All will be just fine long after these treasurers' bones have disintegrated and faded away. Michael knows that he is One within All. And therefore, he too will be just fine. Michael wishes peace for those treasurers. Michael knows that they do not have the foundations in their minds for peace to endure. Because circumstances in their lives have Unfolded as such, they are slaves to that which they treasure. Michael wishes a hope for them.

Michael knows that All are Seekers in Life. Michael also knows that for better or for worse, All have passions and desires which each One will seek to attain or proclaim. And Now, Here they All are, within this world.

These attainments and proclamations of passions and desires have always been present since the dawn of humanity. And it shall linger on. Much will be gained and lost by Many before all these accounts and affairs will be said and done. Many will fight and die to defend their principles and beliefs. The Self has Lead Many astray. Michael's Self was once held back, Lead astray and Controlled within this world. Michael Truly sees that the self is no more.

Michael ponders those who emerge from an upheaval. Michael wonders inwardly whose circumstance would be fairer. The Ones who, through no Control or will of their own, pass on with a Warmth which resides within the Body.

And in so doing, passing on to a Peace which they have never known, like Michael once did at his End. Or the Ones who kill in cold blood to satisfy an urge in their search for what has Now been found by Those who have passed on as a consequence of that cold-blooded urge. Michael knows not to be afraid to die. As he has been put to death and the End, he knows that there is nothing to fear.

Michael knows it is arduous to live in doubt, Many in the world live as such. Due to their fear and doubt, these Many will sometimes victimize Others. Michael was once so very certain of a particular truth, standing by it with fervent assuredness. And yet, Time has showed it to be a misguided ideal. How then will he know Truth from falsehoods in the future? How can One such as Michael, who in being that loathsomely wicked, stumble upon such unconstrained soundness, which can be just so generously integral to Peace? The uncertainty mounts. Michael surely feels unworthy of the Moment.

But ultimately, his finding of Peace within Forever has put everything into perspective. It is a calm perspective. Peace within, it is the most useful feeling that One can harbor. So powerful that it has conquered all pain, fear and doubt in Michael's Mind.

> *"Take what you want, kill any who dares to betray*
> *or steal from you. Amass riches by any means*
> *necessary. Close your heart to pity, act brutally."*

That was Michael's old mantra. To be merciless and destroy Another when there is a tantalizing reward promised in return of those actions. To amass great power so that enemies will fear his might. The keen rule and Control which fear allows for, makes all the efforts worth it. It is hard to turn away from such an ideal situation. The Mind feels a form of assuredness. Outright and attainable power as such, is addictive. Michael held true to this mantra of his, he continually exerted and tested all his boundaries and limits. At least those which he was consciously aware of, Michael persisted as such all so that he could fulfill every last tangible and definitive essence of this mantra. Michael did so because he sought to pacify the strife which bothered him within every waking night and day. Michael sought to pacify the strife, for he found no sleep. There was no rest granted to Michael.

Having gone through the End and having returned, Michael knows that he had rested in Peace, a Peace which he had never known. And as Time has Unfolded, it has led Michael down a path to Completion. The answer to many previously unanswered questions has come to him. Questions which used to gnaw at his existence. And most critically of all, the reasons for those answers came upon Michael in Time and free of doubt. Every occurrence is Now affirmed in Michael's Mind. His heart is no longer closed as such, it is Now turned upwards and welcomingly facing the open skies.

Michael thinks of his closed heart under that old mantra. He also thinks of his closed heart and all of which it had attained, accomplished and amassed. What comes to his Mind as well, are his past thoughts of what should have been and what could have been. He remembers quite clearly that at the time of attainment, accomplishment and amassment, he withheld many regrets about how his potential gains were not maximized. Certain events did not Unfold as he thought it should have at the time. He shut in a great degree of angst for any Moment in Time. Even in Moments of satisfaction,

Michael ponders the reason for the indulging or abandoning of causes. He realizes Now that many a times, it is and always was the fragility within the combinations of sentiments held by One's Mind which then, ultimately initiates One's reasoning and actions.

No matter the sentiment held by his Mind at the time, Michael truly rues what has transpired. He feels for those moments in its effectuality upon Forever, all that had passed played a crucial role. Those regrets have awakened his ability to see Forever and Truly comprehend what he has found.

Michael suffered a tragic betrayal which set him right. One Man indulged in a cause, and another Man abandoned a cause. Life to a Man is uncertain. All possibilities have a credence and justification. All uncertainties can and might Unfold or materialize. Michael knows that sentiments and feelings have ruled All's Unfolding. Michael knows All have this Gift to use those sentiments and thereby, not be Divided or Provoked by it.

Michael Now sees that the Provoked are in fact, not incited by Another at all. Their mercurial disposition and frame of Mind brings them to irascibility and displeasure, leaving them provoked. In Michael's End, he recalls a feeling of sublime content. In his memory, he cannot recall a Moment of greater Peace. He no longer mourns the dead. He Now sees that if he lets it, this Gift which he has been entrusted with can and will acclimate him to the way of the world thereby, bringing him to Peace within it, as it had done before. And it could have done so many times before that as well, Michael just could not and would not allow himself to see it, for he had within himself far too much angst for One to even attempt to bear or carry as an encumbrance in Time. Michael placed a disproportionate amount of importance upon many fleeting, transient and singular Moments in Forever. It has all passed. Like everything else before it. So much has passed him by.

There are many Moments that run through Michael's Mind. He is not surprised by what comes to him again, the fatefulness of that night when tragedy struck, and struck hard it did. In that Moment, he thought it to be his greatest travesty. He thought this world had left him in desolation. He was full of regret, fear and doubt. Michael remembers it all so clearly. He comes to grasp that he had actually misunderstood what that Moment Truly meant. Michael perceives and recognizes that somehow, his Mind harbored an unlearned adaptability which had allowed him to function and live Life through the Unfolding thus far. Now, the Unfolding of Forever has washed away all the abashing and disconcerting sentiments to reveal the Truth to Michael. In this Truth, his Mind conceptualizes that he had in fact, not lost a single Thing. Rather, he had gained the sight of greed belonging to Another, a greed which had seemingly taken every Thing from him. It was in fact, the same greed which had bonded Michael firmly with these cohorts to Undertake and Guard those series of Events that fateful night. It was also the same greed which in Time, had blinded Michael from the Truth. Coming forth as the same greed which Adam lamented. Which is Now, the same greed that has ultimately given Michael back his humanity.

Greed, the one trait that had caused Michael's downfall. It is ultimately the one trait that led Benjamin, who tried to add to his riches by plundering more, to ignore Michael in that very transition in Time, thereby not slaying Michael, who laid helpless and defenseless on a ground stained by blood. Benjamin's Greed ultimately led Michael to salvation in Time.

The past purposefully forms congruent with the present, ceaselessly Unfolding to make Peace Here and Now. In this Peace, Michael vaguely calls to his memory the scripts which were referenced by a pious man. As Michael recalls, those scripts were the same literatures which comforted that butchering man before he set his mind upon another path, where he then chose to do the deed. Apart from that, Michael recalls the word salvation being used commonly and freely as that pious man addressed an impressive grouping of listeners and spectators. Michael recollects that pious man's words succeeding as a source of strength and vigor for that entire gathering within the room. The selected excerpts and quoted matters which were presented throughout the discussion were ostensibly, from Michael's view, dispensed by the pious man with a mounting and expanding sense of enthusiasm. This enthused ardency grew in vehemence and exuberance with each and every detailed utterance. Those uttered words were all True. Michael knew this. The session's participants clung to it all with a mighty grip. They did not let go. It was a grip which seemed to call for a great deal of stamina and focus with regards to commendation, resolution and determination. The session's participants called upon it all. Michael remembers this all Unfolding before him. The pious man tirelessly and noticeably reminded all of his participants about many considerable and crucial subjects. His tireless and noticeable reminders included the consequences of relenting or allowing mighty grips upon faith to slip or wither. The pious man also asserted what that would increasingly and ultimately shift toward.

These consequences have always shifted toward an aftermath which had never brought any person, culture or community much described balance. Michael remembers Balance. Balance has fulfilled much in this world, Michael knows this to be True. Unfortunately, besides remembering Balance, Michael cannot seem to recall any other contents or matters which developed within that session. Michael takes no delight Here and Now in this Moment, for he clearly recollects that those disclosed contents and matters had so empowered and soothed many Ones who were present within that session. In looking back, Michael Now wants to recapture this soothing empowerment within his Mind to keep and never let go. For Michael, this conceptual recollection is Now hidden in plain sight. The vigor of the pious man has passed Michael by, along with many other matters. Michael's memory of that affair is very much vague. His Mind has failed him. Michael Now knows he wishes for himself to have given more attention and consideration that day.

Michael wants to keep this salvation which he has in Time. He aspires to secure and safeguard this salvation Forever. Even within this, Michael knows very much so that he could get swept away by Another in their anger. His abolition, carrying over as the distinct crystalline consequence of a diverse manner of workings, would bring him to his End. Regardless of when or where his abolition would occur, this End of his had to be met eventually by Michael himself within the Unfolding. The End, no matter the eminence, it will come to Michael in due Time. And just like the End, Michael sees that every last imaginable or practical situation and circumstance eventually attaches visibly and composedly to the world. Yet again, Michael rues this world.

Michael knows he always held within himself a dreadful conflict. Furthermore, Michael also knows that it has been completely unintentional on his part, the way in which he has somehow quieted the strife within and found Peace gathered all around Here. To say the least, his Mind was an infertile environment for Peace to grow or thrive. Now there is Peace. Having gone through it all and having lost much, all these situations and circumstances show to Michael the purposeful neutrality and the crystallizing methods of Forever. It pacifies any situation or circumstance that can and will Unfold in Life.

Michael has found Peace in this world. Forever and Time continues to come congruently to Michael. This world is sure and not obscured in any manner to Michael. No matter the world's state, there is only the world's natural form. There is a Trust that exists, and it has been entrusted to each and every individual's Body and Mind. Michael is sure of this. All Michael has to do is to hold True to this Trust he has with Forever, it has given him everything. To renounce Trust in this Gift which he has been presented with, will ruin its very everlasting nature. Michael realizes this.

As he arrives Here, Michael remains receptive and perceptive to an integral concept, that there can and will be future occurrences where All or Some will not seem right. Michael recognizes this through the broadening and expanding of positions concerning strength and Control upon his Mind by Another. These doubtful occurrences will unquestionably have consequences that will leave him struggling in his regard of All within Forever. This struggle is where fear and doubt will begin to creep and crawl back into his being time and time again. Within Michael's Mind however, lays preemptive counsel that will take away his fears and doubts. Michael Now knows that Moments of weaknesses can be triggered within Forever. And Forever's Unfolding is not affected by those weaknesses, fears and doubts. It will continue to Unfold as it should, Michael is to go along with this Unfolding, as well as All who come and go within it. Thus, Michael too, will continue to progress through Time. As Life continues to progress, even if he carries fears and doubts with him, any Moment is redeemable within Time. Michael knows this.

Hate and pain have been comprehensively blunted, as well as stripped away in the capacity of substantial weapons which persist. Michael knows these weapons have formerly overwhelmed and desolated his Mind through Controlled onslaughts. Michael continues to regard and behold this world. He can see Now that it is Here, Completion for him in Forever. Michael is aware that in Times past, he had previously discovered Forever. The sheer presence of Forever had him in a state of marvel. And as Michael marveled, he simply renounced the prevalence which past Moments of his Life had held. This renouncement was accomplished quite doubtlessly. For in doing so, both hate and pain were blunted and stripped away even more so and much further than before. Michael concedes that he himself had endorsed and brought forth that prevalence. Moreover, this renouncement swept away and expelled any past Moments where he was pierced and stung by the frost of grief. As that frost came to be diminished through Time, Michael recognized that this reversal in course, in regards to his continuing vitality, arose from his ordinarily witnessing of the Unfolding.

There is a warmth which he experiences in renouncing and letting go. He has hope for the future. Forever, to Michael has seemingly begun again. Michael embraces it. Michael knows he will always see steps and endings which are fitting for this world. All baneful instances have and will be converted to the world's continuance and progression. Past and present delights of fellowship, even if it did turn bitter and horrid, leave Michael knowing Now that determinable portions of it had brought him joy. He did not always have the sight and perception of this joy within his Mind. And that is the reason why he had suffered so deeply at the Time of his great travesty. This is yet another discovery which Michael has made. He met Darcy at a period of desolation in his life. The companionship which she provided him with saved him from total and utter collapse. That is why she means so much to Michael. At long last, Michael stumbles upon an answer as to why he always thinks of her so fondly.

The world's Unfolding has brought him yet another few Moments of Peace. There is nothing more that Michael can ask from Life. His Body and Mind have held up until Now. Michael's Life is Complete.

Much of what Life has brought to Michael has changed him. Michael looks to his thoughts. He considers how he has come through Time. He thinks to himself, he recognizes that all he knows Now is so very much attainable. Especially if he had paid a closer watch upon his very own Life in days past, particularly in how he reacted to all that surrounded him. It had always been clear and plain to see. It had always Unfolded before him. Michael sees it Now, the way his Body reacted in the face of both heightened and abated emotions. Michael also sees how simplicities and complexities have and continue to elicit certain reactions on his part, which distinguishes many senses of worth within him and his Mind.

As it is all Here and Now for him to see, Michael is glad that this time around, he is able to identify, recognize and understand how circumstances and people shift endlessly in their resolve and determination. Michael knows Now that his stewardship and guardianship over himself is and always was the way it should have been. All the circumstances and people which Michael had seen through his Life, whether fair or foul, he feels an earnest Trust forged within them all, for they too are a part of this world. He is grateful for them all. For they have all made True his journey in Forever.

Michael has watched this world Unfold and coalesce in Time, Time that is a part of Forever. Michael sees Now, that All have been dealt with wills within Forever. And All have a place in this world, a place that is defined by the many Acts. Michael realizes that he has been removed from this Controlled exchange that has its clutches upon All. He has been given Completion, he has achieved this through no will of his own. Michael knew where he was in Time and yet, throughout his path to Completion, it all seemed out of his control. Michael thinks, he still has no clue what is Occurring. Michael is certain and yet, in slight doubt of Forever. Michael knows Forever. No person can help him. He knows Some are There. He will search for a way to get There. A Way that is free of mockery. The Way which he hopes to find shall be True and will harbor neither pride nor deception. Michael will search for it and he will know it when he sees it, for he has felt what is True to Forever. He is very thankful to know this.

Michael knows to stay away from all that is Offered by Few. He also knows to diverge clear, entirely clear of deeds where he would be participating in Acts which are Provoked. Michael will search for that which is absolutely True. In this path ahead where he will be searching, Michael foresees that he will witness many Alignments of Acts, deeds and passions which will resemble, associate and extend back and forth through many present and historical days. Much will be there to delude him. Michael knows this. Many Truths will be hidden from him. Michael also knows that when there are no contortions of Truths, a definitive Feel and composition to sentiments prevails within Time. This Feel and composition is that which does not seem tense, hurried or labored. And such are these sentiments, which have objectives that are plain to see. Wills and intentions within these sentiments are easily found and uncovered, for that which is True, is not interfered with or concealed. The way it is fashioned is not troubled. Through Time and the Unfolding, Michael has been exposed to that which is plain to see. He has found certain Truths in his Life. In his numerous meetings with various sincerities, Michael has discovered that Truths are defiantly Opposed and markedly surrounded by Those who will defend their lies and beliefs with unending and ceaseless violence. Michael recognizes that Those besmirching and disgracing Truths to defend their very ways are indeed the very same collection and gathering who will attempt to Intrude upon and Control One. Michael knows there will be difficulties to be experienced, he has been There before, he knows this. That which he had experienced, Michael remembers it, he sees it all Now as being unable to hinder him in Time's Unfolding.

Michael sees that Many have not been able to avoid the methods meant to mislead and Control. Innumerable amounts of contents have Lead so Many astray. Michael has watched a Few Many Others Lead Another to the very ruin of this world.

Michael ponders the good number of different ways to treat Another. His Mind ultimately concedes that there is much to snatch away from Another, especially if One so desired to prey upon and steal from Another. Michael's Mind also perceives that there will be a significant body of dignity to consider, once the Moment arrives where One chooses to no longer impede upon Another. Michael knows this choice would have Another deliberately remain or be restored with that which is conclusively and distinctly theirs.

Michael has it in his Mind to be True and remain sincere to this Gift. Michael sees the path before him coming to be unsnarled and void of impediments. Michael Watches his Life continue to Unfold. He realizes that the odds and Opposition in Time have not Provoked him to be Turned back from what has and what will.

Michael catches sight of it Now, Provocation will always serve Cycles which are Adversarial. It is that which is decidedly not with All.

And then within Michael's thoughts and memories, there is and was this man who buried his collection of victims away in a large private field. Michael remembers each confirmed murder which this man committed. It was all a set of connecting deeds where this man chose to Oppose Another. All the murders were committed at separate and independent Times. But it was all initiated by one desire, and it is the desire to be Adversarial. To be an Adversary is to Oppose this Gift. Michael sees that Now.

Michael thought he knew Completion. The totality of that confidence Now falters and wavers in skepticism. Michael searches his Mind in order to validate what he formerly knew. He once considered his former knowledge to be trusted, certain and sure. Michael's urgency mounts as he frantically searches with no attainment, obtainment, procurement or fulfillment. Alas, his Mind fails to recall many Truths. This casts gloom and cheerlessness upon Michael, for confidence in his former knowledge of Completion had quieted much strife within him. Michael grasps that these Truths, which are currently beyond attainment or obtainment, have also once brought him Peace. He remembers feeling this Peace. His Mind's retention has Now suppressed these very Truths. Peace as well, is Now faltering and wavering. Over and over again, Michael's Mind abandons him. This causes Michael much disturbance and unsettlement.

It is Here and Now, where he finds himself in doubt once more. This doubt gnaws and bores deep within him. As it continues to sink and fester within his Mind, Michael begins to envisage that this strife and disorder will never end. He begins to recall how he has never been able to carry forth resolutions settled from earlier Moments. Even if those resolutions have proven to have brought stability to his Mind. This failure to carry forth and Act disconcerts him. It is another sentiment that begins to gnaw at his Mind. Presently, Michael realizes that he is to calm and steady these volatile swings which he experiences far too often.

Through the Act of attempting to steady his Mind, Michael realizes that he already knows that Step which is the End. He begins to settle with this memory and recognition. This memory and recognition is yet another volatile swing. However, this memory and recognition prevails and comes Now as a welcomed swing. For it is a swing away from doubt.

Michael deduces that he must not be the only person to feel this way. In fact, Michael begins to gather that at any point in history, he definitely must not have been the only person to have ever felt this way. This deduction and gathering extends and reaches through Time, it matters not whether it was in days past, or the Here and Now. This Peace of Mind which he is feeling, Others have tried to put it into words toward him before, Some have even tried to grab him and forcibly show him the way. All those attempts were reduced to whispers and deflected impetuses through Michael's many limitations in days past. This memory Now expands the swing away from doubt even more so for Michael.

There are so many memories.

And so he continues to push away all forms of desirable Offerings supplied to the Divided, Offerings which leave All in disillusion. As continues to push, his knowledge continues to grow from the sincerity he occupies his Mind with. Michal thinks that without these transpirations, he will be nothing. He allows doubt to crawl back into his Mind. And so the unsettling happens again.

Michael then proceeds to search his own Mind. As he searches, Michael identifies that his Mind has decisively absorbed and coalesced many familiarities. However, there still is no resolution which can be effectively declared or set forth Here and Now. Michael reckons that he remains despairingly helpless and defenseless in this world. He has not overcome this world. He is certain of this. Torturously and atrociously, Michael is to be Controlled by much strife in this world. Many Others will resign the Self of One under this torture and atrocity as well. Michael begins to recall the revelation which he had discovered all those days ago. He remembers that the Unfolding of that discernment within the Mind was and is effortless. As he recalls that resolution, there is an ease which rises within his Mind. He then remembers a particular Saturation. Indeed, Life does go on. Michael feels a reserve of will and energy within his Mind and Body, he has developed this through his constant progression of both

Mind and Body. In Time, it has been carelessly left untapped and forgotten once more. Michael knows that there are Acts to be brought upon by Another. These Acts are great and can overtake him.

It is all in Time. It is coming for him. Moreover, Michael's Mind Now chooses to reason even further. Michael ascertains that as pressing and desperate as many undulations can and will Unfold to be, the Balance between Peace and Asperity would always come back to this Gift of his. This Gift does indeed, bring him relief. It settles him. And as those undulations approach, Michael decisively embraces the concept of searching within his Mind. Michael seeks comfort. His hope is to strengthen and expand upon the existing reserves within this Gift. He remains keen to Watch and witness what these reserves could possibly bring forth from Here on out. Michael will then use past familiarities received from previous encounters as a shield against what Opposes him Now. Those many previous encounters have fittingly brought him the ability to verify Truths from falsehoods, Michael is eager to become accustomed to this Gift's reserves as Time continues to Unfold.

Michael recognizes that and appreciates this settling Moment. This time however, he resolves to carry forth what has settled within his Mind.

Michael distinctly remembers being overtaken. As he reflects upon that awareness more and more, he begins to distinguish that his Mind will always function as an unmistakable reflection of any intense strife or surging discord which torments and envelops this world. Michael finds the Self to be dreadful and awful. Michael knows that there is much need for restoration.

Despite being Divided and disconcerted, his Mind gathers scarcely enough adequacy to sense that this insight could just happen to be True. As a matter of fact, his Mind fully conceptualizes and identifies this all around by Watching. Day after day within this world, Michael Watches transformations, denials and conversions occur over and over again. Such occurrences cause Many to lose significant grips upon Life itself. Michael grasps this. At this instant, it is beyond any doubt that these occurrences are thoroughly tormenting and enveloping this world. Michael recognizes this. This Now reminds Michael of his own Mind. Michael had been subjected to these tormenting and enveloping perils. This Mind of his had undergone great despair and desperation within that confusion and disturbance. Hope is being cornered and squeezed. It is almost lost.

Michael will always want to hold onto hope. He thinks of what is real and True within this world, he can see clearly that there is and always will be that which Opposes. And then there is and always will be that which is Complete Here and Now. One is a Gift, the other is a curse. One is True, the other is false. Falsehood and deception, through it, Some will seek to scheme, contradict, convince, dominate, impose and subvert. Subversion has taken place quite often within this world. Michael can see that All, and all is not well.

There is so much deception. There is so much Greed. Within All, Many will choose to serve these ardent tendencies and preferences. In acknowledgement of the Truth, Michael remembers serving those tendencies and preferences under the banner of passion himself. Here and Now, Michael sees what continues to come to him in Life. As he gathers all his recollections from Watching the Unfolding, numerous salient sentiments are effectively and profoundly comprehended to become One with his Mind. The very Mind which Michael has seen himself let slip away again and again. Michael sees how he continues to carry himself in Time. He envisages being kept away, far away from all these troubles. For there is nothing he can do. Fear and doubt is Here again. It has arrived.

For Michael, plenty of certainty had hinged and rested upon his Mind. Presently, he sees that once again, his mind does not know Truths from falsehoods. He sees Now that he still has the same mind. The very mind which Michael has seen himself let slip away again and again.

In this Moment however, Michael is no longer afraid. His mind has never been clearer. To Michael, all these gradual and subtle changes do not symbolize coincidence. Rather, Michael sees the Alignments and associations of Foretold motivations. And there are plenty. Michael also beholds the Provocations caught between All of a Few Many Others. That which was Foretold, it had come to Another bringing comfort many times before in Forever. That which was Foretold, it had been communicated, passed, quoted, expounded, followed, inscribed, remembered and referenced. It is all Here for Michael to Watch Now. In recognizing this coming and going of Acts and occurrences concerning All, Michael's mind is even clearer. He Now resolves to set out and reaffirm what he thinks are familiarities. These familiarities have remained within his thoughts. Through Watching, these thoughts have come to him. Here and Now, Michael chooses to search for the source of this Gift. A search for That which has Given.

15

Salesperson: Come up here!

Michael looks in the voice's direction and finds the salesperson who he had previously lost track of after initially inquiring her help. While approaching the salesperson, Michael finds himself thinking,

Michael: I cannot wait for the End.

He tells himself this as he looks at the world around him.

Michael: I can't do this anymore. I want out.

Michael feels no will to go on.

Michael: Life is such a struggle

Nevertheless, Michael moves on. Michael has come to this bookstore seeking more resources in his search for that which has Given. The revelation of Greed continues to stand preeminent and firm within his Mind.

In his search, Michael had frequented many pious establishments. These establishments held gatherings of both large and small numbers. Some establishments involved techniques of conscious control centered around sensations and perceptions to bring about mindfulness. Then there were other establishments which held sessions of edification over foundational and elemental concepts of that which has Given. Michael always departed from those sessions with a Perspective Given to him anew. His Mind just had to hold onto that Perspective.

These foundational and elemental concepts included studies of the Giver, how the Giver comes to the world, his messengers, those who the Giver fashioned in his own image, writings which the Giver inspired, worshippers of the Giver, the world's End, depravity committed within this world, amends for that depravity and techniques regarding devotion to the Giver.

Michael would also intermittently take the time to read and Watch materials that came his way while keeping those concepts in Mind. Through Michael's search, he sees that the world's Unfolding events fall in line with the description of Creation's beginning and End in many writings which represent those foundational and elemental concepts. Michael sees that these foundational and elemental writings are testable to be True. And the many fanciful theories conceived by worldly imaginations contradict the Truth.

In these writings, Few were found by the Giver. In these writings, Few were loved and adored by the Giver. In these writings, Few were Given much.

Michael Watches the Unfolding of many establishments within the world. Michael also reviews many historical records of countless subversions and expulsions. Michael also maintains focus upon recorded and witnessed restorations. These historical events arrived in cycles. Michael knows that All have Acted in those many cycles. All are no longer Here. Michael knows that eventually, he too will no longer be Here.

Michael also Watches the Few and some of the Provoked reconcile and come back together after much bloodshed. It is not the first reconciliation between the two. Cyclically, the two did so when a death occurred. The Few and the Provoked are two vast nations. Michael had read about it in these writings.

Their first reconciliation was during the death of their father. The Giver gave these two nations to their father. The Gift of these two nations were recorded in these writings. Along with many promises, predictions and proclamations which were made and fulfilled.

However, this reconciliation only includes some of the Provoked. The remaining hostile factions continue to Oppose the Few. In seeing their tumultuous relationship, Michael knows that the End is secure. For in these writings, this tumultuous relationship had been promised, predicted and proclaimed to be as such at the End.

In the world however, Michael can also see that there are certain splinters of Few who Oppose those writings. They are Overlords who create new Systems of Leadership to overthrow Some who have found Peace. Those who have found Peace, their tolerance of the world around them has allowed those splinters of Few who Oppose to spread and grow into an entity of great strength. Those who have found Peace did not destroy those splinters of Few who Oppose in Time. And Now, this entity is ready to kill and Hunt.

In attending the many gatherings of pious establishments and in reading many materials which came his way, Michael can see that there is so much deception surrounding the Truth.

Michael recalls the devastation of deception. It comes to Michael that the Giver has no need to deceive. For in the many writings, deception and depravity had ruined this Gift over and over again. This deception and depravity has victimized All. And in this assault upon All, Some have recorded many cries for help and lamentation within those writings. Through those arduous times, there have also been many realizations. Michael reads about those many of those realizations in those writings. Amongst those realizations is the knowledge of the fact that his every breath is in the Giver's hand. And the Giver's hand is described to have Controlled many Unfoldings.

This realization takes an especially strong hold of Michael, for his body and his breath had once abandoned him in Time.

Michael continues to search within available establishments. He joins Adam one day for a traditional wedding ceremony which follows all the customs of which were ordained by Adam's culture. Michael Watches the pageantry of the ceremony. Through it all, he talks to another pious man. This other pious man explains all the ritualistic ceremonies which were Unfolding at the wedding. There was the Act where the groom would propose to the bride with the Offering of bread and wine. The bride would show her acceptance by drinking of the cup of wine and eating the bread. This other pious man then explains that in ancient Times, following the acceptance of the proposal, the groom would then part from the woman temporarily so as to prepare his Father's house to accommodate the newlyweds. Eventually, the groom would return for the bride at an appointed Time. The bride is to exercise patience and keep herself ready for the groom all throughout that period. The prepared segment of the Father's house would be where the newlyweds would celebrate their marriage for seven days.

The bride and the groom would then return to their guests after those seven days of celebration, where the wedding would Unfold. Michael sees parallels in the described events of those writings which he read and the Unfolding of events which this other pious man had explained. There are several weddings described within those writings which are within Michael's Mind. Michael is Truly growing to appreciate this culture which Adam calls his own. The way Adam's culture kept track of Time was distinct from all other cultures. Especially in the proclamation of the new year. This other pious man explains to Michael that the most integral part of that ancient civilization was the agriculture. This other pious man made sure to let Michael know that this meant the harvest and the utilities of livestock. This other pious man explains the stages of the harvest to Michael, as well as the sacrificing of faultless and spotless livestock as many atonements for the people's depravity. The many significances of that civilization's agriculture ultimately surrounded their solemn and joyous feasts. As this other pious man explains these topics to Michael, Michael cannot help but think that all those entire writings' topics of discussion had to have hinged upon this culture which Michael is Now learning about.

This culture is described in great detail in those many writings. This culture was Given to this world by the Giver's mighty hand. The Giver which holds everything in his hand. Michael resonates with that fact.

Michael had always admired the work ethic of farmers as they meticulously tend to the grounds. Not to mention how they strive endlessly to make the best of their instruments and devices which they use to collect that which sprouts from the grounds. Furthermore, how they tirelessly toil to reinforce their storage structures in preparation and anticipation of the harvest.

As Michael continues to enjoy the Truth within those

many writings, there are Many in the world who let Michael know that those many writings place many limitations upon All. The Many find these limitations to be annoying and aggravating. Some have even come to Oppose those many writings.

Michael: I still want out. All this is just not worth it.

Michael tells himself inwardly. The uprising of strife in this world makes Michael weary. Michael recalls what his Mind once came to know about Greed. This brings some Moments of tranquility in Time. Michael continues to enjoy even more Truths within those many writings, those many writings describe Peace and Comfort. This gives rise to Michael recalling his time spent on the constabulary team, he remembers what this man described as comfort. This man had many pleasures in bloodlust. It was not a Comfort at all.

Michael attends several seminars of Some who have come to Oppose those many writings. Michael also attends numerous sessions of Those who accept this Gift. Michael understands both sides. He also sees that those who Oppose have simply dismissed Given doctrines because their own formulas mean more to them. Within those those many writings are proclamations of what is to come. The way Time has Unfolded has been predicted in those many writings.

Michael has Watched Leaders and Overlords use their own Control and authority to stimulate and influence the strengthening of the Provoked. Michael has Watched Leaders do so by creating and enhancing their own narratives which have subtleties that directly and indirectly takes torturous shots at One's pride, Ones who have a resentment against Control.

These Ones do not know it, but they are in actuality being Controlled by the many implementations of those

Leaders, Manufacturers, Hunters, Agents and Overlords. These stimulating and influencing Systems steer Alignments which are Provoked. These splinters of Few, they have a dominant cultural heritage. Their domination is intensified with the installation of institutions and outlets. They also have many techniques which are used to steer their own agenda.

Michael wonders how is it possible that Few can persist. Those many writings reveal that the Few, even as they Oppose a Gift, have been shielded in Time as a Gift. There are many weaknesses in the world's Systems which are then exploited to be used as shields. These shielding exploitations have come to the world as legislation, incorporation, invention, innovation, formulation, corruption, exemption and absolution.

Within those many writings, Michael has read of those individuals who have been shielded despite certain circumstances. It was all chances Given to Few. In this world, Few have capitalized upon those chances which were Given.

Michael reviews those materials he came across while on his constabulary duties which comforted this man. As Michael reads those materials, he remains cognizant of all those visions' symbolisms which were recorded within those promises, predictions and proclamations. Those symbolisms allow Michael to understand much of the world's Few Provocations. That absolutely nothing in Creation is left to chance. It is all Truly in the Giver's hands. Michael Now sees that. Michael is Comforted by this unyielding Truth which is all around.

Within those many writings, there are so many parallels to be drawn amongst the separate and prevailing subject matters. These many subject matters Unfold in cycles which continuously come and go. Within those many writings, there is a serpent which keeps coming back. This serpent ceaselessly attempts to veil and twist Truths. This serpent ceaselessly makes efforts to deceive and Provoke. And in so doing, errors in some writings have occurred.

Michael continues to delve into those many writings. There are so many promises, proclamations and predictions. Throughout history, it has always provided much Comfort in Times of pain. At certain Times within those many writings, those many promises, proclamations and predictions allowed Few and Some to know that even in captivity, they were not forgotten. That an event was coming which would set them free. Those many promises, proclamations and predictions enabled them to know that their captors were ultimately, powerless against the mighty strength which Gives. Those many promises, proclamations and predictions placed into their Minds the Truth. They will be avenged.

There are timelines within those many writings which allows any reader to know where One is and was in Time. Those who record those timelines were Ones who stood firm and Watched kings and kingdoms rise and fall. Archeology can also be used as a complementary tool to date events. Some stories and accounts within those many writings serve as warnings of what Unfolds when Minds stray away from Truths. Those stories and accounts retell events that occur when Minds trust their own ability in independence from this Gift and flock to their banners of passion. There is no confusion within those many writings as all symbols within visions are explained earnestly.

Michael's Mind places history alongside those many promises, proclamations and predictions. And as the contents are comprehended by Michael's Mind, Michael sees that those many writings have answered many obscure and inconclusive matters which were brought up in earlier sections of those many writings. Michael also sees that Agents will either intentionally or unintentionally dismiss subject matters of doctrines all while imposing their own formulas and conceptualizations just to allow a certain narration and portrayal to come forth.

This dismissive nature has always been Here in Time within the Acts and deeds of All. It is born out of impatience and petulance. Michael was once as such. Those dismissive natures have also come forth due to the inability to understand the original language which those many writings were transcribed in. In looking into those ancient languages, Michael learns the meaning which his name holds. Michael now knows this meaning, it will stay in his Mind. In fact, Michael learns that all names have distinct meanings. And that the many specific arrangements of names, when translated, often tell a Truth. Upon learning some of those Truths, Michael feels like he is indeed ready to embrace what Gives.

Those many writings' promises, proclamations and predictions Offer Comfort and allows One to persist through pain. That despite the pain, the Few will always be Here. This is due to many mercies. Those many writings' promises, proclamations and predictions also records castigation to enable One to grasp and acquire understandings from their mistakes and shortcomings. Through the accounts recorded in those many writings, Few experience a cycle of captivity, war, subversion, dispersion, comfort, liberation and back to captivity. This cycle is continuously Unfolding til this day.

There are some symbols which have been translated and do not coalesce with the rest of those many writings. As Michael delves a little deeper into the culture of the Provoked with the help of a Provoked fellow who has found Peace, it is shown to Michael with the help of this fellow that those symbols were not transcribed as words, rather, those symbols were and are artistic renditions of unavoidable mosaics within the Provoked culture representing honor.

Some of those who were in captivity allowed themselves

to see and understand the past and present writings in their Time for Comfort. As events in their Time Unfolded, the past writings' promises, proclamations and predictions came as substantiating evidence that these writings are Truly Given. This proves that the Creator was and is responsible for the Creation of everything. For there it is, the Truth of Creation standing at the very commencement of those many writings. The Creator steered Creation, just like how the Unfolding of affairs too, were always steered in Time. The steering of the Unfolding was proven in the promises, proclamations and predictions of those many writings. If One were to understand those many promises, proclamations and predictions Now as it arrives, One will allow for One's Completion. Some of those in captivity allowed themselves to not just know the Giver's mighty hand, but to embrace the Giver's countenance.

There was a crisis involving All and that serpent shortly after the occurrence of Creation. The Creator had to hide the unsightliness of All with the covering of sacrificed livestock in order to enable the tolerance of what had happened. In those many writings, it is clearly stated that the Giver's intent is not to tolerate the crisis, but rather to forget it. In order to forget what had happened, the Act had to be hidden and covered. Plenty of blood will be shed in Time due to this crisis. And therefore, blood must be spilt in order to attain that covering from livestock. The livestock are innocent. However, this is the only way to enable All to atone for that crisis. The Creator has been patiently suffering the serpent throughout all the Unfolding of those many writings. Michael knows it is due to the Creator's will to show All the extent of favor that is to be extended.

Through much of those writings' symbolism, this Completion which One can allow for is entirely possible. Like names, the symbolic arrangements and sequences of objects have distinct significances in their placements. Those many writings are all explained if One views all the writings together as a single continuous narrative. If topics arrive to the Mind as an obscure and inconclusive matter, Time's Unfolding has shown Michael that it is because the Time of those obscure and inconclusive matters had not come. that the unveiling of those obscure and inconclusive matters were prepared as such to allow for the leniency to All.

Mighty feats have been strategically willed so as to erase the serpent's wickedness and thus, allow for Peace. Since the Creation of All, All were Given instruction and direction to fulfill that strategic will. All have continuously failed to participate in the will to erase the serpent's wickedness. The Minds of All have continuously strayed and trusted their own ability in independence from this Gift. Michael then reads of this feat which is the last resort to make All right. This feat has been Completed so that the Giver can Now Live within and alongside All Forever.

In being Given leniency, the world continues to receive Time. However, in this Time, Michael sees that splinters of both Few and Provoked have brought much pain and suffering. Nevertheless, he will occupy the Mind with the accepting of leniency Given. Michael knows he has been Lead astray. For when he read over the feat of sacrifice for atonement, all Michael's Mind could conceptualize was the images and portrayals of heathen rituals within modern works and products. The Act of this feat seemed like such a distant reality in his Mind. There is only one sacrifice that stands True in this world. And Michael will stand witness of this sacrifice's Truth.

Fallen ways are erased, the acts and deeds of assaults and achievements within this world are to be eradicated. Michael has found that Hope which George told him about. Peace is within Michael's Mind.

It has been Given. Not just to Michael. But also to those in the Times of those promises, proclamations and predictions. This Gift is more that what Michael thought it was. Amongst the ubiquitous greenery which is within those many writings, it shields and protects. It hides unsightliness of damnable acts and deeds. It eases all pain. it Comforts Michael. Michael knows that there is so much more to unlock. And so Michael continues to read.